GLOBALISING CHINESE ACTORS AND INTERNALISING THE BELT AND ROAD

IMPLICATIONS FOR GLOBAL AND DOMESTIC GOVERNANCE

GLOBALISING CHINESE ACTORS AND INTERNALISING THE BELT AND ROAD

IMPLICATIONS FOR GLOBAL AND DOMESTIC GOVERNANCE

EDITED BY
MIWA HIRONO

Australian
National
University

ANU PRESS

Australian National University

ANU PRESS

Published by ANU Press
The Australian National University
Canberra ACT 2600, Australia
Email: anupress@anu.edu.au

Available to download for free at press.anu.edu.au

ISBN (print): 9781760466893
ISBN (online): 9781760466909

WorldCat (print): 1502087781
WorldCat (online): 1502091285

DOI: 10.22459/GCAIBR.2025

Cover design and layout by ANU Press

This book is published under the aegis of the China in the World editorial board of ANU Press.

Contents

Part III: Conclusion

List of illustrations

Maps

Figures

Tables

List of contributors

Miwa Hirono is an associate dean at the College of Global Liberal Arts and a professor at the Graduate School of International Relations, Ritsumeikan University, Osaka/Kyoto. Her current research focuses on China's global affairs with particular attention to China's actions in the developing world.

Kenki Adachi is a professor in the College of International Relations and director of the Institute of International Relations and Area Studies at Ritsumeikan University, Kyoto. His research interests include international politics, disarmament and arms control, global governance and civil society.

Rumi Aoyama is a professor at the Graduate School of Asia-Pacific Studies at Waseda University, Shinjuku. Her research interests include Chinese foreign policy and foreign policy decision-making and Japan–China–United States relations.

Takeshi Sato-Daimon is a professor in the Faculty of International Research and Education at Waseda University, Tokyo. His research interests include economic development and law and economics.

Masaki Mori is a professor in the College of Business Administration at Ritsumeikan University, Kyoto. His research interests include international business administration and overseas Chinese networks and company management.

Nimid Ang is an assistant professor at Ramkhamhaeng University, Bangkok, and a doctoral student at the Graduate School of International Relations at Ritsumeikan University, Kyoto. His research interest is China's international relations.

Trissia Wijaya is a McKenzie postdoctoral fellow at the Asia Institute at the University of Melbourne, Melbourne. Her current research focuses on Chinese and Japanese–led green infrastructure financing and energy transition politics in South-East Asia.

Lwin Cho Latt is an associate professor in the Department of International Relations and Political Science at the University of Yangon and a doctoral student in the Graduate School of International Relations at Ritsumeikan University, Kyoto. Her research focuses on Myanmar's cooperation with China under the Belt and Road Initiative and her field of study is peace and security.

Filippo Boni is a senior lecturer in Politics and International Studies at The Open University, United Kingdom. His research interests concern the international relations of South Asia and the politics of Chinese investments in South Asia and Europe.

Mina Tadrous Milad Tadrous is a doctoral student in the Graduate School of International Relations at Ritsumeikan University, Kyoto. His research interest is China's foreign policy in the Middle East.

Acknowledgements

This volume is a collaboration involving China scholars and international relations scholars with expert knowledge about Japan or countries that host Belt and Road Initiative projects. We began our discussions at a workshop in 2019 at Ritsumeikan University's Institute of International Relations and Area Studies (IIRAS) in Kyoto and continued our exploration during the Covid-19 pandemic in online international workshops and symposiums.

Institutional and financial support from the IIRAS have made this book possible. Heartfelt encouragement from colleagues at the institute, especially director Kenki Adachi and China research group leader Ryoji Nakagawa, has been indispensable to the project. I take this opportunity to again express my sincere gratitude for their continuous support since the inception of this project.

I am also very grateful for the support of the Asia–Japan Research Institute of Ritsumeikan University, especially director Yasushi Kosugi, in the process of developing this book. The Ritsumeikan Advanced Research Academy has also been vital to ensuring my research environment remains intact— something necessary for me to continue pursuing my burning research questions on the nature of China's global presence in the twenty-first century. In addition, I have been very fortunate to have worked with the contributing authors of this book, who not only offered insights gathered from their respective fields but also showed extraordinary patience and perseverance in continuing with this project.

I am immeasurably indebted to everyone involved in the project, including those who generously contributed their time, providing knowledge and offering comments on the Belt and Road Initiative and on the role of Japan. I would like to express my deepest appreciation for the highly relevant and wonderfully rich insights provided at various stages in the project, all of which further strengthen this volume, to Timur Dadabaev, Kai Kajitani, Djalilova

Niora, Jun Xue, Pengchao Yang, Qiuli Yang, Saeeda Batool, Jun Honna, Juichi Inada, Ken Inoue, Naohiro Kitano, Masahisa Koyama, Cheng-Chwee Kwik, Shuji Matsuno, Keiichi Shirato, Hiroshi Tanaka and Denghua Zhang.

The original book derived from these workshops was first published in Japan as *Ittai Ichiro ha naniwo motarashitaka: Chugoku Mondai to Toshi no Jirenma* (*What Has the Belt and Road Brought? The China Question and the Investment Dilemma*) in 2021. I would like to thank Masanobu Uehara at the Keisho Shobo in Japan, who carefully and with great attention to detail proofread the book in the process of revising it in Japanese. This book, published in English, is the result of updates since the publication of the book in Japanese.

The process of translating the book from Japanese into English, which has required not only translation but also consideration of the differences in rendering it in a suitable way for international readers, would not have been possible without the work of Rene Bailey and Stephen Bailey. I am very grateful for their tireless, meticulous and first-class editorial work on our original manuscript in English, and to Jan Borrie for outstanding copyediting.

I would also like to thank very much Ben Hillman, who offered excellent service as an executive editor, and the CIW Editorial Board, which supported this book project from the outset. I am grateful to the anonymous reviewers for their very thoughtful and engaging reviews. My endless thanks also go to Natsuki Koto, who managed project operations with constant care and kindness not only to me but also to the contributing authors, as well as to Natsuko Kawamura, who advised me on many aspects of the various projects I undertook directly and indirectly related to this book.

Lastly, this book would not have been possible without the enormous help of all those people in China and the case study countries who helped the authors conduct field research, enabling them to observe the reality of various BRI projects. Listening to those who work in and around project sites on the ground made this project possible. This book is dedicated to all the kind people who enabled our academic fieldwork to make sense of the extensive research we undertook to arrive at this book. Thank you all.

I hope this book does justice to the tremendous support from all the people mentioned above, by offering important correctives to the often-misunderstood nature of the Belt and Road Initiative.

Miwa Hirono

Abbreviations

21CP Conference	Twenty-First-Century Panglong Conference
AA	Arakan Army
AIIB	Asian Infrastructure Investment Bank
ASEAN	Association of Southeast Asian Nations
BRI	Belt and Road Initiative
CCCs	Chinese Chambers of Commerce
CDB	China Development Bank
CEE	Central and Eastern Europe
CEEC	Central and Eastern European countries
CGCC	Chinese General Chamber of Commerce
CIDCA	China International Development Cooperation Agency
CMEC	China–Myanmar Economic Corridor
CP Group	Charoen Pokphand Group
CPC	Communist Party of China
CPEC	China–Pakistan Economic Corridor
CRCC	China Railway Construction Corporation
DAC	Development Assistance Committee
EAGs	ethnic armed groups
EEC	Eastern Economic Corridor
FPNCC	Federal Political Negotiation and Consultative Committee
GDP	gross domestic product
HKGCC	Hong Kong General Chamber of Commerce
HSR	high-speed railway

IMF	International Monetary Fund
JICA	Japan International Cooperation Agency
KCIC	Kereta Cepat Indonesia–China
KIA	Kachin Independence Army
KNPP	Karenni National Progressive Party
KNU	Karen National Union
MNDAA	Myanmar National Democratic Alliance Army
MoFA	Ministry of Foreign Affairs
MoU	memorandum of understanding
MSDP	Myanmar Sustainable Development Plan
NCA	Nationwide Ceasefire Agreement (Myanmar)
NDAA	National Democratic Alliance Army
NDRC	National Development and Reform Commission
NGO	nongovernmental organisation
NLD	National League for Democracy
ODA	Official Development Assistance
OECD	Organisation for Economic Co-operation and Development
PML-N	Pakistan Muslim League (Nawaz)
PTI	Pakistan Tehreek-e-Insaf ('Pakistan Justice Movement')
RCSS	Restoration Council of Shan State
RMB	renminbi
SCCCI	Singapore Chinese Chamber of Commerce & Industry
SEZ	special economic zone
SOE	state-owned enterprise
TNLA	Ta'ang National Liberation Army
UN	United Nations
US	United States
USDP	Union Solidarity and Development Party
UWSA	United Wa State Army
WCEC	World Chinese Entrepreneurs Convention

1

Introduction: The Belt and Road Initiative from bottom-up perspectives

Miwa Hirono[1]

Introduction

Debates about China's influence on the future of the world order have dominated international discussion for some time. Evaluations of this influence, however, are generally dichotomous. Western democracies, for example, tend to take the view that China's influence will be negative because its authoritarian regime will weaken not only the world's democratic international institutions but also those of the many developing countries that receive political and economic assistance from China. In contrast, most analysts in China, as well as those in many developing countries, evaluate China's influence more positively, mainly because they regard its economic power as offering a means to ensure these countries' economic development.

A similar dichotomy is apparent in discussions about China's Belt and Road Initiative (BRI). Many Western analysts point out the negative impacts of the BRI on developing countries. One example is the so-called debt trap, by which investment projects launched under the BRI have resulted in levels of debt that developing countries can never hope to repay. China's 99-year

1   The research used in this chapter was supported by JSPS Grant-in-Aid for Scientific Research JP17K03606 and JP21K01380.

lease of the port of Hambantota which it helped build in Sri Lanka is a case in point, whereby the long-term lease of the port goes some way to repaying the country's debt. In addition, China's disregard for human rights and environmental considerations in countries where its development projects are undertaken is often cited as an example of the detrimental impacts of the BRI on people in those countries. On the other hand, supporters of the BRI claim that the initiative lowers the cost of global trade and boosts economic activity by encouraging investment and the construction of public infrastructure. Such economic development, so the Chinese argument goes, brings about peace and helps to build 'a community with a shared future for humankind'. How, then, are we to understand this dichotomy in discussions about China and the BRI? This is a major question facing many policymakers around the world today.

This book critically assesses the concept of the Belt and Road Initiative by focusing on two aspects: actors and projects. Some of the chapters present an in-depth empirical analysis of the Chinese and/or non-Chinese actors who implement and manage the BRI. Others focus on projects that China is undertaking around the world as part of the BRI, paying particular attention to how each is situated, interpreted, utilised and coopted within its local context.

Research on the BRI has been an important field of Chinese studies over the past few years. However, there is still a lack of empirical research on what exactly the BRI involves, and debate is often premised on the assumptions made by each scholar about the possible scope of the initiative. For example, some argue that China is using the BRI as a tool to establish geopolitical hegemony or, as in the case of Sri Lanka, for neo-colonisation by creating a massive debt obligation. Yet, there is no clear publicly available definition of the BRI; even the Chinese Government's own definition and descriptions are somewhat opaque. With the definition of the BRI unclear, it is imperative to take a deductive approach and examine how the initiative is operationalised on the ground. What does that tell us about the nature of the BRI and what do local interpretations of its impact tell us about the relationship between the projects, the people they serve and China's contribution to development? While it is important to explore the strategic intentions of the Chinese state to understand what lies behind today's emergent challenges, it is also necessary to focus on the actors and projects that may—or may not—represent those intentions.

This book contributes to the study of the BRI in two ways. First, by analysing the nature of the BRI empirically, focusing on the actors and projects involved, this book offers the perspectives of not just key Chinese actors, but also the people on the ground in receipt of China's investment. The literature tends to take a top-down approach to analysis by focusing on China's geostrategic intentions and their implications for the countries that accept China's investment in the BRI. Instead, this book takes a bottom-up approach by exploring how the Chinese actors and people in recipient countries make sense of the BRI.

The second contribution this book makes is its consideration of Japan's roles vis-a-vis China's international aid and investments specifically, and global and domestic governance, generally. Japan matters not only because it was the largest international donor in the world by the end of the 1990s (see Chapter 4) and remained the third largest in 2023, but also because it offers a unique dimension to the frequently dichotomous discussion of the Belt and Road Initiative's apparent failure to meet international standards. As one of the key non-Western donors, Japan's position in the world of aid and investment is somewhat 'in between' the Development Assistance Committee (DAC) of the Organisation for Economic Co-operation and Development (OECD) and non-Western donors. While it strives to work to meet the so-called international standards for development aid as a member of the DAC, it also once deployed the 'trinity' of investment, trade and aid activities from which China developed its own 'trinity' of development assistance (Brautigam 2011). Today, Japan is highly critical of the BRI. Its criticism frequently derives from what Japanese media describes as China's strategic intentions and is quite strong due to Japan's sense of geostrategic rivalry with China (Hirono 2019). With likeminded countries in the G7 and the Quadrilateral Security Dialogue (the Quad), Japan is vocal about the Belt and Road Initiative's adverse ramifications for the financial health of the countries that receive Chinese investment. Facing the scale of BRI investment and the significance of international criticism, how has Japan understood the BRI? How does Japan contribute to the dichotomised discussion of global governance when adding its own perspective as an aid recipient before its rapid economic development in the 1960s, and when offering aid to developing countries with a rationale different from its Western counterparts? What challenges and opportunities does the BRI bring to Japan's position in global and domestic governance?

Against this background, the book sets out to answer the following three research questions:

1. How have the key Chinese actors operationalised their transition from local to global actors?
2. How have the key actors in the host countries interpreted, utilised or coopted BRI projects into the political, economic and social environments of their countries, and how have the BRI projects been established as domestic issues within the host countries as a result?
3. What are the implications of the BRI for global and domestic governance generally, and for Japan's role in countries where the BRI projects take place, in particular?

This book makes a two-pronged argument. First, the BRI represents an intricate dynamic with two contradictory tendencies. One is President of China Xi Jinping's top-down and centralised approach to policymaking, with its focus on producing robust Chinese actors who can succeed in the competitive global economy. The other is a fragmented and decentralised reality made up of an expanding range of actors engaged in realising a plethora of BRI projects on the ground, all of whom are pursuing their own interests, which are often quite different from those of the Chinese state. To understand this fragmented and decentralised reality better, the book highlights the importance of taking local agency seriously. From the perspective of actors in the recipient countries, the BRI is not necessarily what has been imposed on them by the communist giant. In other words, a structure-oriented discussion—the kind that assumes that great powers determine the lives of small countries—misses the reality on the ground. All the recipient states have their own internal political and economic dynamics, within which various local actors attempt to interpret, utilise and coopt the BRI projects for their own interests. These internal dynamics in the recipient countries add to the increasingly fragmented nature of the BRI. The idea of the BRI may depart from China, but once a project arrives at its destination, a critical metamorphosis takes place. The now-local project is no longer simply a Chinese actor's investment project. It becomes a domestic issue around which different local actors compete, utilising the activity to shore up their own competitive legitimacy.

The coexistence of these two contradictory tendencies implies that the BRI has a multifaceted impact on global and domestic governance. Globally, the promotion of the BRI has strengthened the 'open economy' aspect of global governance while, at the same time, it has fostered China's particular twist on the 'planned economy'. Domestically, therefore, while a Chinese-style approach to state management and investment without political conditions may set back democratisation efforts in emerging countries, the BRI has also given rise to a renewed sense of democracy in these countries.

The second part of the argument regards the roles that Japan plays in countries where the BRI projects take place. This book argues that while Japan remains hesitant to cooperate with the BRI based on its broader geopolitical position, including its perception of an underlying threat from China's geopolitical ambitions, it is important to put such perceptions aside and identify the on-the-ground complementarity of China's and Japan's approaches to development aid. This argument derives from two observations made in this book. First, the history of Japan's official development assistance—especially international criticism of its infrastructure-centric aid model in the 1980s and the resultant transformation of the aid model from the 2000s—has much in common with current criticism of the BRI in the literature (see Chapter 4). While Japan's aid has changed to include various soft elements such as capacity-building, infrastructure is still a major component. In this regard, Japan has much experience and a lesson or two to offer China for the benefit of developing countries, potentially better aligning the infrastructure projects of the two countries. Furthermore, some global issues commonly faced by China, Japan and aid-recipient countries may provide opportunities for cooperation.

The second observation that leads to the abovementioned argument is related to the process of internalisation of the BRI—in other words, the process by which various actors in recipient states attempt to interpret, utilise and coopt BRI projects for their own interests. This process offers important lessons for other donors including Japan, Australia and the United States. The fact that actors in host states utilise the BRI to benefit their political and economic status means that those actors' rivals may utilise other aid and investment programs, including those of China, Japan, Australia and the United States, to benefit themselves and gain local status. This could lead to a 'reproduction' of great-power politics. Seeking complementarity in donors' aid approaches goes well beyond looking for compatibility among specific aid projects. It is about finding where donors are situated in the domestic context, and carefully planning aid and investment in a way to avoid being drawn into domestic politics.

The rest of this chapter will set the scene within which the BRI is taking place. The first section reviews the development of the BRI since 2013, highlighting that its contours are still very unclear, and presenting some arguments as to why China decided to launch it in the first place. The second section discusses the kind of research needed to analyse the issues that are often reported in the recipient countries and argues for the importance of looking at the interplay between China's domestic politics and local politics in the Belt and Road Initiative's destination countries. The third section introduces each of the chapters in the book. The book's theoretical base is provided in Chapter 2, in which Kenki Adachi presents a discussion of how the BRI can be understood in the context of global and domestic governance.

What is the BRI?

The development process of the BRI

The concept of the BRI was announced by Xi Jinping as the main plan for China's foreign relations after he became general secretary of the Communist Party of China (CPC) in November 2012 and launched the 'Chinese Dream' as the party's stewardship philosophy. During Xi's visit to Kazakhstan in September 2013 and while at the Nazarbayev University in the capital, Astana, he proposed the joint construction of the 'economic belt along the Silk Road'. This was the first mention of the 'Belt' in the Silk Road project—a concept that would later become the basis for all of China's foreign relations (Xi 2013a). In October of the next year, President Xi addressed the Indonesian parliament and said that China hoped to develop a partnership of maritime cooperation with the Association of Southeast Asian Nations (ASEAN) countries and jointly build the twenty-first-century 'Maritime Silk Road' (Xi 2013b). This introduced the 'Road' part of the BRI. As of October 2024, more than 150 countries and more than 30 international organisations had signed memorandums of understanding (MoUs) to cooperate with the BRI and join the framework (Wu and Bao 2024). It would have been difficult to predict at its launch in 2013 how substantial the concept would become (Sano 2017: 26). More than a decade has passed since this major concept was first announced, during trips to Astana and Jakarta; however, a great deal remains unclear about the substance of the BRI.

What do open sources tell us about the initiative? Its two main objectives, as announced by the Chinese Government, are to 'focus on interconnection and deepen practical cooperation' and to 'realise mutually beneficial schemes and achieve joint development' (NDRC et al. 2015). The BRI is supposed to encompass a vast area of the globe—described as 'six corridors, six routes, multiple countries and multiple ports'. The six economic corridors are shown in Map 1.1, while the six routes are rail, road, water, air, pipelines and the internet. The number of Silk Roads has been increasing ever since the inception of the BRI: in addition to the two mentioned above, in 2017, China and Russia jointly proposed construction of an Ice Silk Road in the Arctic Ocean, and China has also proposed a Digital Silk Road and a Space Silk Road. In addition to Latin America and Oceania, some African countries that are not on the route of the Maritime Silk Road have signed agreements to join the construction of the BRI.

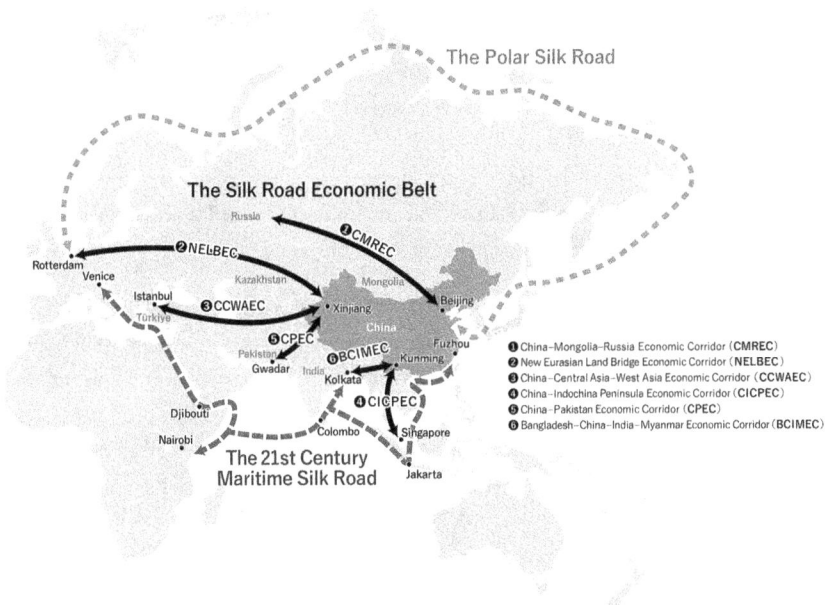

Map 1.1 Three Silk Roads and six economic corridors in the BRI
Sources: Prepared by the author from Hielscher and Ibold (n.d.); Luft (2016).

In December 2014, the Silk Road Fund for the Realisation of the BRI was established with a total capital of USD40 billion and, in March 2015, China's National Development and Reform Commission (NDRC), the Ministry of Foreign Affairs and the Ministry of Commerce jointly issued the 'Vision and Actions on Jointly Building the Silk Road Economic Belt and the 21st Century Maritime Silk Road' (NDRC et al. 2015). This was the first time the government had published a clear definition for and interpretation of the BRI, covering the following topics: 'Background', 'Principles', 'Framework', 'Cooperation Priorities', 'Cooperation Mechanisms', 'China's Regions in Pursuing Opening-Up', 'China in Action' and 'Embracing a Brighter Future Together'.

The cooperation theme focuses on five priority areas: policy coordination, facilities connectivity, unimpeded trade, financial integration and people-to-people bonds. Through these priorities and mechanisms, the BRI aims to 'achieve connectivity between the Asian, European and African continents and the surrounding oceans, and build and strengthen interconnected partnerships among countries along the route' (NDRC et al. 2015). The aim is to achieve global connectivity of infrastructural facilities to link China and Europe, as well as investment and trade, people-to-people understanding and policy coordination. Based on these five priority areas, the Chinese Government has set up the online Belt and Road Portal (www.yidaiyilu.gov.cn), which is constantly updated with relevant news and publicity.

In January 2016, the Asian Infrastructure Investment Bank (AIIB), the backbone of the BRI, opened its doors with USD100 billion in funding and the support of 57 founding members. At the time there was talk of Japan signing up, but the idea of joining an international bank originating in China raised concerns, so it chose not to. This was followed by the establishment of the New Development Bank, led by the BRICS countries (Brazil, Russia, India, China and South Africa), and the establishment of financial 'multilateral institutions' by China. In addition, in 2015, Chinese local governments began to draw up development plans in line with the BRI, which has become increasingly important as a domestic policy (see the discussion by Aoyama in Chapter 3). The amount of investment has since increased every year and, by September 2023, the cumulative investment by Chinese companies in the countries along the route had reached USD1 trillion, while investment in China by these same countries amounted to USD48 billion (SCIO 2023).

The first BRI International Forum was held in Beijing in 2017, with a second in April 2019 and a third in October 2023. The first forum, which attracted about 5,000 people, brought together heads of state to discuss future directions and policy coordination of the BRI. It was an important opportunity not only to demonstrate China's central position on the international stage but also to highlight its international strength domestically. The second forum was an important stepping stone from which President Xi was able to consolidate his power base in China six months later at the Nineteenth National Congress of the CPC, in October 2019. China was facing economic problems when the third forum was held. While it promised to continue major investments, it also advocated 'small yet smart' livelihood programs by other countries and promoted more cooperation on green development and scientific and technological innovation.

Originally just a proposal announced during Xi's foreign trips, the BRI has become a major national program: by July 2024, there were 151 central government regulations, including 88 at the ministerial level, and 646 local regulations with 'Belt and Road Initiative' in their title,[2] and many projects conceived under the BRI have made steady progress.

Uncertainties about the BRI

At the same time, it is apparent that there are still many unknowns. For example, the cost and duration of investment in the BRI have not been declared by the Chinese Government and remain unclear. Estimates of the overall cost range from USD1 trillion to USD8 trillion (Hillman 2018). The media often cites the figure of USD1 trillion, but given that USD100 billion had been invested by 2019, it is not clear to what timespan this refers to in the period from 2013. The figure of USD8 trillion is said to originate in a quote by a Chinese State Council finance official in 2016, reported in the *Hong Kong Economic Journal*, that if Xi Jinping's BRI were to be fully implemented, it would cost USD8 trillion (Lam 2016). Jonathan Hillman (2018), a senior fellow at the Center for Strategic and International Studies in Washington, DC, speculates that this figure may have been taken from the Asian Development Bank, which stated in 2009 that USD8 trillion should be invested in development in Asia between 2010 and 2020, but it is not clear what is included in this amount. In addition to

---

2   According to the PKU Law database.

investment by state-owned enterprises (SOEs), the figure could also include investment by private enterprises, trade agreements and 'human exchanges' for educational and cultural purposes, but the details are vague. In short, we do not yet have a clear idea of the scale of the project.

It is also uncertain how long the BRI will last. It had been argued that, as the poster child of President Xi, it would terminate with the end of his term in 2022, but with his tenure as president made indefinite in May 2018, it can be assumed that the BRI will continue into the future. Or, if the BRI contributes to Xi Jinping's goal of making China a 'wealthy, democratic, civilised, harmonious and beautiful socialist modernising powerhouse' by the one-hundredth anniversary of the People's Republic of China, 2049 can be considered a potential endpoint. If, however, another pandemic causes a series of economic collapses and defaults on loans, and if it is deemed that the BRI cannot solve the problems in the Chinese economy, the possibility of a major change of direction cannot be ruled out.

Nor is it clear how the projects within the BRI relate to existing policies such as the outward investment projects that China implemented before the BRI, particularly the 'Going Out Policy' (*Zou Chu Qu*) of 2000. Many Chinese companies have since expanded and invested overseas, but what has happened to these projects since the launch of the BRI? There is still no consistent agreement as to whether the Going Out Policy was simply rebranded as the BRI or whether the policy led to the overseas expansion of both state-owned and privately owned enterprises, with only those related to SOEs renamed as 'BRI projects'.[3]

What are the benefits of the BRI? In Chapter 3, Aoyama shows that the Chinese provinces that have been identified as key project areas for the BRI have also been given state support in various areas, including negotiations with foreign countries, but it is not clear what the difference is between these projects and others undertaken by enterprises elsewhere. What, then, should we call a project undertaken by an enterprise in a province that is not formally involved in the BRI? Similarly, is there a difference between projects undertaken by Chinese enterprises in BRI regions and those in other regions, and are projects undertaken by Chinese private enterprises in countries along the route of the BRI classified as BRI projects? According to current understanding, there is no policy or research that addresses these issues.

---

3   Author's interview with a Chinese diplomat, September 2019.

In addition, it is unclear whether the BRI is a 'strategy', a 'concept', a 'proposal' or a 'project' since the term can be translated into English in several ways. The Chinese Government has stated that 'Belt and Road Initiative' is the preferred English translation.[4] It is particularly interesting that the word 'strategy', which evokes more geopolitical and global economic ambitions, is not used, whereas 'proposal' and 'concept' imply nothing more than ideas. In fact, in Chinese domestic documents published before 2015, even the Chinese Government used the term 'Belt and Road Initiative Strategy' (for example, Gu 2015). Since then, however, the word 'strategy' has disappeared and only 'Belt and Road' has been used or 'construction of one belt and one road'. Around the same time as the change in terminology from 'One Belt, One Road' in 2015, the Chinese Government made the following statement about the English translation of 'Belt and Road Initiative': 'The word "proposal" is translated as "initiative" and uses the singular form. Words not used are "strategy", "project", "programme", "agenda", etc.' (NDRC Western Division 2015). In addition, at the second BRI International Forum in 2019, Xi Jinping himself stated that 'the Belt and Road Initiative is not a closed bloc or "China club" run by China' (Xi 2019). The use of the term 'initiative' shows that the Chinese Government is anxious to ensure that the BRI does not fuel the 'China threat' argument. However, regardless of how the Chinese Government and President Xi want to describe it, the reality is that we have only the phrase 'Belt and Road Initiative' and we do not yet know whether the noun to which it relates is a 'concept', a 'strategy', a 'project' or an 'agenda'.

In this book, we use the term 'Belt and Road Initiative' for convenience, in accordance with the terminology of the Chinese Government and international practice, but we do not attempt to draw any conclusions about whether it is a 'concept' or a 'strategy'. By so doing, we aim to eliminate as much as possible any preconceptions about the nature of the BRI and to concentrate instead on the characteristics of its activities. As mentioned, the emphasis in this book is on the local context as the object of study, so, when describing the policy position of the Chinese Government, we will refer to the BRI, but when referring to specific investment or aid projects, we will refer to BRI projects.

---

4   The English translation used to be 'One Belt, One Road', but in 2015, a formal announcement changed it to 'Belt and Road'. For informal use, it is suggested that the Belt and Road Initiative or the land and maritime Silk Road initiative could also be used (NDRC Western Division 2015).

Why the BRI?

As discussed, there are many unanswered questions about the BRI. Previous studies have discussed China's reasons for promoting the BRI, raising three main suggestions. The first is that the BRI is intended to improve the Chinese economy by enabling China to confront the 'new normal'— the end of the high economic growth rate of more than 10 per cent that followed the period of reform and opening up—and to maintain a growth rate of about 6 per cent for some time. This would help China avoid a rapid decline in economic growth by aiming for a gradual slowdown in the growth rate. China cannot hope to continue its economic development in the future unless it seeks new routes, mainly through market-based reforms and a move away from resource-dependent development. The BRI will allow China to invest its substantial domestic capital and huge foreign exchange reserves abroad to develop new investment opportunities, escape excessive dependence on exports, reduce its domestic overcapacity and solve production surplus problems.

Of course, other measures are also necessary, such as expanding domestic demand and correcting the economic gap between urban and rural areas, as well as moving away from the manufacturing-centred economic model (also known as the middle-income trap) by promoting China's own technological innovation, as represented in the slogan 'China Manufacturing 2025' (Breslin 2020). The BRI is one of the blueprints for China's future economic development. However, the success of the project is not yet clear, and this uncertainty has given rise to concerns about domestic macroeconomic policy. Problems such as China's economic slowdown, factory closures because of the Covid-19 pandemic and the non-repayment of loans, as well as the state of international financial policy (including the monetary policy of the United States), could increase uncertainty around the BRI, and the future trend in exports of foreign capital will be greatly affected.

The second reason China is promoting the BRI so determinedly is to strengthen resource procurement and secure and enhance access to international markets. This is why it is seeking more 'connectivity' through the development of the initiative. Energy procurement in Central Asia, South-East Asia and the Middle East is the lifeblood of China's economy, and even as it seeks to move away from a dependence on exports, it must also achieve lower costs for the raw materials it imports and the manufactured goods it exports.

In the 1950s, the Marshall Plan created a huge European market for US companies as well as bolstering infrastructure development in Western Europe (Kan 2015). After the global financial crisis in 2008, China's aid plan and other proposals for emerging countries were inextricably linked with the expansion of foreign demand through aid and the resolution of various international economic issues. Xu Shanda, a member of China's National Political Consultative Conference and former deputy director of the State Administration of Taxation, stressed the need for a China-led version of the Marshall Plan to provide funds, at a special meeting of the conference in July 2009 (Kan 2015; Tang 2009):

> The core of the plan is the trinity of 'state bearing of lending risks', 'elimination of excess production capacity of enterprises' and 'internationalisation of the renminbi [RMB]', as [a China-led version of the Marshall Plan] will boost the internationalisation of the RMB, reduce the huge amount of foreign exchange reserves and reduce the risk of dollar depreciation over the medium to long term. (Xu, cited in Kan 2015)

Taken together with the establishment of China's first international financial institutions—such as the AIIB, the Silk Road Fund and the New Development Bank—the BRI provides a glimpse of how China is establishing itself as a central player in the international economic order. The extent to which this order differs from the US-centric one of the past must be examined in more detail. While the internationalisation of the renminbi is of course a new aspect, it should be noted that the AIIB has signed MoUs with the international financial institutions that underpin the existing international order—that is, the World Bank and the International Monetary Fund (IMF)—for its co-financing. Nonetheless, aspects of the IMF's work that focus on supporting democracy and human rights have not been followed by the AIIB to date, and this has led to fears that the BRI will roll back developments relating to democracy and human rights protection.

The third reason for the BRI is China's position in the international community as a 'revisionist state' that is modifying the international order and wants to create its own through the BRI (for more on this possibility, see Chapter 2 by Adachi). In short, the argument is that the BRI is a stepping stone to global hegemony, which China is developing against a background of declining US hegemony and power. This is often referred to as a '*Pax Sinica*' or 'neo-colonialism'. There are also those who see the BRI as a battle for control over the formation of an economic trading bloc to rival the Trans-Pacific Partnership.

However, as already indicated, given there are many unknowns about fundamental aspects of the BRI, any discussion of the true intentions of the Chinese Government cannot be regarded as empirical, and it is difficult to go beyond speculation and interpretation. Takahara Akio (2018) describes the BRI as a 'multidimensional' constellation and maintains that the overall picture is often incomprehensible. He argues that the scattered pointers are in the category of 'ideas' rather than evidence-based 'facts'. In other words, it is an undeniable fact that there are countless stars in the sky, but connecting the dots to form constellations is based on human interpretation, therefore constellations do not really exist; the problem with understanding the Belt and Road concept is that it is often discussed based on such an interpretation.

In sum, it is an almost impossible task to fully clarify China's strategic intentions for the BRI through empirical means, especially when information on China's foreign policymaking process is scarce. However, we must separate the demonstrable 'reality' from the interpretation; otherwise, there is a danger that only the concept of the BRI will prevail and interpretations with a pro-Chinese or anti-Chinese bias will be regarded as 'research'. This book therefore focuses on those parts of the BRI that can be properly verified and aims to analyse the situation objectively, focusing on the main actors and activities that are the 'stars' of the BRI, as well as the political and economic dynamics of the main investment destinations.

Clarifying the problems of the BRI

A frequent theme in discussions about the BRI is its problems. These are mainly concerns about debt, environmental issues, human rights and corruption, but also include issues in relation to China's political interventions and increasing influence in the countries concerned, its growing military power and the adverse impact of the Covid-19 pandemic on investment activity.

Most of the studies detailing the problems of the BRI to date contain three major drawbacks. The first is that such studies usually analyse the issue only at the system and the national levels, and rarely at the actor level. In other words, they are mainly debates about the impact on the international system of 'hegemonic struggle' and 'neo-colonialism', as well as about China's national interests as a unitary actor, based on the premise that the state's policymaking process is a 'black box'. Many China scholars also emphasise the importance of the subnational level in policymaking—specifically, the individuals, diplomatic corps and corporations involved (Liberthal and Lampton 1992; Mertha 2009; Jakobson and Knox 2010). Despite all this, there is still insufficient analysis considering the existence of a variety of actors below the state level. With the concentration of power in the hands of the CPC under Xi Jinping it has become increasingly necessary to consider China as a 'single actor'. At the same time, there has been a move towards decentralisation and the diversification of actors, which means there is an equal and opposite need to focus on a more detailed actor perspective rather than considering only the national level.

The second weakness lies with the kind of analysis that neglects what lies at the heart of China's foreign policymaking process—that is, China's foreign policy seems to have two fundamental objectives: to maintain and strengthen the legitimacy of one-party rule by the CPC and to support China's economic development. However, a common problem is that these fundamental issues are not adequately considered. For example, it is frequently argued that China supports undemocratic regimes abroad through investment projects aimed at achieving hegemony. However, given that economic development is one of China's main goals, it is unlikely that its foreign policy is based on a strategic intention to achieve hegemony, as that could have a negative impact on the global economy.

Finally, several studies have been published in the past few years that focus on the impact of the BRI on the investment destination states (for example, Garlick 2019). While these studies are undeniably important, the impact perspective is problematic, because it is one-sided and considers only the impact of powerful members of the international community on weaker members. A similar criticism has been raised about previous studies of Asian history. For example, in understanding the transformation of Asia in the nineteenth century, the view that Asia was transformed by the impact of Western imperialism has been criticised as Western-centric. If we instead consider Asia as the centre, we can argue that the pressure of Western imperialism represented a powerful element in the internal dynamics of Asia, that this was incorporated into the internal political and socioeconomic dynamics of Asia and that Asia was transformed as a result. This view seems more in line with reality (Cohen 1988). The impact of the BRI overlaps exactly with this approach to historical research, whereas the impact theory on its own is limited to the analysis of a one-way vector of impact from China to the countries in which it invests. By considering the BRI as part of the domestic situation of these countries, we can study its impact in a more empirical way, using a two-way vector.

These three issues have been identified as serious drawbacks in previous studies of the BRI. We must therefore establish what kind of perspective is needed to overcome these limitations. The guiding principle in this book is to identify the problems with the BRI by starting from what can be demonstrated. In other words, it is essential to explore the roots of the problems inductively by focusing on issues with the BRI that have arisen in places where projects have already been implemented. This is because, although the overall contours of the BRI remain unclear, there are already enough empirical data and evidence about the relevant actors in each of the projects along the route and in relation to the domestic situations in those countries where investment is taking place to draw new conclusions. Focusing on specific actors and events therefore offers a window through which to identify the drawbacks and lacunae in previous studies of the BRI.

Based on the above, there are two major issues that this book wishes to address. The first is the globalisation of the Chinese actors involved in the BRI. That is, how have the various Chinese actors—the CPC, the Chinese Government, foreign aid agencies, SOEs, private enterprises and local Chinese networks—interacted with the BRI and how has it evolved? In other words, to what extent has the BRI impacted Chinese Government policies and Chinese actors and to what extent have their activities become globalised? The second issue relates to the domestic consequences of the BRI, given that it is essentially an aspect of foreign policy. Here it will be necessary to consider carefully how the BRI is perceived and used by local actors in the host countries. It is only by applying these two approaches that we can begin to examine the third key question of the book, which is the implications of the BRI for future global governance and the challenges they present for Japan. I return to this in the final chapter.

The structure of the book

The book is divided into three parts. Part I, 'The challenges of the Belt and Road Initiative—Implications for global and domestic governance and Japan', discusses the challenges posed by the BRI from the perspectives of Belt and Road studies and global governance theory and of Japan. In this introductory chapter, I have already discussed the obstacles to deeper analysis in terms of previous research in the field of BRI studies and Chinese international relations theory.

Chapter 2, by Kenki Adachi, considers how the BRI could affect global and domestic governance. On the international front, there are fears that China's perceived lack of shared liberal values could shake up global governance, and Adachi considers the extent to which the promotion of the BRI is disrupting open economies, multilateralism and liberal democracy, calling for an empirical examination of all these effects. While there are concerns that China's infrastructure projects are having a negative impact on corruption, human rights abuses and financial sustainability in the host countries, Adachi also points out that 'if the lenders do not demand accountability, the voters will'. Hence, the chapter focuses on how the BRI becomes a domestic issue rather than offering a one-way discussion of its 'impact' on the countries concerned. In my concluding chapter, I return to the research questions raised by Adachi's thesis and provide some answers drawn from the discussions in this book.

Chapter 3, by Rumi Aoyama, focuses on the combination of two seemingly contradictory elements of Chinese foreign policy—planning, and decentralisation and fragmentation—and discusses the implications of China's centre–local relations in the context of the implementation of the BRI. The planned diplomacy of Xi Jinping's administration, based on decentralisation, is strongly at work in China's centre–local relations, with the central government encouraging competitive relations between local governments, which are key to building a national system for promoting the BRI. At the same time, local governments that have not been included in the plan are making efforts of their own, which are in effect leading to 'decentralisation and fragmentation', although it is noted that without the support of the central government, their efforts remain limited.

In Chapter 4, Takeshi Sato-Daimon turns his attention to Japan and considers the possibility of creating a 'grand coalition' between China, Japan and aid-recipient countries in a 'win-win-win' scenario. The chapter begins by pointing out that Japan's development aid shares some features with that of China. Japan has developed its basic philosophy of development assistance since the 1960s when it viewed trade, investment and aid as a set of activities—the so-called trinity model. This is now a feature of the global development of the BRI. China's trade, investment and aid practices approximate those of Japan (Brautigam 2011), suggesting the possibility of cooperation between the two countries. However, according to Sato-Daimon, in the current context, South-East Asia has become 'the front line' in a 'Sino-Japanese aid race', in which Japanese economic assistance has in many ways failed to match that of China. The competition between China and Japan over mutually exclusive gains makes cooperation between the two challenging. Particularly in the context of the post-Covid reconstruction of South-East Asia, the gap between Japan and China in terms of their aid performance will only widen, unless Japan looks beyond itself to help other countries. The chapter, however, makes the point that some global issues commonly faced by China, Japan and aid-recipient countries—Covid-19 being a quintessential example—may provide opportunities for cooperation in the future.

Chapter 5 moves to an analysis of the bridging function played by Chinese networks in their relations with different organisations. Here, Masaki Mori analyses the importance of the Chinese General Chamber of Commerce in the destination country (using the example of Singapore) for strengthening the relationship between China and BRI investing companies, thanks to the interorganisational networks and exchanges it has built with China's central and local governments and different commercial and industrial organisations.

The importance of this Chinese network also provides a crucial perspective for the analysis in Part II of how the BRI is being 'internalised' in the countries along the route. This is particularly evident in Chapter 6, in which Nimid Ang analyses how the Chinese in Thailand have been closely connected to the political and economic power of the country and played a central role in the financing of the Eastern Economic Corridor (EEC) as part of the process of receiving Chinese capital through the BRI. In particular, Ang shows how the Charoen Pokphand Group, which has a central presence among ethnic Thai-Chinese and strong ties to China, has persuaded the Thai Government that China is an essential source of investment for EEC projects.

This is followed in Chapter 7 by Trissia Wijaya's examination of the Jakarta–Bandung high-speed railway, which analyses how strong links between Chinese capital and local forces have made the BRI possible in Indonesia. Wijaya describes how Chinese capital has formed a kind of alliance with the four Indonesian state-owned companies involved in the railway project, as well as with the regent of Karawang Regency and the governor of West Java province, to suppress social discontent and provide a political and social base for the project to proceed.

What is depicted in both chapters is the fact that the BRI is driven by powerful collaborators in the destination countries who dominate the political and social debate about issues such as anti-elite movements

(Chapter 6) and anti-Chinese sentiment (Chapter 7), and thus the BRI becomes part of these dynamics. In contrast to previous studies of the BRI that have focused on the major powers, Part II uses developing countries as the main stage to highlight the processes through which the BRI is incorporated into the local political and social context and hence becomes a 'domestic issue'.

Chapters 8–10 also portray the BRI in local contexts—in Myanmar, Pakistan and the Middle East, respectively—showing how it has become a 'domestic issue' in these places, embedded in a complex mechanism of interlocking interests. In Chapter 8, Lwin Cho Latt questions why Myanmar's National League for Democracy (NLD), led by Aung San Suu Kyi, promoted the China–Myanmar Economic Corridor (CMEC), despite growing criticism of Chinese investment by the people of Myanmar. The author argues that this is because the benefits offered by the CMEC outweighed the risks posed by anti-Chinese sentiment, for two reasons. First, it was hoped that, given its location in an area of frequent conflict with armed ethnic minority groups, the development of the CMEC would increase the prospects of a ceasefire. Second, the NLD government believed it could strengthen its legitimacy and power to govern through the economic development introduced by the BRI.

In Chapter 9, Filippo Boni focuses on the China–Pakistan Economic Corridor (CPEC) and the impact on its implementation of a change in leadership after Pakistan's 2018 general election. In that election, the Pakistan Muslim League (Nawaz) was defeated and the Pakistan Justice Movement became the leading party. As a result, the focus on the CPEC began to shift away from energy production and connectivity towards social development. Ultimately, the priorities of local leaders determined not only whether Pakistan could attract BRI investment, but also the extent to which its operation changed to benefit the lives of local people.

Chapter 10 narrows the scope of analysis, reflecting on the regional rather than the national level—and this is something of an experimental analysis with a promising future research direction. Most studies of the BRI in developing countries take a country-based perspective. While this is integral to studying the 'internalisation' of BRI projects, regions also offer another dimension of internalisation. How do regional actors utilise and coopt the BRI projects for their benefit in the context of regional rivalry? The book selects the Middle East for regional analysis because of the intensity and significance of regional rivalry and the potential instability that the BRI might bring to the region. Mina Tadrous Milad Tadrous focuses on the three main rivalries that currently exist in the Middle East—Saudi Arabia versus Iran, Iraq versus Syria and Egypt versus Türkiye—and uses the features of China's investment patterns to examine whether BRI projects in the region have benefited both or just one of the actors in each of these relationships. He discusses the characteristics of the investments made so far and notes that implementation of the BRI has the potential to fuel existing conflicts, exacerbate instability in the region and foster antagonistic relationships because of China's investment preferences in relation to individual countries. The chapter provides a useful perspective on how the BRI is incorporated into a regional balance of power, as well as power relations within nations.

Finally, Chapter 11 summarises how all these analyses provide answers to the book's overarching questions and examines the implications of the BRI for global and domestic governance and the possible implications for Japan.

References

Asian Development Bank (ADB). 2019. 'ADB and AIIB Presidents Discuss Strategic and Operational Issues.' News release, 21 March. Manila: ADB. www.adb.org/news/adb-and-aiib-presidents-discuss-strategic-and-operational-issues.

Brautigam, Deborah. 2011. *The Dragon's Gift: The Real Story of China in Africa.* New York: Oxford University Press.

Breslin, Shaun. 2020. 'China in 2019: Party for the Party.' *Asian Survey* 60, no. 1: 21–33. doi.org/10.1525/as.2020.60.1.21.

Central Committee of the Communist Party of China and State Council. 2015. *Zhonggongzhongyang, guowuyuan guanyu jianshe kaifangxing jingji xintizhi de ruogan yijian* [*Several Opinions of the Central Committee of the Communist Party of China and the State Council on Building an Open New Economic System*]. 5 May. Retrieved from ChinaLawInfo database.

China News Service. 2020. 'Zhongguo yiyu 138ge guojia he 30 ge guoji zuzhi qianshu gongjian "yidaiyilu" hezuo wenjian [China Has Signed Cooperation Documents with 138 Countries and 30 International Organisations to Jointly Build the "Belt and Road"].' *China News Service*, 9 October. fec.mofcom.gov.cn/article/fwydyl/zgzx/202010/20201003006299.shtml [Page discontinued].

Cohen, Paul A. 1988. *Discovering History in China: American Historical Writing on the Recent Chinese Past.* New York: Columbia University Press.

Garlick, Jeremy. 2019. *The Impact of China's Belt and Road Initiative: From Asia to Europe*. London: Routledge. doi.org/10.4324/9781351182768.

Gu, Xiaoyu. 2015. *Quanguo renmin daibiao dahui changwu weiyuanhui bangongshi guanyu dishierjie quanguo renmin daibiao dahui disanci huiyi daibiao jianyi, piping he yijian banli qingkuang de baogao* [*Report of the Office of the Standing Committee of the National People's Congress on the Handling of Suggestions, Criticisms, and Opinions of Representatives at the Third Session of the 12th National People's Congress*]. 24 December. Retrieved from ChinaLawInfo database.

Hielscher, Lisa, and Sebastian Ibold. n.d. *Belt and Road Initiative*. www.beltroad-initiative.com/belt-and-road.

Hillman, Jonathan E. 2018. 'How Big Is China's Belt and Road?' *Commentary*, 3 April. Washington, DC: Center for Strategic and International Studies. www.csis.org/analysis/how-big-chinas-belt-and-road.

Hirono, Miwa. 2019. 'Asymmetrical Rivalry between China and Japan in Africa: To What Extent Has Sino-Japan Rivalry Become a Global Phenomenon?' *The Pacific Review* 32, no. 5: 831–62. doi.org/10.1080/09512748.2019.1569118.

Jakobson, Linda, and Dean Knox. 2010. *New Foreign Policy Actors in China*. SIPRI Policy Paper 26, September. Solna: Stockholm International Peace Research Institute. www.sipri.org/publications/2010/sipri-policy-papers/new-foreign-policy-actors-china.

Kan, Shiyū. 2015. *Ugokidashita 'ittai ichiro' kōsō: Chūgoku ban māsharu puran no jitsugen ni mukete* [*'Belt and Road Initiative' Began Its Work: Towards the Realization of Chinese Version of Marshall Plan*]. Paper, 8 April. Tokyo: Dokuritsu gyōsei hōjin keizai sangyō kenkyūsho [Research Institute of Economy, Trade and Industry].

Lam, Willy Wo-lap. 2016. 'Getting Lost in "One Belt, One Road".' *Ejinsight*, 12 April. www.ejinsight.com/20160412-getting-lost-one-belt-one-road [Page discontinued].

Lieberthal, Kenneth G., and David G. Lampton. 1992. *Bureaucracy, Politics, and Decision Making in Post-Mao China*. Berkeley: University of California Press.

Luft, Gal. 2016. *It Takes a Road: China's One Belt One Road Initiative—An American Response to the New Silk Road*. November. Gaithersburg: Institute for the Analysis of Global Security. www.iags.org/Luft_BRI.pdf.

Mertha, Andrew. 2009. '"Fragmented Authoritarianism 2.0": Political Pluralization in the Chinese Policy Process.' *The China Quarterly*, no. 200 (December): 995–1012. www.jstor.org/stable/27756540. doi.org/10.1017/S0305741009990592.

National Development and Reform Commission (NDRC), Ministry of Foreign Affairs and Ministry of Commerce. 2015. 'Tuidong gongjian sichouzhilujingjidai he 21shijihaishangsichouzhilu de yuanjing yu xingdong [Vision and Actions on Jointly Building the Silk Road Economic Belt and the 21st Century Maritime Silk Road].' 'Yidaiyilu' guoji hezuo gaofeng luntan [Belt and Road Forum for International Cooperation], Beijing, March 2015. policy.asiapacificenergy.org/sites/default/files/Vision%20and%20Actions%20on%20Jointly%20Building%20Silk%20Road%20Economic%20Belt%20and%2021st-Century%20Maritime%20Silk%20Road%20%28EN%29.pdf.

National Development and Reform Commission (NDRC) Western Division. 2015. 'Yidaiyilu zhongyu youle guanfang yingyi: jiancheng "B&R" ["Belt and Road" Finally Has an Official English Translation: "B&R" for Short].' *Guancha*, 24 September. www.guancha.cn/politics/2015_09_24_335434.shtml.

Sano, Junya. 2017. 'Ittai ichiro no shinten de kawaru Chugoku to ensen shokoku tono keizai kankei [Economic Relations between China and Countries on the Belt and Road Routes That Change as the BRI Advances].' *JRI Rebyu* [*JRI Review*] 4, no. 43: 24–39. www.jri.co.jp/MediaLibrary/file/report/jrireview/pdf/9832.pdf.

State Council Information Office (SCIO). 2023. 'BRI Mobilises US$1T in Investment, Lifts 40M People Out of Poverty.' News release, 1 November. Beijing: State Council Information Office of the People's Republic of China. english.scio.gov.cn/m/pressroom/2023-11/01/content_116787821.htm#:~:text=Since%20the%20launch%20of%20the,China%20International%20Development%20Cooperation%20Agency.

Takahara, Akio. 2018. 'Ittai ichiro kōsō ha "seiza": Kadona kitai ha kinmotsu [Belt and Road Initiative Is a Constellation: One Should Not Expect Too Much].' *Shūkan Toyo keizai Plus* [*Weekly Toyo Keizai Plus*], 27 January. premium.toyokeizai.net/articles/-/17364.

Tang, Wei. 2009. 'Xushanda pao zhongguoban "maxieer jihua" 5000 yi meiyuan touxiang yafeila jie zhongguo kunju [Xu Shanda Throws a Chinese Version of the "Marshall Plan" 500 Billion US Dollars into Asia, Africa and Latin America to Solve China's Predicament].' *China Times*, 7 August. www.chinatimes.net.cn/article/6769.html.

World Bank. 2016. 'World Bank and AIIB Sign First Co-Financing Framework Agreement.' News release, 13 April. Washington, DC: World Bank Group. www.worldbank.org/en/news/press-release/2016/04/13/world-bank-and-aiib-sign-first-co-financing-framework-agreement.

Wu, Lejun and Han Bao. 2024. '150 duoge guojia, 30 duoge guoji zuzhi gongtong canyu gaozhiliang gongjian "yidai yilu" zhashi tuijin (fenjin qiangguo lu kuobu xin zhengcheng) [More than 150 Countries and over 30 International Organizations are Jointly Participating in the High-Quality Co-Construction of the "Belt and Road Initiative", Making Solid Progress (Striving on the Path to a Strong Nation, Taking Big Strides on a New Journey)].' *Renmin Wang*, 9 October. politics.people. com.cn/n1/2024/1009/c459405-40335200.html.

Xi, Jinping. 2013a. 'Xi Jinping zai nazhaerbayefudaxue de yanjiang [Chinese President Xi Jinping's Lecture at Nazarbayev University].' Speech, 7 September. Beijing: Ministry of Foreign Affairs of the People's Republic of China. www. fmprc.gov.cn/web/ziliao_674904/zt_674979/dnzt_674981/qtzt/ydyl_675049/ zyxw_675051/t1074151.shtml [Page discontinued].

Xi, Jinping. 2013b. 'Working Together to Build a China—ASEAN Community with a Shared Future: Speech at the Indonesian Parliament, Jakarta, 3 October.' Beijing: Ministry of Foreign Affairs of the People's Republic of China. www.gov. cn/ldhd/2013-10/03/content_2500118.htm.

Xi, Jinping. 2019. 'Working Together to Deliver a Brighter Future for Belt and Road Cooperation: Keynote Speech at the Opening Ceremony of the Second Belt and Road Forum for International Cooperation.' *China Daily*, 26 April. www. chinadaily.com.cn/a/201904/26/WS5d9c5a05a310cf3e3556f38b.html.

Xinhua. 2014. 'Zhongguo gongchandang dishibajie Zhongyang weiyuanhui disici quanti huiyi gongbao [Communiqué of the Fourth Plenary Session of the Eighteenth CPC Central Committee].' *Xinhua*, 23 October. cpc.people.com. cn/n/2014/1023/c64094-25896724.html.

Xinhua. 2019. 'Zhongguo qiye dui "yidaiyilu" yanxian guojia touzi leiji chao 1000 yi meiyuan [Chinese Companies' Cumulative Investment in Countries along the "Belt and Road Initiative" Exceeds US\$100 Billion].' *Xinhua*, 30 September. www.gov.cn/xinwen/2019-09/30/content_5435149.htm.

Yang, Jing. 2014. *Guowuyuan guanyu shenhua xingzheng shenpi zhidu gaige jiakuai zhengfu zhineng zhuanbian gongzuo qingkuang de baogao* [*Report of the State Council on Deepening the Reform of the Administrative Approval System and Accelerating the Transformation of Government Functions*]. 27 August. Retrieved from ChinaLawInfo database.

Part I: The challenges of the BRI—Implications for global and domestic governance and Japan

2

The BRI and its implications for global and domestic governance

Kenki Adachi[1]

Introduction

Since President of China Xi Jinping proposed the Belt and Road Initiative (BRI) in 2013, there has been much debate about how it should be evaluated. The BRI is essentially a plan to increase global connectivity and boost the economy by promoting investment and the construction of public infrastructure. However, as Miwa Hirono (Chapter 1) points out, the BRI also seeks to deepen cooperation between the countries involved in the initiative, not only in terms of logistics and trade, but also in areas such as finance, politics and public research. This means that the BRI can be understood as a policy package that aims to expand China's influence in the international community beyond direct investment, encompassing a full range of political, economic, military and soft-power policies. One trillion dollars has been invested in the BRI since 2013 (SCIO 2023), which has been received with both anticipation and caution due to the sheer scale of the investment and the broad geographical and policy reach of the initiative.

1   The research used in this chapter was supported by JSPS Grant-in-Aid for Scientific Research JP22K01367 and JP23H00792.

Concerns and warnings about the BRI can be broadly divided into two types: concern about its impact on the state of the global order, or *global governance*; and concern about its impact on the political stability of the countries participating in the BRI, or *domestic governance*. The concern about its impact on global governance is that the BRI will challenge the liberal international order that has been established by the West. This refers to the US-led post–World War II order, based on open economies, multilateral organisations, security cooperation and liberal democracy (Ikenberry 2018a: 7). The second concern is that the BRI will make the domestic political governance of each country less transparent, thereby promoting corruption and reducing the quality of governance. In other words, analysts are worried that the BRI will upset the liberal values–based order at both the global and the national levels. Leaving aside the (possible) intentions behind the BRI, it is necessary to consider whether its projects have any impact on the way global and domestic governance is conducted.

Governance at the global level

First, let us review global governance in relation to the concept of governance. The debate about global governance focuses on how to achieve a state of order in a world where there is no global government. The end of the Cold War and the accelerating pace of globalisation have led to the emergence of several urgent global issues that cannot be addressed by one country alone. Hence, the increasing attention on the concept of global governance, which considers how to shape and maintain the global order by including not only national governments, but also global actors such as international institutions (for example, the United Nations and the World Health Organization), multinational corporations and nongovernmental organisations (NGOs).

The Commission on Global Governance defines global governance as 'the sum of the many ways individuals and institutions, public and private, manage their common affairs' (Shridath and Carlsson 1995). The concept of global governance provides a more comprehensive understanding of the formation and maintenance of order, which has been proposed given the reality of accelerating globalisation and the increasing capacity of nonstate actors to be involved. Global governance as a concept attempts to capture the reality that a variety of actors are increasingly involved in the management and administration of global affairs. However, even if several initiatives exist in a particular area of contention, it is difficult to say that 'order' is being formed and maintained in that area if these initiatives do not share underlying principles and norms or if there is overlap between several initiatives that are mutually contradictory and in opposition to each other. Therefore, this chapter defines global governance as 'the way in which various actors manage and administer a common set of global issues in a variety of ways under a set of principles' (Adachi 2011: 9).

In the absence of a central government, the international community has always been sensitive to the question of how to form and maintain order through the cooperation (and competition) of diverse actors. This problem is not limited to the global order and includes the creation and maintenance of national and local order. These factors lie behind the gradual development of a theory of governance that is not limited to global issues—one that increasingly considers how different actors, whether at the global, regional or national level, can be involved in the formation and maintenance of order.

The dominant view in the debate on global governance has been that of a liberal international order based on liberal democracy and open economies, shaped and maintained by collaboration between diverse actors. The Commission on Global Governance was a leading advocate of this view. In fact, a variety of actors, including Western countries, international organisations and NGOs, have attempted to form and maintain a global order based on shared liberal values. Similarly, in the debate on domestic governance, since 2000, there has been an increasing emphasis on the importance of liberal democracy, the rule of law, public participation, and transparency and accountability in the formation and maintenance of order. Western countries and international organisations have tried to promote domestic governance based on liberal values by imposing conditions for the implementation of such practices whenever they provide aid (Goldsmith 2007: 165).[2]

---

2   A state of governance based on liberal values is called good governance. This expression also suggests the normative aspect of the desirability of governance based on these values. Although in relation to the principle of non-interference in the internal affairs of countries it was prohibited to interfere in the national governance of other countries, the Millennium Declaration of 2000 clearly stated that the achievement of the Millennium Development Goals would depend on the good governance of countries (OHCHR 2000: para. 13). There has since been widespread agreement that good governance (that is, national governance based on liberal values) is necessary for development assistance to work. See Goldsmith (2007).

The BRI and the global order

Does the BRI have any impact on global governance based on liberal principles or on the governance of individual countries? The BRI concept itself is elusive, but it is distinctive in its emphasis on increased connectivity. At the same time, it is unclear what principles and norms it is based on or what kind of order it seeks to create. Increasing connectivity and stimulating the economy do not in themselves necessarily conflict with an order based on liberal principles. It is not an attempt to deny liberal democracy or to close the open economy. On the contrary, improved connectivity could reinvigorate open economies and strengthen the liberal international order.

Why, then, are there fears that the BRI will upset global governance as it currently operates? One reason may be the suspicion that, because China does not itself share the West's liberal values, the BRI as promoted by China does not share these values either. This is exemplified, for example, by the perception in the National Security Strategy published by the US Trump administration that China wants 'to shape a world antithetical to US values and interests' (The White House 2017: 25). But even if China does not share liberal values, it does not necessarily follow that the BRI projects it promotes will upset the liberal international order, even less so if the initiative itself does not have illiberal principles embedded in it.

China has also been a beneficiary of the liberal international order—in particular, it has reaped many economic benefits from an open economy. Since the 1990s, China has been proclaiming slogans such as the 'New International Political and Economic Order' and 'New International Order', but these mostly emphasise that China has no intention of challenging the existing international order and underline the importance of the United Nations (Zhang 2018: 324). At the very least, such slogans do not oppose the key principles of liberal governance, such as an open economy, multilateralism and democracy. Hence, it has been argued that with its own economic development, China has come to embrace 'much of the current constellation of international institutions, rules, and norms as a means to promote its national interests' (Medeiros and Fravel 2003: 22). Many believe that for the foreseeable future, China intends to remain within the current international system (for example, Ikenberry 2018b). Despite the understandable wariness about the BRI, it is necessary to examine empirically how the promotion of related projects is (or is not) shaking the principles of an open economy, multilateralism and liberal democracy.

The BRI and domestic politics

There is a persistent view that the BRI and the projects within it may not *directly* threaten the global order, but they do pose an *indirect* threat. In other words, BRI projects may damage liberal elements of governance in the countries involved and thus undermine the global liberal order.

In some respects, BRI projects are 'perceived to be faster, more responsive to the needs of local elites, and have fewer conditions attached' than development aid from traditional development partners (Rajah et al. 2019: 5). This could increase China's attractiveness as a development assistance partner in many countries struggling to finance infrastructure development. Clearly, funding that does not impose conditions regarding corruption, human rights or financial sustainability could accelerate corruption in the countries borrowing these funds. Excessive borrowing could result in non-repayment. It has also been argued that the BRI is an attempt to influence the borrowing countries by placing them in debt (Parker and Chefitz 2018). Such was the case when former US secretary of state Mike Pompeo said that 'China peddles corrupt infrastructure deals in exchange for political influence' and its 'bribe-fueled dept-trap diplomacy undermines good governance and upends the free-market economic model' (US Department of State 2019). Concerns about the negative impact of the BRI on the countries involved were heightened when examples of what appears to be a classic 'debt trap' were highlighted, such as the Hambantota Port project in Sri Lanka.[3]

However, there are indications that only eight of the countries involved in the BRI have significantly high debt repayment risks (Hurley et al. 2018).[4] Lending beyond the ability to repay is a major risk for both the borrower and the lender. Therefore, no matter how geopolitically important a project may be in a country, it is not easy for either the borrower or the lender to initiate such a project. It is also important to note that the case of Hambantota Port has led to a better understanding on the part of borrowing countries of the risks associated with the BRI, which imposes few conditions on lending (Balding 2018).

---

3   However, it is necessary to look at the actual impact of the BRI on Sri Lanka in a dispassionate way. For such a discussion, see, for example, Inada (2019).

4   The eight countries identified as being at high risk of debt non-repayment are Djibouti, Kyrgyzstan, Laos, the Maldives, Mongolia, Montenegro, Pakistan and Tajikistan.

The fact that there are very few standards or conditions for receiving BRI loans does not necessarily encourage corruption and human rights abuses in borrowing countries. Of course, lenders have a responsibility to ensure that the funds are not used in undesirable ways or for undesirable purposes. Nevertheless, whether human rights abuses and corruption are fostered in the country to which the funds are channelled is essentially a matter for that country. Indeed, it is not uncommon for citizens of those countries that have received loans with few conditions to demand transparency from their government to prevent corruption and abuse. In Malaysia, the May 2018 elections were won by the League of Hope led by Mahathir Mohamad, who pledged to conduct in-depth investigations into major projects funded by foreign countries as one of his election promises. Subsequently, a review of all BRI projects was conducted and three major projects were cancelled (Berger 2018). Other countries, such as Kenya, Zambia, Pakistan and the Maldives, have also seen increased domestic scrutiny and evaluation of projects. In some cases, 'with Chinese lenders unwilling to demand accountability, voters are doing it for them' (Balding 2018).

It is therefore important to look not at how the BRI itself affects domestic politics in each country, but rather at how the BRI has become a domestic political issue in countries where it is being implemented. This is why the analysis of country cases in this volume focuses on the domestication of BRI projects. However, it is only in countries where there is a degree of democratic control over government that one can say, 'with Chinese lenders unwilling to demand accountability, voters are doing it for them'. In autocratic or authoritarian countries, such control is less effective, and it is therefore more likely that the BRI projects will proceed without scrutiny or monitoring. This could encourage corruption and human rights abuses, and lead to more authoritarian tendencies. Alternatively, it could lead to a 'debt trap' and increase China's influence in domestic politics. As a result, it is possible that the BRI could lead to the expansion of an 'illiberal Chinese sphere of influence' (for example, Ratner 2018). In recent years, which have seen the retreat of democracy and the return of authoritarianism in many parts of the world (Diamond 2015; Kawanaka 2018), this aspect may be one of the reasons there are more doubts than before about the BRI.

Conclusion

As outlined in this chapter, concerns about the BRI are at present largely impressionistic. Global governance is unlikely to be directly affected by the BRI, but it is likely to affect domestic governance in various ways. How it does will depend more on the way that countries promoting the BRI turn the project into a domestic issue than on the impact of the BRI itself. That is why this book empirically explores how the projects of the BRI have become domestic issues in the countries involved. The final chapter, based on an analysis of the empirical chapters, provides some observations on how the BRI projects are affecting the national governance of the countries concerned and, consequently, whether they are having any impact on global governance as well.

References

Adachi, Kenki. 2011. *Rejīmu kan sōgosayō to gurōbaru gabanansu* [*Institutional Interplay and Global Governance*]. Tokyo: Yūshindō.

Balding, Christopher. 2018. 'Why Democracies Are Turning against Belt and Road: Corruption, Debt, and Backlash.' *Foreign Affairs*, 24 October. www.foreignaffairs.com/articles/china/2018-10-24/why-democracies-are-turning-against-belt-and-road.

Berger, Blake H. 2018. 'Malaysia's Canceled Belt and Road Initiative Projects and the Implications for China.' *The Diplomat*, 27 August. thediplomat.com/2018/08/malaysias-canceled-belt-and-road-initiative-projects-and-the-implications-for-china/.

Diamond, Larry. 2015. 'Facing Up to the Democratic Recession.' *Journal of Democracy* 26, no. 1: 141–55. doi.org/10.1353/jod.2015.0009.

Goldsmith, Arthur A. 2007. 'Is Governance Reform a Catalyst for Development?' *Governance: An International Journal of Policy, Administration, and Institutions* 20, no. 2: 165–86. doi.org/10.1111/j.1468-0491.2007.00352.x.

Hurley, John, Scott Morris, and Gailyn Portelance. 2018. *Examining the Debt Implications of the Belt and Road Initiative from a Policy Perspective*. CGD Policy Paper 121 (March). Washington, DC: Center for Global Development. www.cgdev.org/sites/default/files/examining-debt-implications-belt-and-road-initiative-policy-perspective.pdf. doi.org/10.24294/jipd.v3i1.1123.

Ikenberry, John G. 2018a. 'The End of Liberal International Order?' *International Affairs* 94, no. 1: 7–23. doi.org/10.1093/ia/iix241.

Ikenberry, John G. 2018b. 'A New Order of Things? China, America and the Struggle over World Order.' In *Will China's Rise Be Peaceful? Security, Stability, and Legitimacy*, edited by Asle Toje, 68–95. New York: Oxford University Press.

Inada, Jyūichi. 2019. 'Chūgoku no ittai ichiro jigyō no suriranka he no inpakuto to sono hyōka [The Impact of China's "Belt and Road" Project on Sri Lanka: An Evaluation].' In *Senshū daigaku shakaikagaku kenkyūjo geppō [Monthly Report of the Institute of Social Science]*, 675–76. Tokyo: Senshu University.

Kawanaka, Takeshi. 2018. *Kōtaisuru minshushugi, kyōkasareru kenishugi [Democracy in Retreat, Authoritarianism on the Rise]*. Kyoto: Minerva Shobō.

Medeiros, Evan S., and Taylor M. Fravel. 2003. 'China's New Diplomacy.' *Foreign Affairs* 82, no. 6: 22–35. doi.org/10.2307/20033754.

Office of the High Commissioner for Human Rights (OHCHR). 2000. *United Nations Millennium Declaration*. Adopted 8 September. General Assembly Resolution 55/2. New York: OHCHR. www.ohchr.org/en/instruments-mechanisms/instruments/united-nations-millennium-declaration.

Parker, Sam, and Gabrielle Chefitz. 2018. *Debtbook Diplomacy: China's Strategic Leveraging of Its Newfound Economic Influence and the Consequences for U.S. Foreign Policy*. Paper, 24 May. Cambridge: Belfer Center for Science and International Affairs, Harvard Kennedy School. www.belfercenter.org/publication/debtbook-diplomacy.

Rajah, Roland, Alexandre Dayant, and Jonathan Pryke. 2019. 'Ocean of Debt? Belt and Road and Debt Diplomacy in the Pacific.' *Lowy Institute Analysis*: 1–30.

Ratner, Ely. 2018. 'There Is No Grand Bargain with China: Why Trump and Xi Can't Meet Each Other Halfway.' *Foreign Affairs*, 27 November. www.foreignaffairs.com/articles/china/2018-11-27/there-no-grand-bargain-china.

Shridath, Ramphal S., and Ingvar Carlsson. 1995. *Our Global Neighborhood: The Report of the Commission on Global Governance*. Oxford: Oxford University Press.

State Council Information Office (SCIO). 2023. 'BRI Mobilises US$1T in Investment, Lifts 40M People Out of Poverty.' News release, 1 November. Beijing: State Council Information Office of the People's Republic of China. english.scio.gov.cn/m/pressroom/2023-11/01/content_116787821.htm#:~:text=Since%20the%20launch%20of%20the,China%20International%20Development%20Cooperation%20Agency.

The White House. 2017. *National Security Strategy of the United States of America*. December. Washington, DC: The White House. trumpwhitehouse.archives.gov/wp-content/uploads/2017/12/NSS-Final-12-18-2017-0905.pdf.

US Department of State. 2019. 'Press Availability with British Foreign Secretary Jeremy Hunt: Remarks to the Press.' UK Foreign and Commonwealth Office, London, 8 May. 2017-2021. 2017-2021.state.gov/press-availability-with-british-foreign-secretary-jeremy-hunt/.

Zhang, Ruizhuang. 2018. 'Despite the "New Assertiveness", China Is Not up for Challenging the Global Order.' In *Will China's Rise Be Peaceful? Security, Stability, and Legitimacy*, edited by Asle Toje, 309–24. New York: Oxford University Press. doi.org/10.1093/oso/9780190675387.003.0012.

3

The BRI under China's 'planned diplomacy': Sino-Russian relations and China–Central and Eastern Europe relations

Rumi Aoyama

Introduction: 'Planning' and 'decentralisation and fragmentation' within the BRI

The Belt and Road Initiative (BRI) is a foreign policy initiative of China's Xi Jinping administration. Through it, China aims to expand its sphere of influence within the international community through cooperation with the countries involved in respect of logistics, trade, finance, politics and public research. In other words, the BRI is a policy package that encompasses the full range of political, economic, military and soft-power policies.

Various studies have already been published on the BRI, which is President Xi's signature foreign policy strategy. Generally, it is perceived as a top-down policymaking strategy through which China aims to solve several structural problems in its own economy and to gain influence internationally (Wang 2012; Lai 2020). Nonetheless, an increasing number of studies have instead highlighted the fact that the BRI is merely a policy mobilisation vehicle for the central government and not a well-thought-out national strategy at all. These studies focus on the 'decentralisation and fragmentation' aspects of China's policymaking since the 1980s and argue that the BRI is not particularly coherent as a strategy (He 2019; Jones and Zeng 2019; Ye 2019).

In the context of the foreign policymaking process under Xi Jinping, the perception that the BRI is a top-down strategy and that it has a 'policy mobilisation' aspect is reasonable. On the one hand, decentralisation and fragmentation have been major features of China's foreign policymaking since the 1980s, with ministries, state-owned enterprises (SOEs) and local governments independently interpreting central government policy and implementing their own foreign policies in competition with one another. This trend has continued under President Xi and, consequently, not all the policies related to the BRI are necessarily aimed in the same direction. On the other hand, given that China is a one-party state, new policies are always integrated into state planning. Nor has the central government loosened its control over the key sectors and basic industries that underpin the nation's politics and economy. As Mark Wu (2016) has pointed out, China is indeed a massive 'state-led corporatist regime'.

Since the start of Xi's presidency, China's political society has undergone a major structural change known as the 'Third Revolution' (Economy 2018) and has seen a rapid increase in centralisation. As will be argued here, there has also been a move towards centralisation in foreign affairs, with the central government increasing its control over the various actors involved in foreign policy. The central government 'sets policy in a top-down manner with a comprehensive view of all elements and implementation processes' (*dingceng sheji*, 'top-level design') (People's China 2013). Under Xi, as the importance of top-level design is emphasised, the central government's intentions are strongly reflected in the implementation process of the BRI (Aoyama 2022).

Consequently, two key (though contradictory) elements of the BRI must be considered: 'planning' and 'decentralisation and fragmentation'. We must therefore ask how BRI planning is carried out under President Xi and to what extent local governments are involved because of decentralisation and fragmentation. To shed some light on these issues, the chapter first analyses the trend towards centralisation under Xi Jinping and considers what measures have been adopted to ensure that the policies of the central government are implemented. It then examines the impact of the twin elements of planning and decentralisation/fragmentation on the policy direction of the BRI, taking as examples the Sino-Russian relationship, which has become an important pillar of the BRI, and the relationship between China and Central and Eastern European countries (CEEC). On this basis, it will be possible to elucidate the role of both the central and local governments in China's policymaking process.

From decentralisation to centralisation

Throughout the period from the adoption of reforms and China's opening-up policy in 1978 to former president Hu Jintao's regime of collective leadership from 2002 to 2012, the most significant features of policymaking in China have been the concentration of political power and the sharing of decision-making power (Aoyama 2013). The party-state system has given the CPC tremendous power, but at the policy level, its power has been decentralised to the ministries and local governments that both make and implement government policy. Under this 'fragmented authoritarian regime', various actors such as local governments and SOEs have emerged as foreign policy participants, making it difficult for foreign policy coordination to function effectively (Jakobson and Knox 2011).

In 2006, under Hu Jintao, the Central Conference on Work Related to Foreign Affairs was a national event. At the time, it was regarded as one of the most important meetings on foreign affairs since the 1990s and was widely reported on in China. The central topic of the meeting was a discussion about strategic planning and uniform implementation of foreign relations, and all organisations involved in foreign policy were called on to ensure that foreign policies at the local level were implemented in accordance with the strategy set at the central level. However, despite calls by the Hu administration for upper-level strategic planning and uniformity in policy implementation, the situation whereby 'policies formulated in Zhongnanhai never leave Zhongnanhai [*Zhengling bu chu Zhongnanhai*]' had not improved. Against this backdrop, voices advocating the importance of top-level design continued to grow.

Since Xi Jinping came to power in late 2012, sweeping reforms have been undertaken to ensure the absolute authority of the CPC's Central Committee in policymaking, policy execution and resource allocation (Yang 2013). To eliminate the negative effects of decentralisation and fragmentation, such as the central government's policies not being implemented at the grassroots level or fierce competition among the relevant ministries and local governments that care only about their own interests, Xi Jinping's leadership has moved towards centralisation. This has led to a situation of 'planned diplomacy' in foreign relations.

This chapter defines planned diplomacy as a way of promoting foreign policy whereby the central leadership formulates strategy from a broad perspective and allocates resources strategically and the relevant domestic ministries and local governments then strictly implement that strategy. In promoting planned diplomacy, Xi's administration has advanced two main reforms. One is to ensure that all actors involved in foreign policy implementation act according to the top-level design. The other is to enforce policy coordination among the relevant organisations.

A series of moves to increase the absolute authority of the CPC's Central Committee in determining, executing and allocating resources for foreign policy began to take shape in 2012, with a range of measures taken to ensure that 'the party is in control of foreign relations [*dang guan waishi*]'. At the Eighteenth National Congress of the CPC in November 2012, it was proposed to 'defend the authority of the Party's Central Committee and strengthen the unified leadership of the [party] in foreign policy'. The first and second Five-Year Plans on the formulation of internal party regulations explicitly stipulated that the party would 'rectify internal Party regulations on foreign policy in order to strengthen the Party's leadership' (Xinhua 2013).

To consolidate the leadership of the CPC, Xi's administration has further empowered party committees and tightened the central leadership's control over them. In January 2019, Qi Yu, deputy minister of the CPC Committee of the Central Organisation Department, was appointed party secretary of the CPC Committee of the Ministry of Foreign Affairs (MoFA). In May, Zhang Ji, a former member of the Ministry of Commerce, a member of the CPC's Central Commission for Discipline Inspection and head of MoFA's Discipline Prosecution Team, also became a member of that ministry's party committee. This process was repeated in other ministries and local governments, whereby everything to do with foreign affairs was placed under the jurisdiction of the CPC Central Committee, and a new Party Committee Leading Group on Foreign Affairs was established to strengthen the party's authority in this key policy area.

To ensure that the central government's policies are implemented appropriately across the different organisations involved in foreign relations, the MoFA has given lectures and presentations by senior officials at the national level, the main purpose of which is to familiarise the public with the conduct of foreign affairs, to explain the central government's perspective on the international situation and set out the foreign policy it has formulated. Senior MoFA officials visit other ministries, major SOEs, universities, local party schools and local governments to make presentations, and it is the responsibility of all the individuals and organisations who attend the lectures to ensure they have a correct understanding of the central government's strategy and use their own diplomatic resources to serve that strategy.

Coordination among the various organisations has been facilitated through the implementation of a system of regular meetings, resource-sharing mechanisms and event co-hosting between ministries and local governments and between the foreign affairs offices within local governments. For example, in May 2018, the foreign affairs offices of the three municipalities and provinces of Beijing, Tianjin and Hebei signed an MoU on cooperation mechanisms and agreed to meet regularly, cooperate on important national projects and events, jointly train new cadres and establish a liaison mechanism for emergencies (Li 2018). Similar coordination mechanisms have been established in other provinces and cities. Through these, Xi's regime is trying to share diplomatic resources and strengthen the coordination function among the relevant organisations.

In addition, the training of cadres in foreign relations who can adhere to the party's discipline is also promoted under the guidance of the MoFA, which set up the China Diplomatic Academy in March 2016 under its jurisdiction. State Councillor Yang Jiechi made a speech at the opening ceremony, emphasising the political direction of the institute and the discipline of the cadres it trains (Wang 2016).

Thus, since the start of the Xi Jinping regime, there has been a move towards centralisation of foreign relations. The regime has formulated the party's internal regulations and policy documents that clearly state the CPC's absolute power over foreign affairs and has strengthened the authority of the Central Party Committees within each organisation over foreign relations. Efforts have also been made to counter the negative effects of decentralisation and fragmentation, to ensure the implementation of policies emanating from the centre and to strengthen the coordination function between the various organisations in respect of foreign relations, in which the MoFA plays a central role. In this way, in terms of moving from decentralisation to centralisation, a mechanism has been established whereby the central government formulates foreign policy and allocates resources effectively, but the organisations involved in foreign relations also ensure that the central government's policy is implemented and that coordination is achieved between them.

In the context of this planned diplomacy, state capitalism in China[1] has become more pronounced. In a system in which local governments are involved in the central government's foreign policy strategy and are expected to ensure their policies are always implemented in accordance with the central government's plans, the role of the MoFA as coordinator is becoming increasingly important. Under Xi Jinping, MoFA has been holding events to introduce China's provinces to the international community and promote local exports. Between 2016 and July 2019, it carried out promotional activities for 19 provinces. In addition, MoFA plays a coordinating role in the foreign relations of provincial cities. To promote cooperation between Guangxi and the Shanghai Cooperation Organisation, especially with Russia and India, an international medical innovation cooperation forum was held in Guangxi in May 2019. Under MoFA's leadership, about 20 major Chinese financial and medical enterprises participated in the forum. Thus, in external relations, new cooperative relationships have been established between MoFA, other ministries, SOEs and local governments.

Just as the role of the MoFA has become far more important in the process of centralisation, China's other major external relations organisation, the International Liaison Department of the CPC, is likewise playing an important role in the process of strengthening party leadership. While the MoFA oversees the foreign relations machinery, the International Liaison Department is responsible for party propaganda, promoting President Xi's blueprint and the CPC's governance experience through party diplomacy and promoting the party's story at the local level.

---

1   State capitalism is a form of capitalism driven by the state, where the state takes the lead in all economic activity (see 'State Capitalism' in the *Digital Daijisen Dictionary*, at: kotobank.jp/word/%E5%9 B%BD%E5%AE%B6%E8%B3%87%E6%9C%AC%E4%B8%BB%E7%BE%A9-502389).

Sino-Russian relations driven by planned diplomacy

As the trend towards greater confrontation between the United States and China becomes more pronounced, it has become increasingly important for China to strengthen its relations with Russia. Equally, since the Russian annexation of the Crimean Peninsula from Ukraine in 2014, which has led to deteriorating relations with Western countries, Russia has been keen to improve its relations with China.

In recent years, Sino-Russian relations have become much closer. President Xi explicitly praised the good relations between the two countries, saying they 'have the greatest trust, cooperation has reached the highest level, and they share the highest strategic values' (Xinhua 2019). In 2015, China and Russia signed a joint statement fostering cooperation between the China-led Silk Road Economic Belt and the Russia-led Eurasian Economic Union (EAEU). When the EAEU–China trade and economic cooperation agreement came into effect in October 2019, China lauded it by saying it 'laid the foundation for a free trade zone with the EAEU' (MofCOM 2019). The period 2020–21 was declared the 'Sino-Russian Year of Science and Technology Innovation' and, during former Chinese premier Li Keqiang's visit to Russia in September 2019, the two governments issued a joint statement to promote relations and signed several bilateral cooperation agreements in high-tech fields such as lunar and space exploration (Zheng 2019).

Today, the two countries cooperate not only on energy and infrastructure but also in a wide range of other areas such as data communications, e-commerce, space and Arctic development. Cooperation between China and Russia in the financial sector is also being promoted. The United States often imposes economic sanctions on other countries through the international interbank communications association known as the Society for Worldwide Interbank Financial Telecommunication (SWIFT) and, as the US–China standoff intensifies, China fears that US sanctions could cut Chinese banks out of SWIFT, making international remittances impossible. This has led to discussions in China about a gold-backed digital currency aimed at weakening the dominance of the US dollar and reducing risk (Xinhua 2019). As a result, China has begun promoting settlements in renminbi[2] when trading with other countries: in June 2019, China and Russia signed an agreement to denominate Sino-Russian trade in their respective currencies and to establish a renminbi international payment system, the Cross-Border Interbank Payment System,[3] and a Russian remittance network, the System for Transfer of Financial Messages, in an effort to circumvent the US-led SWIFT (Xinhua Finance 2019).

However, the two countries also face significant difficulties when it comes to promoting economic relations. Despite the enthusiasm of the two leaders, trade between China and Russia has been sluggish and the 'hot politics and cold economics' situation persists. To overcome this and further improve Sino-Russian relations, Xi Jinping's regime has devised two mechanisms for regional cooperation: the north-east and Far East regional cooperation mechanism and the Yangtze River–Volga regional cooperation mechanism.

The north-east and Far East regional cooperation mechanism emphasises cooperation between China's three north-eastern provinces and Russia's Primorsky Territory, focusing on agriculture, forestry, infrastructure and trade. Economic development of China's three north-eastern provinces is one of the key policy issues of the current regime, as exemplified by President Xi's visits to Liaoning in August 2013, Jilin in July 2015 and Heilongjiang, in both May 2016 and September 2018. In November 2016, the 'Opinions of the State Council on the Comprehensive Promotion of the Old Industrial Bases in the Three Northeastern Provinces' and the *Thirteenth Five-Year Plan for the Promotion of the Northeast* were promulgated. All these policies demonstrate a development strategy to promote the economy of the three north-eastern provinces under the framework of the BRI, combining regional development with the development strategy of the Russian Far East.

Based on this strategic plan, the revitalisation of the three north-eastern provinces is promoted through Sino-Russian cooperation. The Intergovernmental Cooperation Committee for the Northeast and Far East Regions held its first meetings in 2017. In April of that year, the fourth meeting of the Sino-Russian Intergovernmental Investment Cooperation Committee was held in Beijing, at which 73 priority development projects with a total value of USD100 billion were selected (Jin 2019). In November 2018, the 'China–Russia Cooperation and Development Plan in the Russian Far East (2018–2024)' and the 'Agricultural Cooperation Plan between

---

2   Oil trade between China and Russia has been settled in renminbi since 2015.
3   Which became operational in 2015.

Northeast China and the Russian Far East and Baikal Region' were publicly promulgated. Meanwhile, construction is underway for three border bridges (Heilongjiang Bridge, Heihe Bridge and Dongning Bridge), one island (Heixiazi Island), one road (Binhai No. 1 and No. 2) and one port (Vladivostok), which will connect Heilongjiang to the Far East. In other words, in its present stage, the regional cooperation mechanism for the north-east and Far East is being developed mainly through infrastructural facilities, although cooperation in agriculture and energy is regarded as important as well.

The Yangtze River–Volga regional cooperation mechanism was set up by the two governments during premier Li Keqiang's visit to Russia in 2013. The agreement involves six provinces and cities in the middle and upper reaches of the Yangtze River (Anhui, Jiangxi, Hubei, Chongqing, Sichuan and Wuhan) and 14 Russian federations, with the total gross domestic product (GDP) of the participating Chinese provinces and cities accounting for 22 per cent of national GDP. This regional cooperation mechanism is known as 'Non-Border Adjacent Sub-Regional Economic Cooperation' in China—a new form of international cooperation for promoting the BRI.

The first meeting of the Cooperation Council of the Russian Volga Federal District and the Middle and Upper Yangtze River Region was held in July 2016. At the second meeting in June 2017,[4] 21 priority projects for investment cooperation were selected, covering a wide range of sectors including agriculture, tourism and communications technology (Sheng 2019). The six provinces and cities in the middle and upper reaches of the Yangtze River had previously carried out only 7 per cent of their total trade with Russia (Jiang 2020), but through this mechanism, trade with Russia reached USD5 billion in 2018—an increase of 30 per cent compared with the previous year (Ma and Qiang 2019).

The Yangtze River–Volga Regional Cooperation Board meets regularly and a parallel forum for cooperation between universities has been organised in conjunction with these meetings. MoUs for cooperation have also been signed by local governments. For example, Jiangxi Province signed a full cooperation agreement with Russia's Perm region in 2014 and an MoU on deepening cooperation in September 2018. Such cooperation covers agriculture, aircraft manufacturing, renewable energy, forestry, tourism, education and youth exchanges (Liu et al. 2018).

---

4   The third meeting took place in May 2019.

To develop Sino-Russian trade and promote Sino-Russian relations over and above the two regional cooperation mechanisms, other Chinese local governments that are geographically distant from Russia have also been mobilised. The Chinese Government designated 2018 the 'Year of Regional Cooperation and Exchange between China and Russia' to encourage the development of cooperation at the local government level. In line with this policy, by the end of October 2017, 140 twinning agreements had been signed between Chinese and Russian cities, and many Chinese provinces had signed agreements with Russian local governments to strengthen economic and trade ties (Jin 2019). In July 2018, the first meeting of the Sino-Russian Regional Cooperation Forum was held in Yekaterinburg, Russia.

In terms of regional governments, the cooperation established between the Republic of Tatarstan and China is considered the most successful case. Among others, the refrigerator company Haier began trading in Tatarstan in 2016 and developed its brand successfully; it now holds one-quarter of the Russian market for refrigerators.

As already noted, the administration of Xi Jinping aims to utilise a combination of the north-eastern region (which borders Russia), the Yangtze River Basin (which does not) and local diplomacy to improve Sino-Russian relations, and it has set a goal of raising bilateral trade volumes to USD200 billion by 2024. As shown in Figure 3.1, thanks to the efforts of the two governments, the volume of trade between China and Russia already exceeds USD100 billion. In particular, the promotion of major projects in energy, nuclear power and aerospace technology by the two governments has contributed greatly to the growth of trade since 2017.

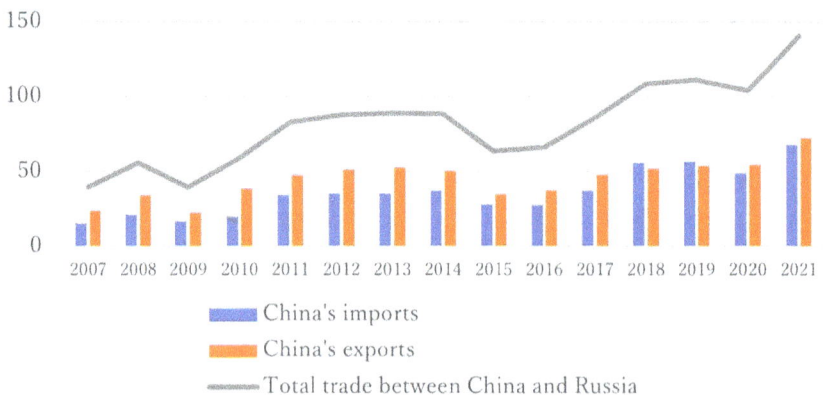

Figure 3.1 China–Russia trade (USD billion)
Source: Compiled by the author based on data from Statista.com.

In promoting Sino-Russian relations, Xi Jinping's regime attaches great importance to top-level design. Under the decentralised system of the Hu Jintao era, local governments exploited their individual geopolitical advantages to compete against one another in developing foreign relations, with the three north-eastern provinces emphasising exchanges with Russia, while Guangxi in the south and Yunnan in the south-east developed ties with ASEAN countries. However, under the new concept of 'subregional economic cooperation without adjacent borders', which led to the implementation of the Yangtze River–Volga regional cooperation mechanism, Chongqing is now regarded as an important BRI hub and occupies an important position in central policy by promoting exchanges with Russia and Central Asian countries. Consequently, the 2019 Shanghai Cooperation Organisation regional leaders' meeting was held in Chongqing. New external relations are being established by local governments very much in accordance with this central design.

The Yangtze River–Volga regional cooperation mechanism is not a bottom-up framework, but one planned by the central government. In the execution of such planned diplomacy, the division of labour among ministries and agencies has not changed significantly since the Hu administration. The point of contact for Sino-Russian negotiations is the MoFA (at the level of assistant foreign minister), with the NDRC and the State-Owned Assets Supervision and Administration Commission of the State Council also playing a leadership role. The Chinese Government has established a Sino-Russian regional cooperation and development investment fund with a total value of RMB100 billion (approximately USD14.5 billion), 10 per cent of which (RMB10 billion or approximately USD1.45 billion) will be released in the first phase (Consulate-General of the People's Republic of China in Vladivostok 2018). The fund will be managed by the China Development Bank (Lin 2018).

At the same time, the central–local relationship in the implementation of planned diplomacy has undergone a major change under Xi Jinping. Whereas the Ministry of Commerce used to coordinate international cooperation on economic matters, the MoFA is now taking the lead. In 2012, during the consultative stage of the Yangtze River–Volga regional cooperation mechanism, MoFA hosted a roundtable in Beijing between China and Russia. Likewise, it was the MoFA that signed the minutes of the first Yangtze River–Volga regional cooperation meeting in Chongqing in

February 2014. Subsequent meetings of the working groups on economic and trade cooperation and cultural exchanges were regularly attended by the deputy minister of foreign affairs.[5]

Nonetheless, the planned diplomacy promoted by Xi Jinping's regime has not always produced significant results. The perception in Russia of China as a threat is not uncommon, with 46 per cent of respondents to a 2017–18 Russian public opinion poll saying China was a threat to Russia's territorial integrity (Yu 2019). There are also economic concerns that opening the Russian market to China will result in a massive influx of Chinese products into the country (Yang 2020). Some projects contracted with China have not gone according to plan and frequently projects are being abandoned. Also, as it became clear that the target of USD200 billion in bilateral trade by 2020 (Sina Finance 2016) would not be achieved, the deadline was postponed to 2024.

The Yangtze River–Volga regional cooperation mechanism was originally conceived with the strategic aim of linking Sino-Russian relations into the BRI to strengthen ties with Europe and with Russia. However, it was an ambitious idea that is difficult to implement. At present, the six provinces and municipalities in the Yangtze River Basin have only one railway link with Russia and no direct air links, making the rapid development of trade a practical problem. For this reason, local governments have not been actively involved, and there have been cases where officials involved in the 162 investment projects selected for the agreement have refused to participate (Yang 2020). Meanwhile, the province that holds the top position on the index of participation in the BRI does not feature as part of the government's plan (He 2019). Guangdong, which is not a designated province for promoting ties with Russia, appears to be particularly enthusiastic about trade with Russia and has signed an MoU with the Republic of Sakha (Yakutia) (Ma and Qiang 2019).

Overall, government-led cooperation projects are underway in space and the Arctic, and there are new areas of cooperation such as missile defence (Garamone 2020; Guardian 2019) and weapons development. It goes without saying that the 15 cooperation agreements signed by President Xi and President of Russia Vladimir Putin just days before Russia's invasion of Ukraine are fully in line with a decade of bilateral relations.

---

5   For example, Deputy Minister Zhang Hanhui participated in the meeting of the Working Group on the Yangtze River–Volga Region Economic Trade and Humanities Cooperation held in April 2019.

There is often speculation that China may change or has changed its pro-Russia approach, but by looking at the mechanisms of foreign policy decision-making and implementation at home, China so far has shown no signs of this. However, it seems it will be difficult to increase trade between China and Russia even with planned diplomacy. The 'hot politics and cold economics' in China–Russia relations will likely continue for some years.

Planned diplomacy for strengthening relations with CEEC

In 2012, China and CEEC launched the '16+1' cooperation framework.[6] China has since been making great efforts to strengthen its relations with those countries.[7] The way Xi Jinping's regime promotes cooperation between China and Central and Eastern Europe (CEE) is similar to the mechanism for strengthening Sino-Russian relations. In other words, the central government has laid out a strategic framework for domestic cooperation based on the BRI and the relevant ministries must ensure that the central plan is implemented. At the same time, cooperation between local governments in China and CEE countries is encouraged.

Following the call for cooperation between local governments, twinning agreements for 76 pairs of cities were established between China and CEE countries between 2012 and 2018. The MoFA oversees local exchanges between China and countries in CEE.

At the same time, cooperative frameworks between China and CEEC were developed under a system known as 'Shanghai in the South and Liaoning in the North' (Liaoning Provincial Development and Reform Commission 2016), in accordance with which '16+1' national pavilions were built in Shanghai and Liaoning in 2018. As can be seen from the process of building domestic structures to promote cooperative frameworks with CEE countries, the planned diplomacy promoted under President Xi does not exclude competition between local governments. The central government first presented its plan for strengthening relations with CEE countries to local governments, then selected provinces and cities to interact with CEEC from the nine provinces that signalled their interest. Following this selection

---

6 Greece also joined in 2019, making it '17+1', but Lithuania left in 2021, as did Estonia and Latvia, in 2022, so it is down to '14+1'.
7 Note that 'CEE countries' and 'CEEC' are used interchangeably throughout.

process, Liaoning joined Chongqing and Hebei to host the China–CEE Local Government Working Group Meeting in 2019 and the Fifth China–CEE Local Leaders' Meeting in 2020. In May 2020, Liaoning Province also held an online business meeting with CEE countries to discuss the equipment needed to combat Covid-19.

Strengthening relations with CEE was not a bottom-up initiative generated by Liaoning. While Liaoning's *Thirteenth Five-Year Plan* (2016–20) mentioned the importance of trade with regions along the route of the BRI, the province set the goal of 'consolidating traditional markets such as South Korea, ASEAN, the EU [European Union] and the US and developing international markets such as Russia, Mongolia, India, Africa, South America and the Middle East' (Liaoning Province 2016), with no mention of CEEC. It was only after Liaoning was chosen as the site for the construction of a '16+1' national pavilion that the province really began to focus on exchanges with countries in CEE.

Now Liaoning Province is constructing the 'Liaoning 17+1 Trade Cooperation Pilot Zone' and is trying to expand trade with CEE via land routes (Liaoning–North-East Provinces–Europe and Liaoning–Montgomery–Europe) and sea routes, with Shenyang, Yingkou and Dalian becoming transit points. As a result, in 2018, Liaoning's total trade with CEE countries reached RMB15.7 billion (approximately USD2.28 billion)—up 32 per cent on the previous year—with Poland, the Czech Republic, Hungary and Romania each accounting for more than RMB1 billion (USD150 million) of this trade (Yang 2019). Liaoning Province is also keen to establish sister relationships with local governments in CEE countries and is actively promoting the establishment of Confucius Institutes in the region.

In contrast, in Shanghai, where the other '16+1' national pavilions were constructed, there has been no further development of any significance, although studies on cooperation with CEE countries are underway.

The city of Ningbo in Zhejiang Province, which has had difficulty obtaining the endorsement of the central government, is nonetheless enthusiastic about cooperation with CEE countries and, from an early stage, put forward plans to strengthen relations with the region. Alongside the launch of the BRI, the Chinese Government designated 2014 as the 'China–CEE Investment and Business Promotion Year'. In response, Ningbo targeted countries in Central and Eastern Europe and actively lobbied central ministries and agencies to hold the China–CEEC Investment and Trade Expo and the Meeting of China–CEEC Economic and Trade Ministers in the city (Zhou 2019).

In May 2015, the Ningbo municipal government promulgated 'Some Opinions on Strengthening Overall Cooperation with Central and Eastern European Countries'. This was followed by the 'Ningbo Municipal Subsidy Management Methods on Trade Cooperation with Central and Eastern Europe' in 2016 and the 'Implementation Plan for the Construction of the "16+1" Economic Cooperation Pilot Zone' in 2018. Ningbo has also hosted various meetings, including the China–CEE Forum on Development Cooperation, the China–CEE Trade (e-Commerce) Business Meeting, the China–CEE Ministerial Conference on Economic and Trade Promotion and the China–CEEC Investment and Trade Expo. In sum, the city has emerged as a significant actor in promoting relations with CEE countries.

Ningbo is home to many privately owned enterprises and is keen to support private sector investment in CEE. To this end, it has developed 16 country-specific investment priority areas (Ji and Wang 2016). The city actively promotes e-commerce, using platforms and companies such as KJB2C. com, Taobao and TMALL, and has signed MoUs with Latvia and Hungary. In addition, Ningbo is focusing on cooperation through cultural and educational exchanges and tourism to CEE. Ningbo has been particularly keen to promote trade with CEEC with the aim of ranking as one of the top three cities in China. In 2015 the city therefore set itself a target to increase trade with CEE by 20 per cent annually and to reach a total trade value of USD6 billion by 2020 (although the target was later revised down to USD4.5 billion).

As a result, Ningbo, which was not included in the national plan, has become a major regional city player in promoting relations with CEE countries. Thanks to these efforts, the 2014 expo and ministerial conference were held in the city, while the annual China–CEEC Investment and Trade Expo was upgraded to a national-level exhibition in 2019. China's first 16+1 Pilot Zone for Economic and Trade Cooperation was launched in Ningbo in June 2018.

Currently, although the central government allows Ningbo to promote relations with CEE countries, it has not clearly defined the city's position within China's top-level design. In 2017, Zhejiang Province approved the construction of the BRI Comprehensive Experimental Zone in Ningbo, but this was not approved by the central government. Air transport capacity between Ningbo and CEE is limited and rail transport relies on Yiwu or Suzhou as the first stop. There are also only three or four ship services a month to CEE countries (Ge 2019). In the end, it is difficult for Ningbo to achieve significant diplomatic and economic results with CEE countries using its own financial resources, and it has no choice but to seek to participate in the central government's planned diplomacy. China's setbacks in CEE have also made it more difficult for Liaoning to engage in the country's planned diplomacy.

Conclusion

The BRI is being pursued under the banner of planned diplomacy. After the bitter experience in 2006 of failing to strengthen the supervision of different organisations involved in foreign relations, Xi Jinping's government has introduced several new measures. These include clarifying the authority of the central government and the party in internal CPC regulations and government literature, strengthening supervision by party committees and expanding the party committees' authority over foreign affairs to ensure that the central government's policies are carried out and that a system of coordination is established between all organisations involved in foreign relations.

If we define a planned economy as 'an economic system in which resources are owned by the government under a centralised political system and allocated according to a plan formulated by the government' (Britannica Japan 2013), by extension we can say that the regime of Xi Jinping is pursuing a strategy of planned diplomacy. The central leadership formulates the overall foreign strategy and allocates resources strategically, while the relevant domestic ministries and local governments ensure the strategy is implemented. Xi Jinping's regime believes this is the ideal way to conduct diplomacy.

The way foreign policy is planned in China today and the systematic mobilisation of enterprises and local governments are totally different from the way China's foreign policy first developed after the country's reform and opening up in the late 1970s. Under President Xi, there is a deliberate linkage between foreign relations, propaganda, the economy, trade and foreign investment, and the establishment of government-led economic relations based on a top-level design is explicitly encouraged. The planned diplomacy pursued under such a system of total mobilisation is gradually creating a form of state capitalism that is completely different from that under Hu Jintao.

One of the first instances of planned diplomacy being put into practice is the mechanism for promoting relations between China and Russia. From the above analysis, we can see that the mobilisation of local governments is completely ineffective if the overarching plans are unrealistic. On the other hand, plans for which the central government can mobilise support directly, such as financial and space cooperation, are progressing well.

The domestic mechanisms of planned diplomacy are particularly evident in central–local relations, whereby local governments with a decentralised tendency compete to participate in the planned diplomacy. Yet, as I have argued, the division of labour between ministries has remained intact since the introduction of planned diplomacy. Consequently, the decentralisation and fragmentation between ministries still exert a powerful influence on how China's foreign policy is implemented. In addition, those local governments that have yet to be integrated into the national strategy can potentially have a significant impact on China's foreign relations as well.

References

Aoyama, Rumi. 2013. *Chūgoku no Ajia gaikō [China's Diplomacy in Asia]*. Tokyo: University of Tokyo Press.

Aoyama, Rumi. 2022. 'China's Dichotomous BeiDou Strategy: Led by the Party for National Deployment, Driven by the Market for Global Reach.' *Journal of Contemporary East Asia Studies* 11, no. 2: 282–99. doi.org/10.1080/24761028.2023.2178271.

Britannica Japan. 2013. *Buritanika kokusai dai hyakka jiten [International Encyclopedia Britannica]*. Tokyo: Britannica Japan Co. Ltd.

Consulate-General of the People's Republic of China in Vladivostok. 2018. 'Zhu Fuladiwosituoke zonglingshi Yan Wenbin jieshou Eluosi "Yataizhichuang" zazhi tekan caifang [Yan Wenbin, Consul General in Vladivostok, Accepted an Interview with Russia's "OKHO B ATP" Magazine].' News release, 28 December. Vladivostok: Consulate-General of the People's Republic of China. vladivostok.china-consulate.org/chn/zlgdt/t1625534.htm.

Economy, Elizabeth C. 2018. *The Third Revolution: Xi Jinping and the New Chinese State*. New York: Oxford University Press.

Garamone, Jim. 2020. 'Missile Defense Becomes Part of Great Power Competition.' *DOD News*, 28 July. Arlington: US Department of Defense. www.defense.gov/Explore/News/Article/Article/2291331/missile-defense-becomes-part-of-great-power-petition.

Ge, Honglei. 2019. 'Ningbo: Zhongdongou guoji wuliu tongdao youhua sheji [Ningbo: Central and Eastern Europe International Logistics Channel Optimisation Design].' *Chanye chuangxin yanjiu [Industrial Innovation]* 1.

Guardian. 2019. 'Russia Is Helping China Build a Missile Defence System, Putin Says.' *The Guardian*, 4 October. www.theguardian.com/world/2019/oct/04/russia-is-helping-china-build-a-missile-defence-system-putin-says.

He, Baogang. 2019. 'The Domestic Politics of the Belt and Road Initiative and Its Implications.' *Journal of Contemporary China* 28, no. 116: 180–95. doi.org/10.1080/10670564.2018.1511391.

Jakobson, Linda, and Dean Knox. 2011. *New Foreign Policy Actors in China*. Solna: Stockholm International Peace Research Institute.

Ji, Chunxian, and Fengshan Wang. 2016. 'Jinyibo shenhua Ningbo yu zhongdongou guojia de jingmao hezuo [Going Further and Deepening the Economic and Trade Cooperation between Ningbo and Central and Eastern European Countries].' *Sanjiang luntan [Sanjiang Forum]* 6.

Jiang, Zhenghong. 2020. 'Zhonge "Changjiang–Fuerjiahe" jingji hezuo xingzhi ji lujing de xuanze [China–Russia "Yangtze River–Volga" Economic and Trade Cooperation Nature and Selection of Paths].' *Suzhou keji daxue xuebao (shehui kexue ban) [Journal of the University of Science and Technology of Suzhou (Social Science Edition)]* 37, no. 2.

Jin, Ye. 2019. '"Yidaoyilu" beijingxia woguo Heilongjiang sheng Eluosi yuandong diqu yunshuye fazhan duice yanjiu [Research on the Development Strategy of the Transport Industry in the Far East of Russia in Our Country's Heilongjiang Province under the Background of "The Belt and Road"].' *Lilin guancha [Observation]* 10.

Jones, Lee, and Jinghan Zeng. 2019. 'Understanding China's "Belt and Road Initiative": Beyond "Grand Strategy" to a State Transformation Analysis.' *Third World Quarterly* 40, no. 8: 1415–39. doi.org/10.1080/01436597.2018.1559046.

Lai, Hongyi. 2020. 'The Rationale and Effects of China's Belt and Road Initiative: Reducing Vulnerabilities in Domestic Political Economy.' *The Journal of Contemporary China* 30, no. 128: 330–47. doi.org/10.1080/10670564.2020.1790896.

Li, Hongying. 2018. 'Shouci! Sandi waishiren xieshou rongru jingjingyi xietongfazhan dageju [First Time! Foreign Affairs Personnel from the Three Regions Join Hands to Integrate into the Coordinated Development Pattern for Beijing–Tianjin–Hebei].' News release, 24 May. Beijingshi waishi bangongshi [Beijing Municipal Foreign Affairs Office]. beijing.qianlong.com/2018/0524/2944806.shtml.

Liaoning Provincial Development and Reform Commission. 2016. 'Liaoning sheng guomin jingji he shehui fazhan dishisanci wunian guihua gangyao [National Economic and Social Development of Liaoning Province Outlined in the Thirteenth Five-Year Plan].' News release, 21 March. Shenyang: Liaoning Provincial People's Government. fgw.ln.gov.cn/fgw/zc/zcwjk/EB31DDBD68 FE4E66BF19ECF374B866D4/index.shtml.

Lin, Xiyao. 2018. 'Dudong zhonge "liangqu + Lianghe" defang hezuo [Understand the China–Russia "Two Districts + Two Rivers" Local Cooperation].' *Huanqiu* [*Globe*] 11. paper.news.cn/2018-06/07/c_129889931.htm [page discontinued].

Liu, Yong, Dongming Li, and Ye Bing. 2018. 'Jiangxisheng yu Eluosi biermu bianjiangqu qianshu hezuo beiwanglu [Jiangxi Province and Russia's Perm Territory Signed a Memorandum of Cooperation].' *Jiangxi ribao* [*Jiangxi Daily*], 27 September.

Ma, Xhaocheng, and Yong Qiang. 2019. 'Difang hezuo jiasu tuidong zhonge jingmao fazhan [Local Cooperation Accelerates China–Russia Economic and Trade Development].' *Xinhua*, 6 June. www.gov.cn/xinwen/2019-06/07/content _5398293.htm.

Ministry of Commerce (MofCOM). 2019. 'Liuguo zongli gongtong xuanbu jingji hezuo xieding shengxiao—"yidaiyilu" yu dongya jingji lianmeng duijie hezuo maichu jianzhi yibu [The Prime Ministers of the Six Countries Jointly Announced the Entry into Force of the Economic and Trade Cooperation Agreement—Taking a Solid Step in Cooperation between the "Belt and Road" and the Eurasian Economic Union].' News release, 25 October. Beijing: Ministry of Commerce of the People's Republic of China. www.mofcom.gov.cn/article/i/jyjl/e/201910/20191002908338.shtml.

People's China. 2013. 'Dingceng sheji [Top-Level Design].' *People's China*, 3 December. www.peoplechina.com.cn/home/second/2013-12/03/content_ 581273.htm.

People's Daily. 2018. 'Zhongyang dangnei fagui zhiding gongzuo dierge wunianguihua gangyao (2018–2022) [The Outline of the Second Five-Year Plan for the Formulation of Central Party Regulations (2018–2022)].' *People's Daily*, 24 February. cpc.people.com.cn/n1/2018/0224/c64094-29831349.html.

Shangye Jiandi Wang. 2019. 'Zhonge deng 9 guo gongkai liangjian qumeiyuanhua, yilang yong renmingbi ti meiyuan hou, shiqing you fazhan [After 9 Countries Including China and Russia Publicly De-Dollarised and Iran Replaced the US Dollar with Renminbi, Things Are Progressing].' *Shangye Jiandi Wang*, 3 October. Bank.jrj.com.cn/2019/10/03112328206125.shtml [page discontinued].

Sheng, Haiyan. 2019. '"Yidaiyilu" changyi xiade zhonge diqu hezuo de qianjing [Prospects of China–Russian Regional Cooperation Under the Setting of "Belt and Road"].' *Xiandai jiaoji* [*Modern Communication*] 14.

Sina Finance. 2016. 'Zhonge 2020nian 2000yi meiyuan maoyi mubiao nan shixian [China and Russia's 2020 US$200 Billion Trade Target Is Hard to Achieve].' *Sina Finance*, 17 January. finance.sina.com.cn/stock/usstock/c/20160117/1559 24169892.shtml.

Wang, Huihui. 2016. 'Zhongguowaijiaopeixunxueyuan jiepai chengli yishi ji kaixuedianli juxing yangjiechi wei xueyuan jiepai bing jianghua [China Foreign Affairs University Inauguration Ceremony and Opening Ceremony: Yang Jiechi Unveiled the Academy and Gave a Speech].' *Xinhua*, 2 March. www.gov.cn/ guowuyuan/2016-03/02/content_5047905.htm.

Wang, Jisi. 2012. 'Wangjisi: "Xijing", Zhongguo diyuan zhanlue de zai pingheng [Wang Jisi: "Going West", the Rebalancing of China's Geopolitical Strategy].' *Huanqiu shibao* [*Global Times*], 17 October. opinion.huanqiu.com/article/9Ca KrnJxoLS [page discontinued].

Wu, Mark. 2016. 'The "China, Inc." Challenge to Global Trade Governance.' *Harvard International Law Journal* 57, no. 2: 1001–63.

Xinhua. 2013. 'Zhongyang dangnei fagui zhiding gongzuo wunian guihua gangyao [Outline of the Five-Year Plan for the Establishment of Central Party Regulations (2013–2017)].' *Xinhua*, 27 November. www.gov.cn/jrzg/2013-11/27/content_ 2536600.htm.

Xinhua. 2019. '70nian fengyujiancheng—zhonge guanxi heyi chengjiu "sange zuigao" [Special Report: How Did China–Russia Relations Achieve the "Three Highests" after 70 Years of ups and downs].' *Xinhua*, 2 June. www.xinhuanet. com/world/2019-06/02/c_1124573464.htm.

Xinhua Finance. 2019. 'Zhonge 50%jiaoyi shiyong benbi—ouqi: renmingbi juesuan geng anquan [50% of China–Russia Transactions Use Local Currencies. European Companies: RMB Settlement Is Safer].' *Xinhua Finance*, 3 July. rmb. xinhua08.com/a/20190703/1857926.shtml.

Yang, Jiechi. 2013. 'Xinxingshi xia zhongguo waijiao lilun he shijian chuangxin [China's Diplomatic Theory and Practice Innovation in the New Situation].' *Qiushi* 16.

Yang, Jun. 2020. 'Zhonge changjiang—fuerjiahe liuyu defang hezuo zhong cunzai de zhuyao wenti [Main Problems Existing in Local Cooperation between China and Russia in the Yangtze–Volga River Basin].' *Guoji gongguan* [*PR Magazine*].

Yang, Lei. 2020. 'Zhonge zhanlue xiezuo jizhi de youxiaoxing jiqi gaishan [The Effectiveness and Improvement of the China–Russia Strategic Cooperation Mechanism].' *Guoji luntan* [*International Forum*] 2.

Yang, Lijuan. 2019. 'Dajian gaocengci duiwai hezuo xinpingtai—liaoning yu zhongdongou guojia jiaoliu hezuo zongshu. [Building a New Platform for High-Level Foreign Cooperation: Overview of Exchanges and Cooperation between Liaoning and Central and Eastern European Countries].' *Liaoning Daily*, 12 June.

Ye, Min. 2019. 'Fragmentation and Mobilization: Domestic Politics of the Belt and Road in China.' *Journal of Contemporary China* 28, no. 119: 696–711. doi.org/10.1080/10670564.2019.1580428.

Yu, Xiaoqin. 2019. 'Wukelan weiji yilai Eluosi yuandong duihua hezuo yuqing fenxi [Analysis of Public Opinion on Cooperation in the Russian Far East and China Since the Ukraine Crisis].' *Eluosi Dongou Zhongya yanjiu* [*Russia, Eastern Europe & Central Asian Studies*] 6.

Zheng, Qingting. 2019. 'Zhonge qianshu lianhe gongbao—hezuo cong chuantong lingyu xiang gaokeji tuozhan [China and Russia Sign a Joint Communiqué to Expand Cooperation from Traditional Fields to High-Tech].' *21 Shiji jingji baodao* [*21st Century Business Herald*], 19 September. www.gov.cn/xinwen/2019-09/19/content_5431215.htm.

Zhou, Zhixing. 2019. 'Zhongguo–Zhongdongou guojia bolanhui: Ningbo "yidaiyilu" xinzhanfang [China–Central and Eastern European Countries Expo: Ningbo "Belt and Road" Blooming].' *Ningbo Jingji* [*Ningbo Economy*] 7.

4

The BRI and Japan: Possibilities for mutually beneficial competition over aid diplomacy

Takeshi Sato-Daimon

Introduction

The year 2020 saw the most serious global pandemic in terms of loss of life since the Spanish flu outbreak of 1918–20. During the subsequent shutdown of economic activity, in the silent streets from London to Tokyo, people realised that, like it or not, they could not survive even a day without the masks and toilet paper supplied by China. In response to people's rising fear and the reckless comments of some politicians hoping to take advantage of the uncertain situation, Haruki Murakami, one of Japan's most celebrated authors, spoke on public radio in May 2020 to urge that 'Covid-19 should not be compared with a war. Unlike a war, we must all cooperate and rack our brains to find ways to come through this ordeal.'[1]

---

1   'Murakami Radio Stay Home Special' (Tokyo FM, 22 May 2020).

Despite Murakami's plea to humanity, the post-Covid world is filled with rivalry and conflict between nations. This includes the mutual antagonism between China and the United States, which played out through the World Health Organization (WHO), from which the United States under Republican president Donald Trump threatened to withdraw.

The subsequent Democratic Party administration under President Joe Biden did not bring about major changes to the fundamental structure of the world, in which Beijing is portrayed as an ambitious challenger to the West's power structure and its 'rules of the game'. In the field of economic development alone, where post-Covid-19 recovery and reconstruction are a major concern for both industrialised and industrialising economies, the increasing flow and dominance of Chinese capital seem to be overwriting the West's rules-based model of foreign aid (in terms of emphasis placed on human rights and environmental concerns, for example) for which a consensus had largely been created within the Western donor community of the OECD, of which China is not a member.

Regardless of whether one likes or dislikes the concept of 'international connectivity', Chinese permeation of and expansion within various fields is an undeniable phenomenon of modern society. Its influence on diplomatic policy is considerable, as is its impact on economic policy. For Beijing, the Belt and Road Initiative (BRI) serves as a powerful mechanism to present China as a country promoting peace and prosperity through international trade. The underlying assumption for the initiative seems to be consistent with the type of internationalism or liberalism that supports the free market, as propounded by Adam Smith in *The Wealth of Nations* (1776) and international organisations such as the World Bank and the World Trade Organization. From a competitive free-market point of view, fair economic competition among countries to provide the best quality of aid is therefore highly desirable.

The aim of this chapter is to shed light on the viability of politically motivated Sino-Japanese competition over aid provision to developing countries, as well as the social and economic implications of this competition from the recipients' perspective. One of the central questions is whether it is possible to have a mutually beneficial form of competition based on 'win-win-win' solutions, as it were, for China, Japan and the recipient countries.

Japan's official development assistance: History and key turning points

In the immediate postwar period of the late 1940s, Japan became a major recipient of US aid and World Bank loans, as it could not afford to reconstruct and catch up with the West without external financial resources. Japan remained an aid recipient during the 1950s and 1960s, when it was the World Bank's second largest borrower (after India), with a total of USD863 million spread over 31 loans.[2] By the late 1960s, the Japanese economy had grown to become the second largest in the world after the United States and a 'model case' for World Bank loans, in the sense that the country continued to grow after 'graduating' from external financing and relying instead on its own financial resources.

Japan then started to assist other countries as an emerging donor country. Tokyo had been a good student of the World Bank during the period when growth was the top priority for aid from the two Bretton Woods institutions —the World Bank and the International Monetary Fund—and this affected the way Japan assisted other nations. Having become free of its debts to the World Bank in the 1960s, by the 1980s, Japan had become a major creditor. This pattern of 'adaptation', 'internalisation' and 'externalisation' of the foreign aid process, as learned by Japan through borrowing from the World Bank, is now apparently being reproduced in China.

The first foreign aid from Japan, which came to be known as Official Development Assistance (ODA), can be traced back to the mid-1950s. Intended and conceived of as reparations to South-East Asian countries victimised by Japan during World War II, ODA's official objectives tended to include aspects of international development that varied according to the times and the needs of the recipient countries (Okaido 2019).

In 1954, under Prime Minister Shigeru Yoshida, the Government of Japan extended the first tranche of war reparations, totalling USD200 million, combined with soft loans (which are sometimes referred to as 'quasi' war reparations) of USD50 million. The first recipients were Burma (Myanmar), the Philippines, Indonesia and South Vietnam, followed by Laos, Cambodia, Malaysia, Singapore and, towards the mid-1960s,

---

2   See Abe (2011, 2013) for a complete list and full historical background of World Bank loans to Japan.

Thailand.[3] The Republic of China (Taiwan) renounced war reparations from Japan and no diplomatic relations were established with the People's Republic of China (PRC) or South Korea. However, once diplomatic relations were established, Tokyo started to assist both the PRC and South Korea on a massive scale through quasi-war reparations, particularly in the form of public investment in infrastructure, to the extent that they helped significantly towards industrialising the two recipient countries.

There is no record of the Japanese payment of war reparations to India, as damage there due to Japanese aggression was considered minimal. In this sense, India is one of the few countries in Asia in which Japan began its ODA operations with completely 'clean hands'. The first aid arrived in 1958, when Japan assisted with the heavy industry and steel sectors as part of India's *Second Five-Year Plan*. It was clear that India was following an import substitution policy or de facto Soviet-style planned economy at that time, although diplomatically the country was positioning itself as the non-aligned leader of the so-called Third World.

By the end of the 1990s, Japan had become the largest contributor of ODA in the world. However, the following years saw a reversal of the world order that completely changed the ODA paradigm. On 11 September 2001, the horrific terrorist attacks on US territory shattered American pride in a way similar to the attack on Pearl Harbor by Japan. After this tragedy, the United States and other major countries doubled or tripled their military and non-military assistance to countries such as Iraq and Afghanistan, with Japan eventually ranking as the fourth or fifth highest contributor (largely in response to domestic downward fiscal pressure regarding overseas operations). Like military assistance, ODA came to be recognised as a major diplomatic tool in a return to the political realism of the Cold War era (Morgenthau 1948).

A somewhat abrupt turning point in Japan's ODA policy occurred under the government of Junichiro Koizumi in 2003, when the ODA Charter—the most influential policy instrument adopted by the government—was drastically revised to ensure that peacebuilding became and remained one of the central missions of ODA, alongside poverty reduction, sustainable growth and a focus on global issues. This was a drastic change of direction

---

3   See Okaido (2019: 98) for a complete list of war reparation packages for South-East Asian countries. War reparations in the strict sense were paid to only four countries—Burma (Myanmar), the Philippines, Indonesia and South Vietnam—while other countries received grants or soft loans regarded as 'quasi' war reparations.

from Japan's immediate postwar diplomacy. Japan has since been more explicitly involved in international peace operations through projects in countries like Iraq and Afghanistan (Lancaster 2007). In 2005, the ODA Medium-Term Policy (MoFA 2005) provided some clear operational guidelines. For example, it defined 'peacebuilding' as a process 'to prevent the occurrence and recurrence of conflicts, alleviate the various difficulties that people face during and immediately after conflicts, and subsequently achieve long-term stable development'. It also underlined the importance of 'human security'. In this regard, the Japan Self-Defence Forces became a partner for ODA operations in countries such as Iraq, which were difficult for aid officials to access.

Major changes in aid administration came about in 2008, when the Japan International Cooperation Agency (JICA) became the sole implementing body for Japanese ODA under the leadership of Sadako Ogata, the former United Nations High Commissioner for Refugees (UNHCR), who co-chaired the UN Human Security Commission with Professor Amartya Sen. It is not widely known that Ogata's career as a UN official was influential in forming her rather conservative political position. As a UNHCR co-chair, Ogata had been heavily involved in refugee management and she proposed from her 10 years of hands-on experience (mostly with African refugees) that the peacebuilding programs should be centred on four key policy directives: reconstruction of social capital, reconstruction of the economy, recovery of governance and assurance of security. Ogata broadened the concept of peacebuilding to include various forms of humanitarian assistance for developing countries under the banner of human security—operations that fell within the new jurisdiction of the JICA. As a result, peacebuilding is now concerned with a wide range of human security factors, including poverty and inequality, migration, education and health, and law and governance.

The ODA Charter was updated in 2015 under conservative prime minister Shinzo Abe, who did not shy away from expressing his political views—which were greatly influenced by his grandfather, former prime minister Nobusuke Kishi, who had been imprisoned as a war criminal after World War II and later pardoned. In some senses, then, for Abe, the battle with China over the aid market in Asia was somewhat reminiscent of the real war fought against China under the government of Hideki Tojo (1941–44), when Kishi had been in charge of international trade and industrialisation.

Is mutually beneficial competition over aid possible?

During the summer of 2020, the streets of Ginza in central Tokyo were decorated with 'Tokyo 2020' Olympic Games flags, despite the cancellation of the games due to the Covid-19 pandemic. In retrospect, the Olympics seemed to coincide with significant turning points in modern history—a history characterised by war and conflict. For instance, the Tokyo Olympics have twice been cancelled: the first time in 1940, due to the Second Sino-Japanese War, and the second time in 2020 (although technically they were only postponed), due to the 'war' against Covid-19.

The 1964 Tokyo Games was seen as a turning point in Japan's postwar reconstruction. Its Shinkansen high-speed railway (HSR), which was the world's fastest train at the time (and was mainly financed through loans from the World Bank), began operating just a week before the Olympic Games Opening Ceremony. In the 1960s, China was completely isolated from the rest of the world and its economy had greatly deteriorated during the ideological campaign of the Cultural Revolution. The country launched a process of drastic economic reform in the late 1970s with Deng Xiaoping's Open-Door Policy, which enabled the nation to become a major economic power by the early 2000s. The 2008 Beijing Olympic Games marked another turning point in Sino-Japanese history, after which China overtook Japan as the second largest economic power in the world.

Since the 2008 Beijing Games, China has been playing a growing role in regional leadership. In the eyes of most Western observers, this makes it an emerging hegemonic power that threatens the *Pax Americana* that has characterised, for better or worse, most of the postwar period. For many developing countries, the so-called spirit of Bandung (referencing the Bandung Conference of 1955)[4] survived the Cold War as a set of common values, if not binding principles. At the same time, it was often used as political rhetoric to justify policies of non-interference by donor countries in authoritarian regimes in developing countries. Twenty-nine representative countries from Asia and Africa, including China and Japan, were among the participants of the Bandung Conference. Both countries later became

---

4   At the conference in April 1955 in Bandung, Indonesia, delegates from 29 countries in Asia and Africa met to affirm their refusal to align with the world powers, demanding peaceful coexistence and non-interference in internal affairs.

major donors, remaining loyal to the Bandung spirit of non-interference, whereby the only interests that mattered were economic ones. Sixty years later, Bandung again attracted international attention when China and Japan battled over the building of the Jakarta–Bandung HSR. (For more on this, see Chapter 7 by Trissia Wijaya in this volume.)

In terms of an aid 'menu', it is no surprise that there are more similarities than differences between what Japan and China can offer recipient nations. The two countries' very similar aid models are a version of the Harrod–Domar (HD) model, under which the financing of economic infrastructure projects entices private investors to follow suit and, coupled with a high savings rate, aims to achieve high economic growth. The HD model is also consistent with the Keynesian model of public investment. Long before the shift towards the Washington Consensus paradigm in the 1980s, which claimed the government had no role to play at all, it can be said that this was the World Bank's modus operandi for financing investment, and it became the default model for international financial institutions such as the Asian Development Bank (ADB) as well.

Another, albeit related, point is that Japan and China both use loans as a type of foreign assistance, helping to build infrastructure such as roads, bridges and electric power plants (on an economic basis) in South-East Asia. In line with the HD model, these public investments are intended to have spillover and multiplier effects that result in an increase in private investment, which in turn leads to higher economic growth. Both countries achieved double-digit economic growth in this manner. On the other hand, European and US donors—whose aid policies are centred more on grants than loans—warn that this form of aid can create a 'debt trap'. Both Japan and China must therefore ensure that any assistance they provide for HSR projects and the like will be productive rather than damaging to the recipient countries, and that a debt trap will be avoided.

During the period of rapid economic growth in the 1980s, Japan's aid was criticised internationally as being developmentalist, mercantilist, having strings attached, being anti-environmentalist and having a low grant element. In those days, Japan was pursuing the 'trinity' model of aid, through which the powerful Japanese Ministry of International Trade and Industry (today the Ministry of Economy, Trade and Industry) was playing the role of benign 'broker' for private sector interests. The ministry's main aim was to promote foreign aid as a mechanism for Japanese exports and investments, particularly in the South-East Asian market. Aid was promoted as a catalyst for the private sector–led growth to counter Western criticism. There was even a quasi-religious belief held by Japanese aid professionals and their researchers that the Japanese 'trinity' model was superior to any of the Western models.

After the shift towards a more collaborative form of aid in the 2000s—exemplified by the World Bank and IMF's Poverty Reduction Strategy Papers and the UN Millennium Development Goals and Sustainable Development Goals—Japan followed international calls for debt reduction by increasing the grant element in its aid program (or making its loan menu more concessional) and decreasing the amount of aid provided. Consequently, Japan lost its position as the top aid provider among the G7 nations, falling to fourth or fifth place in terms of the annual ODA amount committed. During this same period, China surpassed Japan's GDP to become the world's second largest economy. Today, China aims to become the largest economic power globally thanks to the BRI, although its ODA is now being criticised in just the same way as was Japan's in the past. Meanwhile, Japanese politicians and experts have started boasting about their qualitative superiority, using somewhat ideological terminology such as 'free and open Indo-Pacific', 'quality infrastructure partnership' and 'international rules'.

Before the 'Tragedy of Bandung' in 2015, when Indonesia rejected Japan's bid to develop the Jakarta–Bandung HSR, Japan was exceedingly confident about its superiority over China for winning the bid. The 'defeat' of Japan was therefore seen as a diplomatic humiliation. However, if the aid had been targeted at something else, such as a highway or toll road network that could be neatly sliced into packages of co-financing projects, there might have been more cooperation between Japan and China. The HSR project was too exclusive to be sliced up between competitors.

What this example seems to show is that some projects are 'zero-sum', while others are 'win-win', depending on the nature of the investment. Nonetheless, it seems that with just a little effort the HSR project could have been at least partly converted into a 'win-win' situation if both countries were willing to work together—by focusing on establishing effective safety guidelines or guidelines for rail transport, for example. In the case of the Jakarta–Bandung HSR, when Indonesia said 'Sayonara to the Shinkansen' (Tempo 2015), it carefully compared the two countries' proposals. The government of Joko

Widodo, which would be re-elected for a second term in 2019, opted for the Chinese menu, which offered a faster schedule, thus making it politically more attractive.

Indonesia now wants to extend its HSR network to Surabaya, the second largest city in East Java, in accordance with the original plan for a line to connect Jakarta with Surabaya. Bandung was not included in the original master plan put forward by Japan, but it was added later to make the project more profitable (by capturing higher than expected demand) rather than connecting Jakarta and Surabaya directly (which would cost more but generate less income). In terms of transportation economics, it became more and more apparent that, despite what is generally believed, HSR is *not* economically viable. First, since neither the Japanese nor the Chinese HSR system could be constructed on the existing rail tracks, the necessary land purchases would require enormous capital investment and social costs. Second, higher speed imposes higher operational and maintenance costs per kilometre; this is often difficult to recover from operational revenue (ticket prices), which tends to be set lower than the marginal cost. For example, it is an open secret that Taiwan's Shinkansen system has been running at an operational loss since its inauguration in 2007.

Even in 1961, the World Bank project appraisal report highlighted the risk of rising operational and maintenance costs when it financed the first Shinkansen in Japan.[5] The report said the HSR (the 'New Tokaido Line') should consider having a dual operating system for 'around the clock' operation (World Bank 1961). This would mean that, for passenger movements during the day, the trains would run faster (at 200 kilometres per hour), while, during the night, for cargo operations, they would go slower (at 150 kilometres per hour) to reduce costs. Japan spent JPY200 billion or USD560 million (at 1961 exchange rates) on developing its first HSR (when the overall national budget at the time was just JPY1.5 trillion, equivalent to USD4.2 billion) of which 50 per cent went towards land purchase costs. Unfortunately, the plan for cargo transport never materialised, due to the high land purchase costs and noise pollution concerns of residents.

In the 1960s, air travel was expensive everywhere and trains were the only means of transportation for most people. In those days, the Shinkansen HSR was run by the Japan Railway Corporation (a 100 per cent state-owned enterprise). It would be more than three decades before the privatisation

---

5   The 2019 World Bank report addresses these same trade-off issues regarding China's HSR system.

of the national railways took place. All ticket prices were therefore heavily subsidised (subject to approval by the Japanese Diet, or parliament), making it difficult to recover costs in full. Even today, train tickets are heavily subsidised in many parts of the developing world. Thailand, for example, gave up on its HSR project because it was financially unviable.

As shown above, competition in the HSR market may not make economic sense. The competition between China and Japan over aid for ASEAN countries has been heavily politicised by their diplomatic rivalry (more than economic profitability) and is directly influenced by the political ambitions of the target country. In the same year that Japan lost the HSR deal in Indonesia to China, it won another with India for its Mumbai–Ahmedabad HSR, with very generous lending conditions for India (JPY2 trillion at an interest rate of 0.1 per cent over 50 years), although tied to Japanese companies for its construction. By 2020, however, both projects had experienced major delays and cost overruns. Clearly, when competition is connected to national pride, it can be a very costly enterprise.

Implications for post-Covid international relations in Asia

Faced with both a domestic administrative need to streamline its aid operations and international demands for increased transparency of China's foreign aid program, in 2015, Beijing established the China International Development Cooperation Agency (CIDCA) to take on the functions that had previously been carried out through a complex network of independent channels alongside the Ministry of Commerce (MofCOM), the MoFA and China's financial institutions. The creation of a separate foreign aid agency represents a significant administrative reform, which is continuing. CIDCA has started promoting its activities online—in English as well as Chinese—thus slowly increasing its international presence as well (CIDCA 2021).

CIDCA acted quickly in response to the Covid-19 pandemic—much more quickly than JICA. One of CIDCA's most significant achievements at this time was the provision of emergency medical aid to countries such as Ethiopia, Angola and Sri Lanka (which already had a history of receiving aid from China). Between March and April 2020, information about CIDCA's emergency medical aid program was updated daily on its website, describing China's response in great detail.

Looking back to the 1990s, we see that JICA was the main actor in the field of international emergency medical aid through the dispatch of the Japan Disaster Relief teams. JICA's modus operandi was to help as quickly as possible with any natural disasters, and then praise Japan's role in overcoming them afterwards. In 2015, an Infectious Disease Response Team was inaugurated, based on the previous year's experience of helping with the Ebola epidemic in West Africa. However, as far as the response to Covid-19 is concerned, JICA has not been as active as CIDCA, and it seems to have been mainly concerned with the infection status of its employees and experts overseas as well as reports about the interrupted dispatch of its volunteers—in the initial stages, at least.

As more and more donors, including the World Bank and the ADB, signal their intention to provide emergency aid, it appears that Japan has lost its position as the main provider of emergency relief. In contrast, China moved quickly in concert with the Alibaba Group (and its founder, Jack Ma) to set up an internet platform for sharing medical information about Covid-19 in Chinese and English. The 'One World One Fight' forum was promptly established, greatly surpassing the efforts of Japan. In his keynote speech to that forum, Jack Ma stated (in English):

> We should cooperate with Africa in fighting infectious diseases. In this field, it should be obvious what is preferable between competition and cooperation among countries, but we are responsible for that decision. In only two weeks, China has been able to provide 50 countries with emergency medical supplies, and this is also thanks to the aid of Ethiopian Airlines. We want to keep strengthening the relationship between China and Africa. (GMCC 2020)

Post-Covid international relations might best be characterised by how much 'social distance' people are prepared to tolerate in terms of a dire dilemma that juxtaposes authoritarianism with democracy. Some European countries achieved more complete security for society by imposing a complete lockdown, albeit with significant limitations on individual freedom. The transfer of personal rights to the state is a trade-off for life security.

In Japan, such limitations were not applied as strictly as elsewhere, thus the economic security obtained was not total. Furthermore, there was no program of contact tracing in Japan using smartphones, as was the case in South Korea, because people were unwilling to give the state their private information due to strong privacy concerns. In practice, local prefectural requests were observed by people just as though they had been administrative orders or laws. As the industries and shops that did not comply with these requests were ruthlessly exposed by the government, the first wave of the pandemic was thought to have subsided. However, in the second wave, the virus spread rapidly, so Japanese society did pay the price for its democracy in the end.

Many developing countries have been unable to limit their citizens' personal freedoms, hence failing to provide complete life security and leaving many citizens (some of whom turned to rioting) without opportunities for employment. This has led not only to financial disaster in some cases, but also to existential threats for some countries and a worsened security situation overall. As developed countries now focus on reconstructing their own economies, it is unlikely that developing countries will receive substantial aid from them in the short term. Considering that China is the largest source of aid for many developing countries, the risk of the authoritarian state model—under which personal freedoms are limited and economic security is low—spreading across the world is relatively high. International relations will therefore be decided by the extent to which people accept the application of the Chinese model.

According to *Our World in Data*,[6] the number of Covid-19 cases in China peaked in February 2020. European countries and the United States have requested that the Chinese Government investigate and provide clarity about the origin of the virus. At the same time, the US Government has been suggesting that the Wuhan Institute of Virology was the source of the virus, whether intentionally or not.

Some believe that the purpose of these criticisms is to deflect complaints about the United States' own poor response to the pandemic (particularly under President Trump), even though it has resulted in a worsening of relations with China. However, leaders of several other Western countries such as France, Germany and Australia, who had previously taken a positive stance towards the BRI, have also been critical of China. This has not gone down well in China and, in an interview with the *Australian Financial Review* in April 2020, China's ambassador to Australia harshly criticised the Australian Government with a not-very-subtle threat, saying:

---

6   *Our World in Data* (ourworldindata.org/).

The investigation that America is requesting [probing into the source of Covid-19] is politically motivated and, as such, I cannot agree with it. We should rely on [the] WHO's investigation. If Australia happened to join America in this request, there is no doubt that the Chinese people would have second thoughts about coming here, as tourists or to study abroad, and about consuming Australian products such as wine and beef. (Embassy of China 2020)

Compared with this, it cannot be said that the Japanese Government has taken an openly negative stance towards China. Traditional print media and television simply repeat the information coming from the office of the prime minister and the Tokyo metropolitan government, without the slightest critique. There are no requests for investigations into China's actions, as there are in the European and US media, nor is there any independent research on the issue.

The situation is similar in South Korea, where the media seems prepared to praise the country's response to Covid (while criticising that of Japan), but again, without criticism of China. The main media outlets in Singapore show a similar affinity for China in their reports.[7] This reluctance to criticise cannot be unrelated to the growing reliance of these countries' economies on China. In May 2020, the *People's Daily* (2020) published an article entitled '10 Doubts Regarding the Disease: The American Government Has a Duty to Take Responsibility and Respond', strengthening the confrontational attitude vis-a-vis the United States.

The 2020 *World Development Report* (World Bank 2020) warned that, while the global value chain is evolving, some countries and people are being left behind, and it is important not to fall prey to the increasing country-level individualism and isolationism. This is a type of idealism that goes against the 'liberal' view[8] on which the global economic consensus is based (Deudney and Ikenberry 1999).

This way of thinking directly confronts the retrospective 'realist' view of considering aid (and trade and investment) as 'a diplomatic tool to pursue the benefit of one's own country' (Morgenthau 1948). While different from the classic realism that saw the United States and the Soviet Union

---

7   For example, Reuters (2020) criticised the Australian prime minister's request for an investigation into China's role in the spread of the virus.

8   It was even suggested (see Mawdsley 2012) that liberalism (and, by extension, internationalism) could counter the threat of a global pandemic. Unfortunately, the reality shows that this view was overly optimistic.

confront each other during the Cold War, this neorealism can be seen as a characteristic of the current 'Ground-Zero period', which is marked by economic competition between the United States and China in particular. Propelled by international relations theory (which focuses on regionality, identity and social norms), constructivism has also positioned itself as part of aid theory—not least by promoting the eradication of poverty and the achievement of the UN Sustainable Development Goals (Fukuda-Parr and Hulme 2011). Seen from this perspective, aid is a tool for diplomatic and political mediation.

There is little doubt that the post-Covid markets for foreign aid in Asia will be influenced by China's power, and that the position of traditional providers of aid—including Japan and the United States—will diminish, at least in the short term. China has been using foreign aid as an important diplomatic tool throughout the world to maintain its influence in recipient countries. Hence, ASEAN countries now face a difficult dilemma: to what extent are they willing to lose their institutionalised democracy in return for resources from China if they wish to kickstart their economic recovery after the shock of Covid?

Conclusion

In terms of international diplomacy, especially in relation to China and South Korea, postwar Japan chose to be silent for a long time. Occasionally these countries have raised historical issues arising from Japan's conduct during World War II, usually for domestic political purposes to reduce internal tensions affecting their own regimes. Consequently, because Japan depends heavily on both China and South Korea for its raw materials and as markets for its manufactured goods, such politically sensitive issues have made Japan an even more passive player in the region. In the eyes of Japanese taxpayers, the massive ODA budget has benefited these countries at their own expense, and usually without any formal recognition.

While Japan's sense of national pride has been greatly impaired through these often-frustrating dealings with China and South Korea, in other parts of the world—especially in countries that have been significant beneficiaries of Japanese ODA and investment—Japan's ambition to regain a 'respectable position in international society' (as the preamble to the 1947 Constitution of Japan stipulates) has been more successful. Since the early 2000s, human security has been a guiding principle of Japanese diplomacy and of Japan's ODA policy under the high-profile leadership of former JICA president Sadako Ogata. By 2020, however, human security was in severe decline across the world. If nothing else, the Covid-19 pandemic has made everyone aware of the importance of aid as a key concept for development.

A central theme of the analysis in this chapter has been to consider the possibility of creating a 'grand coalition' between China, Japan and aid-recipient countries in a 'win-win-win' scenario. However, it is clear this would be very difficult to achieve, in theory and in practice. The main difficulty lies in the fact that a trilateral equilibrium can never be stable, especially when two countries are competing over mutually exclusive gains, as clearly evidenced by the fierce competition between China and Japan to build HSR lines around the world.

This line of thought should not make us too despondent, however, because it provides a glimmer of hope by showing the need for unity in tackling global issues; combating Covid-19 is undeniably a global public good that could benefit us multilaterally rather than unilaterally. Regional security in many parts of the world is on the line, as governments in the developing world desperately require medical supplies, health professionals and financial support. China, India and Japan all have a comparative advantage in terms of the aid they are able to provide, and the net effect would be even more powerful if they pooled their resources and cooperated with one another, given that they are offering complementary forms of support.

A little like the pandemic, perhaps, the 'America First' campaign under the Trump administration was so contagious that it quickly reproduced itself in slogans of 'Japan First', 'Britain First' and 'China First'. Let us hope that humanity can overcome this phase of exclusive isolationism and generate a greater sense of sacrifice from all sides for the global good.

The Japanese economy cannot sustain itself without China because the core industries that maintain it are heavily reliant on materials and food from China. This includes most of the metals used in the automotive industry as well as more than half of all imported vegetables. Similarly, almost all integrated circuit chip exports from Japan are headed to China. Clearly, whatever their political differences, the import/export symbiosis between Japan and China is inescapable.

Competition between China and Japan over aid to developing countries has produced many positive results in the recipient nations, as well as some unforeseen consequences. Despite (or because of) the economic damage caused by the Covid-19 pandemic, we can expect these two countries to play an important role in global post-Covid reconstruction for many years to come—not just as sources of finance, but also as sources of knowledge and experience about how to manage conflicts of interest in both the economic and the political realms.

References

Abe, Yoshiaki. 2011. 'Japan and the World Bank, 1951–1966: Japan as a Borrower.' *Journal of Asia-Pacific Studies* 17 (October): 217–44.

Abe, Yoshiaki. 2013. 'Japan and the World Bank, 1951–1966: Japan as a Borrower (Part 2).' *Journal of Asia-Pacific Studies* 21: 213–57.

China International Development Cooperation Agency (CIDCA). 2021. 'Our Work.' [Online]. en.cidca.gov.cn/ourwork.html.

Deudney, Daniel, and G. John Ikenberry. 1999. 'The Nature and Sources of Liberal International Order.' *Review of International Studies* 25, no. 2: 179–96. doi.org/10.1017/S0260210599001795.

Embassy of China. 2020. 'Transcript of Chinese Ambassador Cheng Jingye's Interview with Australian Financial Review Political Correspondent Andrew Tillett.' 27 April. Canberra: Embassy of the People's Republic of China in the Commonwealth of Australia. au.china-embassy.org/eng/gdtp_16/t1773741.htm.

Fukuda-Parr, Sachiko, and David Hulme. 2011. 'International Norm Dynamics and the "End of Poverty": Understanding the Millennium Development Goals.' *Global Governance* 17, no. 1: 17–36. doi.org/10.1163/19426720-01701002.

Global MediXchange for Combating Covid-19 (GMCC). 2020. 'Alibaba Actions.' [Online]. gmcc.alibabadoctor.com/alibaba-actionsm [Page discontinued].

Lancaster, Carol. 2007. *Foreign Aid: Diplomacy, Development, Domestic Politics*. Chicago: Chicago University Press. doi.org/10.7208/chicago/9780226470627.001.0001.

Mawdsley, Emma. 2012. *From Recipients to Donors: Emerging Powers and the Changing Development Landscape*. London: Zed Books. doi.org/10.5040/9781350220270.

Ministry of Foreign Affairs (MoFA). 2005. *Japan's Medium-Term Policy on Official Development Assistance (Provisional Translation)*. 4 February. Tokyo: Government of Japan. www.mofa.go.jp/policy/oda/mid-term/policy.pdf.

Morgenthau, Hans J. 1948. *Politics among Nations: The Struggle for Power and Peace.* New York: Knopf.

Okaido, Keiko. 2019. *Nihon no tonan ajia enjo seisaku: Nihon gata ODA no keisei [Japan's Foreign Aid Policy for Southeast Asia: Formation of Japanese-Style ODA].* Tokyo: Keio Gijyuku Daigaku Shuppan Kai [Keio University Press].

People's Daily. 2020. 'Kansensho ni kansuru jyu no gimon Beikoku seifu ha sekinin wo mottte kotaeru gimu ga aru [10 Doubts Regarding the Disease: The American Government Has a Duty to Take Responsibility and Respond].' *People's Daily*, 1 May. j.people.com.cn/n3/2020/0501/c94474-9686404.html.

Reuters. 2020. 'Australia PM Morrison's Call for Coronavirus Inquiry May Harm Long-Term China Trade, Say Business Leaders.' *Straits Times*, 4 May. www.straits times.com/asia/australianz/australia-pm-morrisons-call-for-coronavirus-inquiry-may-harm-long-term-china-trade.

Smith, Adam. 1776. *The Wealth of Nations.* Boston: E.P. Dutton.

Tempo. 2015. 'Sayonara to the Shinkansen.' *Tempo English*, 13 October. magz.tempo.co/read/30754/sayonara-to-the-shinkansen.

World Bank. 1961. *Appraisal of the Japanese National Railways: New Tokaido Line Project.* Washington, DC: World Bank Group.

World Bank. 2019. *China's High-Speed Rail Development.* Washington, DC: World Bank Group.

World Bank. 2020. *World Development Report: Trading for Development in the Age of Global Value Chains.* Washington, DC: World Bank Group.

5

Chinese networks: The case of the Chinese General Chamber of Commerce in Asia and the World Chinese Entrepreneurs Convention

Masaki Mori[1]

Introduction

The Belt and Road Initiative (BRI), first proposed in 2013, aims to link the East Asian and European economic spheres by promoting exchange and cooperation in five areas (policy, infrastructure, trade and investment, finance and private sector cooperation) and, through economic aid to developing countries, to establish a global economic zone with China at its centre. In particular, Chinese enterprises[2] in the countries and regions along the route of the BRI are encouraged to build deep and trusting relationships with the Chinese Government and the political and business circles of the countries in which they are located, creating a network of Chinese entrepreneurs who view the BRI as a new business opportunity.

---

1   This work was supported by JSPS KAKENHI grant numbers 15K17133 and 18K01778.
2   Any enterprise established and managed by a Chinese entrepreneur in a country or region outside mainland China.

The Chinese Government therefore attaches great importance to Chinese enterprises overseas and wishes to strengthen cooperation with them to realise the 'Great Revival of the Chinese Nation' through the BRI. Consequently, the ease with which Chinese enterprises can participate in the business activities of the BRI in the country or region in which they reside is due to the existence of extensive Chinese networks. Chinese entrepreneurs have formed relationships based on business ties in their home country and region, through which they have been able to obtain a wide range of information and conduct business. This chapter examines the role of Chinese networking organisations in Asia in relation to the development of the BRI and particularly the economic and business relations between Chinese enterprises in these countries and in China.

The two bridging functions of the Chinese General Chamber of Commerce

To support their business activities, Chinese entrepreneurs have been developing business relationships and connecting them to new networks both inside and outside China. In many countries, the locally established Chinese General Chamber of Commerce (CGCC) has played an active and important role in promoting and protecting these business activities and has many entrepreneurs and business associations of Chinese origin as its members. As the representative body of the Chinese community, the CGCC also plays a leadership role in bringing together different groups from different places within China. The CGCC is an umbrella organisation for a wide network of Chinese enterprises, businesses and commercial organisations that has links not only with the All-China Federation of Industry and Commerce, but also with different Chinese Chambers of Commerce (CCCs) overseas, as well as an extensive network of non-Chinese entrepreneurs, businesses and commercial organisations, government bodies and social organisations in various countries.

In the next section, I will use the Singapore Chinese Chamber of Commerce & Industry (SCCCI) and the Hong Kong General Chamber of Commerce (HKGCC) as case studies to analyse the role played by Chinese networking organisations in relation to the BRI.

The structure of the CGCC presents the characteristics of a linking-pin organisation. Aldrich and Whetten (1981), in their model of network formation, suggest that organisational populations are loosely linked and constantly adapting while maintaining a hierarchically differentiated network structure. They are integrated through many ties into linking-pin organisations that have the following functions: 1) to act as a communication channel between organisations; 2) to link third parties by transferring resources, information and customers; and 3), in the case of dominant organisations, to extract dependence from other organisations by acting as a model to be imitated or by actively directing their actions (Aldrich and Whetten 1981: 391). Such linking-pin organisations are generally dominated by powerful or high-status organisations, which occupy a central position within them. This is because the dominant organisations achieve a linking function by strategically manoeuvring for such a position in the first place, and then by manipulating interorganisational relations to retain power.

In fact, the CGCC is a commercial and industrial association whose main members and board of directors are Chinese enterprises and sectoral organisations and their representatives. Hence, the activities of the CCCs in Singapore and Hong Kong serve not only to facilitate domestic and international exchanges with other Chinese and non-Chinese commercial and industrial organisations, but also to provide social services and cultural activities for communities, such as schools and hospitals, and political activities, such as lobbying the local government. This means that the CGCC benefits from an extensive network of Chinese enterprises and associations as well as links to social organisations, schools, hospitals and the government in the countries in which they are located. Facilitating these interorganisational relationships can be regarded as the first bridging function of the organisation. Furthermore, because Chinese entrepreneurs—who are the decision-makers of Chinese enterprises—participate in the activities of the CGCC themselves, this makes it easier for Chinese enterprises to establish networks with each other, which is the second bridging function of the organisation (for a full conceptual framework of these two bridging functions, see Figure 5.1). In addition, the CGCC uses its own extensive and diverse network to organise activities and provide information to help its members (enterprises) build networks with entrepreneurs connected to various commercial and industrial organisations at home and abroad, as well as with social organisations and government officials.

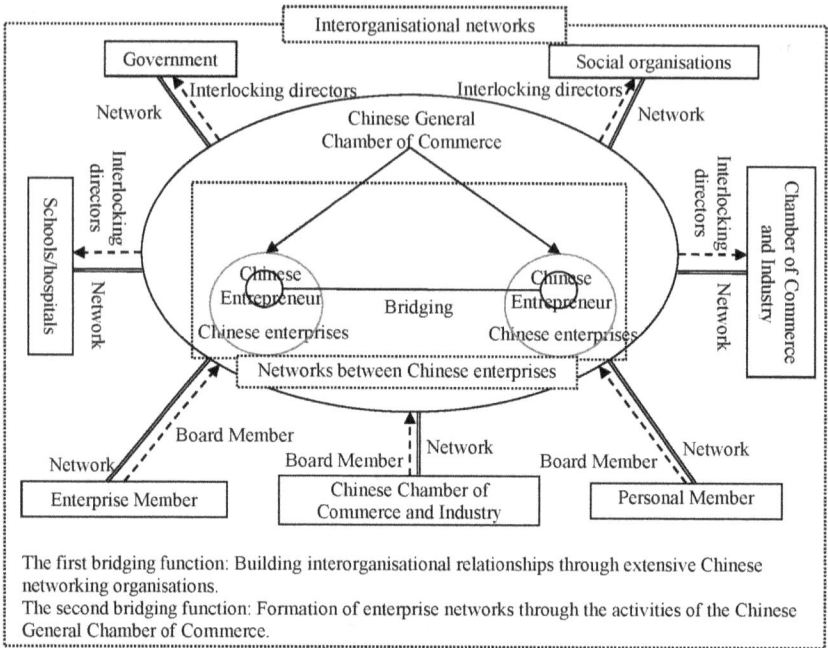

Figure 5.1 The two bridging functions of the CGCC network
Source: Created by the author.

Because it is a consolidated linking-pin organisation, the CGCC provides channels and opportunities for its member enterprises to build networks with other domestic and overseas organisations and enterprises through the formation of interorganisational relationships. Furthermore, as the representative body of Chinese business communities wherever they are located, local chambers of commerce also tend to be politically involved and influential in improving the business environment, as well as working to improve communities through social services and grants. Enterprises that are members of either the SCCCI or the HKGCC expect to increase their reputation, recognition and trust by joining these organisations, enabling them to exchange business experience, develop partnerships with other member companies, and establish overseas networks. As for the CCCs, their activities are mainly related to forming interorganisational networks between themselves and other commercial and industrial organisations and foreign government agencies, as well as internally between their own members. This suggests that the greater the degree of network-building and frequency of organisational activities of the CGCC, the greater its role as an intermediary, bridging the structural gaps in the network for the participating Chinese enterprises.

The activities of the CGCC and its role in the BRI

The purpose of this section is to clarify the role played in the BRI by the CCCs in Singapore and Hong Kong through their organisational activities. Although the BRI was first proposed in 2013, the SCCCI and the HKGCC only began to engage in related activities in earnest in 2015. Consequently, the present study covers the period from 2015 to 2019. The analysis is based on the organisations' annual activity reports (or, in some cases, monthly activity reports) to examine the policies and actions of these CCCs in relation to the BRI.

Activities of the SCCCI and its role in the BRI

The SCCCI initiated activities related to the BRI in 2015, although at the time the initiative was just one of many themes of business exchange with China, providing local companies with information and networking opportunities. However, in 2015, the SCCCI established networking opportunities between top executives of Chinese enterprises and the China Enterprises Association (Singapore), and with the Macau Chamber of Commerce Youth Wing in 2016, to exchange views on several issues, including 'One Belt, One Road' (as the BRI was initially called). Although the organisation engaged in 191 activities in 2015 and 165 in 2016, only a few of these were related to the BRI.

The change came after the appointment of the fifty-ninth board of directors, with Roland Ng San Tiong as the new president, in March 2017. Under the new leadership, the first step was to build the Enterprise Development Centre@SCCCI Proprietary Limited, which was a subsidiary of the SCCCI and had already set up a representative office in Shanghai in 2010 with the support of International Enterprise Singapore. Next, the SCCCI established the Chongqing Representative Office in July 2017 and the Chengdu Representative Office in May 2019 to provide consultative services and support to Singaporean companies expanding into western China, as well as to Chinese enterprises expanding into South-East Asia through Singapore.

Across China, 18 provinces and municipalities were included in the plan for the BRI (mainly in the western and north-eastern regions as well as some coastal areas), linking to the 64 countries it covered. This underlines the fact that China is itself a 'core area' for BRI activity, so it was important to establish representative offices in places like Chongqing and Chengdu, which are the core cities of China's Great Western Development Strategy, to develop relations with the core 'Belt' in mainland China.

BRI-related activities in the period 2017–19 included the organisation of the 'Singapore–China Business Forum: Leveraging China's Belt and Road for Regional Market Opportunities' and the dispatch of a delegation to the Fourteenth World Chinese Entrepreneurs Convention (WCEC) in Myanmar in 2017 (see below for a detailed discussion). In 2018, a delegation visited Sri Lanka to explore BRI-related business opportunities, while, in China, delegations went to Chongqing to attend the event 'Tapping into Opportunities from the Economic Development of Western China', and to Nanning (Guangxi Province) to explore the progress of the BRI and related business opportunities, particularly the Southern Transportation Corridor.[3]

In 2019, Singaporean companies were encouraged to set up businesses in Wuxi (Jiangsu Province) through the 2019 Wuxi (Singapore) Modern Industries Promotion Meeting and to participate in the Ningbo–Belt and Road Countries Trade Cooperation Conference, the signing ceremony for major procurement projects and the BRI Investment Conference, to strengthen cooperation and exchange with local governments and chambers of commerce in China and promote the SCCCI and its SME Centre@SCCCI. Thanks to the cooperation of International Enterprise Singapore, the SCCCI signed the Singapore Overseas Base Agreement with the Chengdu Regulatory Commission of Sichuan's Tianfu New Area as part of its development strategy to develop the BRI and enhance cooperation by promoting business and investment in both locations.

All this shows that the SCCCI has been able to strengthen its relationship with mainland China in relation to the BRI, using the interorganisational networks and exchanges it has built with China's central and local governments and commercial and industrial organisations. According to the SCCCI's annual reports, Chinese VIPs, business delegations and other visitors from mainland China accounted for 76.0 per cent (38 of 50) of visitors hosted by the organisation in 2015; 73.3 per cent (33 of 45) of visitors in 2016;

---

3   A transportation route linking Chongqing with Singapore via Guangxi.

42.5 per cent (17 of 40) in 2017; 65.1 per cent (28 of 43) in 2018; and 46.4 per cent (13 of 28) in 2019. Most of these Chinese visitors were sent by the central government in Beijing, national-level industrial and commercial associations and local commercial organisations. Visitors and delegations came not only from China's economically developed areas in the north-east, east coast and central regions but also from the inland and mid-western regions of Sichuan and Chongqing (where the SCCCI has established representative offices) and the economically developing regions of Guangxi, Yunnan, Xinjiang and Guizhou. It is particularly notable that the number of exchanges with economically developing regions has been increasing since 2016.

To summarise the SCCCI's activities and the role it is playing within the BRI, it is instrumental in fulfilling the first bridging function of developing an interorganisational network with China. Given that a representative office had already been set up in Shanghai in 2010, good economic relations for building a network between Shanghai and the eastern coastal areas and regions already existed. This was further developed by the establishment of representative offices in Chongqing and Chengdu to promote the development of the inland regions of central and western China, which are still developing economically. In terms of the second bridging function (developing networks between Chinese enterprises), the SCCCI provides member enterprises with information to promote their understanding of the BRI. It also sends inspection teams to China and countries along the BRI route to observe developments, and co-hosts and participates in exhibitions and business meetings to form networks with commercial and industrial organisations and enterprises, providing channels of communication and opportunities for cooperation.

Activities of the HKGCC and its role in the BRI

Since 2015, the HKGCC has consistently expressed its policy on the BRI and has been active in related activities, playing a central role in strengthening cooperation with mainland China and surrounding areas. In particular, it aims to keep pace with the Chinese Government's development of the BRI and the Guangdong–Hong Kong–Macau Greater Bay Area Development Plan and to contribute to the economic development of Hong Kong and East Asia.

The HKGCC focuses on the provision of business information and networking opportunities related to the BRI, offering seminars and lectures for its members, such as the Seminar for Committee Members: New Opportunities under the 13th Five-Year Plan and One Belt, One Road in 2015 and the National People's Congress and Chinese People's Political Consultative Conference Exchange and Sharing Meeting: Opportunities Arising from 'Two Sessions' in 2019. These conferences provide opportunities for networking and receiving policy information related to the BRI. The latter element is supported through events such as the Vietnam–China Economic Trade Cooperation Seminar in 2017, the Promoting Regional Cooperation: France–Hong Kong and Mainland China Economic Forum and the Promoting Regional Cooperation: Indonesia–Hong Kong Strategic Partnership on the BRI Seminar and Luncheon in 2018. There were also meetings for networking and information exchange aimed at promoting Hong Kong as a hub to link China and countries along the BRI.

The full network includes the central government of China, which decides BRI policy, the governments of Guangdong Province and Macau, which cooperate with each other in the Guangdong–Hong Kong–Macau Greater Bay Area Development Plan, and the countries along the BRI route, such as Singapore, Vietnam and Indonesia in South-East Asia and Egypt and the United Arab Emirates in the Middle East. Both Russia and the United Kingdom are located in the maritime section of the BRI and some activities are focused on cooperation with Japan.

Even more noteworthy is the Mainland–Hong Kong Belt and Road Business and Professional Services Council, established in December 2018, which is supported by the MofCOM and the Government of the Hong Kong Special Administrative Region (SAR), and led by the HKGCC and the China Council of Foreign Trade and Industry, with more than 40 major business and professional associations and large enterprises from Hong Kong and China represented. It aims to promote cooperation between Hong Kong's industrial and professional service industries and Chinese enterprises and countries along the route of the BRI. Through symposiums, business meetings, inspection tours and other activities, the committee aims to create a platform for exchange and cooperation between Hong Kong and China, so enterprises can expand their business overseas as well as participate in the construction of the BRI and contribute to national development (see CGCC 2018).

In this way, the HKGCC will link the BRI with the Guangdong–Hong Kong–Macau Greater Bay Area Development Plan set up by the Chinese Government and function as an international open city and financial centre by cooperating with the Chinese Government, Guangdong and Macau to build and strengthen the economic relationship with countries along the BRI, so creating new business opportunities.

In summary, like its counterpart in Singapore, the HKGCC fulfils the first bridging function of acting as an intermediary between China and the countries along the BRI and developing interorganisational networks. In particular, based on its good relationship with the Chinese Government, the HKGCC has established a number of bilateral relationships with relevant countries in fulfilment of the economic development strategies of the BRI and the Guangdong–Hong Kong–Macau Greater Bay Area Development Plan, and has established extensive networks with the economic development areas in the east of China (especially south-eastern China), and with Asia, Eurasia, the Middle East and Europe. In addition, the HKGCC is helping to develop the BRI by focusing on regional cooperation with China, especially with Guangdong Province, and using its regional business power as a springboard to form new networks along the route of the BRI and to create business opportunities by taking advantage of the BRI's development.

In fulfilment of the second bridging function (establishing networks between Chinese enterprises), member companies are provided with information on BRI policy and business in the countries along the route to promote greater understanding. They are also provided with channels and opportunities to form networks with commercial and industrial organisations, business associations and commercial enterprises, including sending inquiry teams to countries along the route.

The role of the WCEC in the BRI

This section examines the activities of the Fourteenth WCEC held in Yangon, Myanmar, in 2017. Myanmar is one of the countries along the route of the BRI and therefore provides a useful case study to clarify the role of the WCEC in the initiative.

The WCEC was set up in 1991 following a joint proposal by the SCCCI, the HKGCC and the Thai–Chinese Chamber of Commerce. The aim of establishing the WCEC was to 'contribute to the economic development and social progress of resident countries and regions by promoting the hard work and strong founding spirit of Chinese people, deepening mutual understanding, exchanging experience and information, and discussing issues of mutual concern' (WCEC 2024). The biennial event is organised by the CGCC of the host country and is a forum for Chinese entrepreneurs from all over the world, enabling them to build relationships and interact with one another. It also functions as a business forum at which to discuss important issues in world trade, industry and the economy.

The fourteenth convention was held in Yangon from 15 to 18 September 2017. The theme was 'An Opening Economy in Myanmar: A New Epoch in History'. It was organised against the backdrop of the BRI with the aim of establishing cooperative relationships with Chinese entrepreneurs from around the world and opening a new era of economic development in Myanmar. Organised by the CGCC in Myanmar, the event was attended by 2,300 Chinese entrepreneurs, high-level officials (representing the governments of Myanmar, China and the Hong Kong SAR) and chairpeople of the major CCCs, including 1,500 participants from 90 organisations in 30 countries and 800 representatives from Myanmar.

The congress began with a welcome dinner and opening ceremony, followed by thematic sessions focusing on 1) Myanmar's investment environment and the latest investment regulations, 2) the BRI, and 3) the success and innovation of young Chinese entrepreneurs. Thanks to a program of visits and excursions in Yangon and these social events, participants were able to learn about Myanmar's society, economy and culture as well as get to know other Chinese entrepreneurs.

Alongside the main WCEC program, each of the participating organisations was able to organise its own activities. For example, the China Federation of Overseas Chinese Entrepreneurs held the Myanmar–China Investment and Trade Exchange Meeting, which was attended by 400 people, including ministers and senior officials of the Myanmar Government and more than 200 WCEC participants. The trade exchange meeting included the official signing ceremony for a series of investment projects and joint business ventures.

The Chinese Chamber of Commerce in Japan is also a member of the WCEC Advisory Committee, which comprises major CCCs and member organisations that have hosted conventions in previous years from 14 countries and regions and which plays an important role in the organisation of the WCEC. The Chinese Chamber of Commerce in Japan, headed by Yan Hao, sent 63 delegates to the Yangon convention, including not only Chinese merchants but also academics and representatives of Japanese companies. During their visit to Myanmar, the delegates inspected companies invested in by Japanese-Chinese entrepreneurs and Japanese-affiliated companies.

The Fourteenth WCEC can be characterised in three ways. First, the Myanmar CGCC and the WCEC Secretariat (Thai–Chinese Association of Commerce) played a central role in building new relationships through the various CCCs in South-East Asia, China and other countries. Given the foreign economic policy focus embodied in the BRI and the political and economic cooperation between Myanmar and China, the WCEC provided an opportunity to strengthen ties between the two governments and contributed to improving the business environment for Chinese enterprises in Myanmar.

The second important element was that the Government of Myanmar showed its willingness to support the WCEC and seized the opportunity to develop Myanmar's economy. Senior government officials stated that they hoped to strengthen relations with China by promoting economic cooperation and attracting Chinese and international Chinese businesses to invest in Myanmar. Finally, the convention helped to establish a good relationship between Myanmar's Chinese business community and the Government of Myanmar, which will be beneficial for doing business there in the future.

Watts (2003) argues that while small networks maintain the internal cohesion of a tightly knit community, they also extend their tentacles far and wide to connect with otherwise unconnected long-distance nodes via short paths, and this reduces redundancy. Hence, according to Watts, the system has characteristics that are suitable for the 'search for and propagation and utilisation' of information with little redundancy.

Viewed from this perspective, by organising the Fourteenth WCEC, the CGCC in Myanmar (a linking-pin organisation) was able to respond to the changing environment of the Chinese Government's BRI by building new relationships with the Myanmar Government and local Chinese business circles as well as receiving support from the Chinese Government and the Government of the Hong Kong SAR. Thanks to this support, the network topology is being changed through a process of rewiring (reconnecting information channels) between the Myanmar CGCC and the interlinked local Chinese business community. Through this, Chinese enterprises participating in the WCEC were provided with information on the social, political and economic situation and business environment in Myanmar, where previously there were few relationships and little information. Through the institutional mechanism of the WCEC, this rewiring occurs regularly to enhance the external search capability of enterprises (Figure 5.2). In addition, Chinese enterprises can expect an improved investment environment in Myanmar through the new network connected by the CGCC, leading to business development.

After Bali, Indonesia, in 2015, and Yangon in 2017, the 2019 WCEC was held in London and the sixteenth convention was in Bangkok in 2023. The WCEC is a platform for Chinese enterprises to connect with each other through this international business network. This will enable investment and business development to accelerate as the BRI becomes a reality through the economic cooperation of Chinese-owned enterprises.

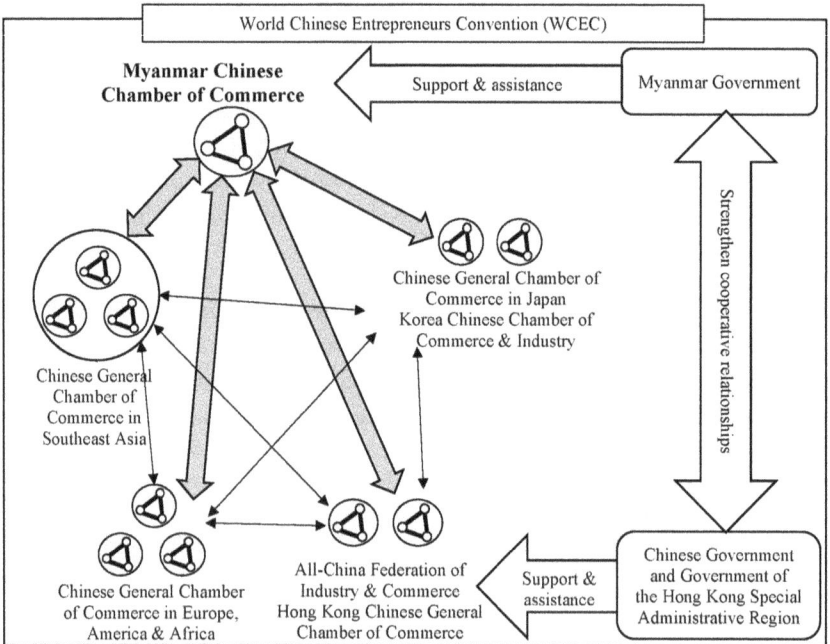

Figure 5.2 The Chinese General Chamber of Commerce's external search power resulting from the Fourteenth World Chinese Entrepreneurs Convention

Source: Created by the author.

Conclusion

This chapter has examined the operations of Chinese networking organisations, the CCCs, in Asia and their role in developing the BRI by establishing economic and business relations between local countries and China.

The chapter began by examining the role of the CGCC in the BRI. Because the CGCC has Chinese overseas enterprises at its core, it has already established an extensive interorganisational network, not only with local Chinese business communities but also with local government bodies and social organisations. In response to their advocacy of the BRI, these organisations have rewired their networks to connect mainland China, the starting point of the BRI, with countries along its route, thereby fulfilling the first bridging function of creating interorganisational networks.

This is exemplified by the SCCCI, which has established representative offices in Shanghai, Chongqing and Chengdu with the support of International Enterprise Singapore, and formed networks with mainland China and Sri Lanka. The HKGCC has also established several bilateral relationships with countries along the BRI route in line with the Chinese Government's national economic development strategies, which include the BRI and the Guangdong–Hong Kong–Macau Greater Bay Area Development Plan, allowing it to form an extensive network with Asia, Eurasia, the Middle East and Europe.

Hence, the CGCC has the characteristics of a small network with two significant features: internal cohesion and external search power. The connection of long-distance nodes across mainland China and the countries along the BRI provides a large network with good information transmission efficiency for the Chinese member enterprises and affiliated Chinese commercial and industrial associations, which can be extremely useful for the search for and propagation and utilisation of information. This will surely lead to the establishment of strong relationships between Chinese enterprises and the development of new investment and business opportunities in connection with the BRI (the second bridging function of developing networks between Chinese enterprises).

In the third part, the chapter discussed the function of the WCEC, demonstrating the small network characteristics of the CGCC as a linking-pin organisation. The good relationship between Myanmar's Chinese business community and its government was observed, as exemplified by the latter's willingness to support the WCEC and its readiness to seize the opportunity to develop the Myanmar economy. It can therefore be expected that the government will contribute to improving the business environment for Chinese enterprises in Myanmar.

Based on this foundation, with the Myanmar CGCC and the WCEC Secretariat (Thai–Chinese Chamber of Commerce) at its core, extensive rewiring is being carried out through the various CCCs in South-East Asia, China and beyond. This has created new opportunities for business development and investment in connection with the BRI and enhanced Myanmar's ability to connect to the outside world.

References

Aldrich, Howard E., and Catherine Zimmer. 1986. 'Entrepreneurship through Social Networks.' In *The Art and Science of Entrepreneurship*, edited by Donald L. Sexton and Raymond W. Smiler, 3–23. Cambridge: Ballinger.

Aldrich, Howard E., and David A. Whetten. 1981. 'Organization Sets, Action-Sets, and Networks: Making the Most of Simplicity.' In *Handbook of Organization Design: Adapting Organizations to their Environment*, edited by Paul Nystrom and William Starbuck, 385–408. New York: Oxford University Press.

Burt, Ronald S. 1992. *Structural Holes: The Social Structure of Competition*. Cambridge: Harvard University Press.

Chin, Tenji [Chen, Tien-shi]. 2001. *Kajin diasupora: Hanashō no nettowaku to aidentiti* [*The Chinese Diaspora: Networks and Identities of Chinese Merchants*]. Tokyo: Akashi Shoten.

Chinese General Chamber of Commerce, Hong Kong (CGCC). 2018. '"Mainland–Hong Kong Belt and Road Business and Professional Services Council" Officially Established.' Media release, 14 December. Hong Kong: CGCC. www.cgcc.org.hk/zh/temp_news.php?cid=8&sid=51&tid=0&id=1225.

Granovetter, Mark S. 1973. 'The Strength of Weak Ties.' *American Journal of Sociology* 78, no. 6: 1360–80.

Hong Kong General Chamber of Commerce (HKGCC). 2015–18. *Xianggang zhonghua zongshanghui nianbao* [*Annual Report of the Chinese General Chamber of Commerce, Hong Kong*]. Hong Kong: HKGCC.

Hong Kong General Chamber of Commerce (HKGCC). 2019. *CGCC Vision, 2019*. Hong Kong: HKGCC.

Kanai, Toshihiro. 1994. *Kigyōsha nettowakingu no sekai: MIT to bosuton kinpen no kigyōsha komuniti no tankyū* [*The World of Entrepreneurial Networking: Exploring the Entrepreneurial Communities of MIT and the Boston Area*]. Tokyo: Hakutō Shobō.

Li, Minghuan. 1995. *Dangdai haiwai huaren shetuan yanjiu* [*Research on Contemporary Overseas Chinese Associations*]. Xiamen: Xiamen University Press.

Mori, Masaki. 2017. 'Nettowāku soshiki no katsudō ni yoru kigyōka nettowāku no keiseini kansuru kenkyū: Honkon chūka sōshōkai to shingapōru chūka sōshōkai no jirēbunseki wo motoni [A Study on the Formation of Entrepreneurial Networks through the Activities of Network Organisations: Based on the Case Study of the Chinese General Chambers of Commerce of Hong Kong and of Singapore].' *Kyūshū keizai gakkai nenpō* [*Kyushu Association of Economic Science*] 55: 149–57.

Mori, Masaki. 2020. 'Ittai ichiro ni okeru ajia no kajin nettowāku soshiki ga hatasu yakuwari: Ajia no chūka sōshōkai to sekai kashō taikai wo jirei ni [The Role of Chinese Network Organisations in Asia in the Belt and Road Initiative: The Case of the Chinese General Chamber of Commerce in Asia and the World Chinese Entrepreneurs Congress].' *Kokusai chīki kenkyū* [*Ritsumeikan Journal of International Relations and Area Studies*] 52: 71–93.

Nishiguchi, Toshihiro, and Motoko Tsujita. 2016. *Enkyori kōsai to kinjyodukiai: Seikōsuru soshiki nettowāku senryaku* [*Distant Relations and Neighbourhood Relations: Successful Organisational Network Strategies*]. Tokyo: NTT Shuppan.

Nishiguchi, Toshihiro, and Motoko Tsujita. 2017. Komyunitī kyapitaru jyosetu: Surikomi, dōitsu shakudo no shinrai, junchūtai no kinō [An Introduction to Community Capital: Imprinting, Same-Scale Trust, and the Function of Quasi-Ties]. *Sosiki kagaku* [*The Academic Association of Organisational Science*] 50, no. 3: 4–15.

Shu, En [Zhu, Yan]. 1995. *Kajin nettowāku no himitsu* [*The Secret of the Chinese Network*]. Tokyo: Tōyō Keizai shinpōsha.

Singapore Chinese Chamber of Commerce & Industry (SCCCI). 2015–19. *Xinjiapo zhonghua zongshanghui changnina baogaoshu* [*Singapore Chinese Chamber of Commerce & Industry Annual Report*]. Singapore: SCCCI.

Watts, Duncan J. 2003. *Six Degrees: The Science of a Connected Age*. New York: W.W. Norton & Co.

Watts, Duncan J., and Steven H. Strogatz. 1988. 'Collective Dynamics of "Small-World" Networks.' *Nature* 393: 440–42.

World Chinese Entrepreneurs Convention (WCEC). 2017. *Di 14jie shijie huashang dahui huiyi zhinan* [*Conference Guide of the 14th World Chinese Entrepreneurs Convention*].

World Chinese Entrepreneurs Convention (WCEC). 2024. 'About WCEC.' [Online]. Hong Kong: WCEC Secretariat. www.wcecofficial.org/en/index.php/about-us/about.

Yamagishi, Toshio. 1998. *Shinrai no kōzō: Kokoro to shakai no shinka gēmu* [*The Structure of Trust: The Evolutionary Game of Heart and Society*]. Tokyo: Tōkyō daigaku shupankai [University of Tokyo Press].

Zhu, Yan. 2018. 'Di 14jie shijie huashang dahui zai miandian yangguang shunli zhaokai [The 14th World Chinese Entrepreneurs Conference Was Successfully Held in Yangon, Myanmar].' In *Report on Development of Overseas Chinese Entrepreneurs 2018*, edited by Wang Hui-Yao and Kang Rong-Ping. Beijing: Social Sciences Academic Press.

Part II: Internalising the BRI projects in emerging countries

6

The Eastern Economic Corridor and the Thai-Chinese business class: The CP Group as a case study

Nimid Ang

Introduction

China's Belt and Road Initiative (BRI) has gained considerable global recognition and Thailand, the second largest economy in South-East Asia, is one of the most important countries involved in it (Zhang 2018). Thailand's involvement in the BRI aligns with its traditional foreign policy approach, which, as Pavin Chachavalpongpun (2010) notes, seeks a balance between powerful nations with interests in South-East Asia. Initially, Thailand sought both Japanese and Chinese investment in its ambitious infrastructure development projects, but over the past few years, many of these contracts have been awarded to Chinese companies. This coincides with the recent development of a close relationship between the Thai and Chinese governments. However, the Thai public has grown increasingly critical of Chinese power and influence in Thailand. Many professionals and academics have started to raise concerns, especially about issues that directly impact on Thailand's economy and natural environment. Such criticisms may ultimately lead to the failure of BRI-related projects in Thailand, which would carry significant political and economic implications.

This study explores how the influence of Sino-Thai businesses—businesses owned by Chinese immigrants to Thailand—has allowed China to exert greater economic and political influence in the country, leading to this widespread criticism. The study investigates the role of one Sino-Thai business, the Charoen Pokphand Group (CP Group), which is the most influential business in Thailand, with strong connections to the country's political elites. The CP Group's dual identity as, on the one hand, a Sino-Thai clan (the Chearavanont family) with roots and familial connections in China and, on the other, a company with significant business interests in China, makes it both a domestic and a multinational actor. With substantial economic and political power, the CP Group dominates many contracts within the Thai Government's Eastern Economic Corridor (EEC) projects in conjunction with China's BRI.

The chapter is divided into five sections. The first briefly presents the constructivist theoretical framework, focusing on three key concepts: historical conditions, cultural identities and elite beliefs, and social norms. It then explains how these concepts can be used to examine the impact of Sino-Thai businesses on the BRI. The second section focuses on the historical conditions of Sino-Thai businesses. The third considers the cultural identities and elite beliefs of Sino-Thai businesses, particularly the CP Group. The fourth section examines how the historical conditions, cultural identities and elite beliefs of the CP Group have shaped the terms of the Thai–Chinese agreement for implementing BRI projects in Thailand. The fifth section discusses new social norms in Thailand over the past few years that have led to a backlash against Sino-Thai businesses. The chapter concludes by discussing the implications of this backlash for the BRI in Thailand.

Analytical framework

Foreign policymaking is a complex process at the intersection of domestic political environments. According to Neack (2008), the leaders of many governments often have a similar political motivation—that is, to get into power and build and maintain coalitions. Domestic politics is especially important, and the goal of foreign policy is ultimately to serve the domestic needs of a country's political elites. Final policy outcomes are the result of complex interactions among myriad factors. Constructivism suggests that: 1) states' behaviours are shaped by a combination of historical narratives, the cultural identities of domestic agents, ideas, discursive practices, elite beliefs and social norms; and 2) analysts should focus on the relationship between domestic interest groups and foreign policy (Wendt 1999). Farnham (2004) states that the political context of the state influences the decision-making of its leaders. Policymaking requires various groups to reach a consensus within a state's unique political context and social constraints. In short, domestic politics always affects the foreign policymaking process. Using this constructivist analytical framework, the chapter aims to establish empirically that a state's foreign policy goal is not independent of domestic factors, and that its end goal is to serve the needs of the most powerful political groups, which could be the elites or the masses, depending on the state's political dynamics.

To study Thailand, the next sections draw on these constructivist insights. Thai politics has always been dominated by domestic issues rooted in its history. The people have very little political clout in Thailand's system, which caters to elites such as Sino-Thai business leaders. The most important issues that drew people into the streets and led to Thailand's cycle of coups d'état were accusations of corruption among the government and big business. Another important grievance in Thai politics is the widening wealth gap. Many people accuse the ruling class of conspiring with big business to keep most people poor and subservient. As China's influence in Thailand grows, there are increasingly frequent accusations—especially from NGOs, academics and opposition political parties—that the ruling class and the Sino-Thai business class are conspiring with China to exploit Thailand both politically and economically.

The history of the Sino-Thai business class

The historical relationship between China and Thailand plays an important role in framing the current situation. Further, this history frames each state's political actors' perception of the other. Thailand's relationship with China dates back to the formation of the Thai States in the 1200s, when Chinese merchants began exerting significant influence in South-East Asia through trade and migration. Over time, the Sino-Thai business class has become one of the most successful minority diasporas in South-East Asia, if not the world (Deng 1992).

During the late nineteenth and early twentieth centuries, South-East Asia saw large-scale migrations of the Chinese population (Zhu 1991). European colonies in the region were facing labour shortages, creating an incentive for Chinese workers to move abroad. In Thailand, for example, official reports in 1932 stated that 12.2 per cent of the population was of Chinese ancestry (Stuart-Fox 2003). The extent of this migration was significant. Today there are approximately 20 million Teochew-speaking people in China and almost 10 million in Thailand (Pisanbutra 2001). A second wave of large-scale Chinese migration followed the collapse of the European colonies in South-East Asia after World War II (Purcell 1965). Thailand was the principal destination for Chinese migrants, followed by Malaysia and Indonesia. Historically, the Chinese in South-East Asia engaged mainly in business and trading activities, which eventually resulted in an economic disparity between the Chinese migrants and the local population. Moreover, in the European colonies, the Chinese often acted as liaison between the European colonisers and the local population. For these reasons, local people had many grievances against the Chinese. For Chinese migrants to survive in this hostile environment, they relied on their social networks, which provided access to capital and economic opportunities (Lim and Gosling 1983).

Sino-Thais enjoy a different social setting from Chinese migrants in other parts of South-East Asia. They are among the most successful migrants anywhere in the world, and there are many underlying reasons for this. First, since the seventeenth century, Thailand's feudal leaders have allowed Chinese merchants to intermingle with the ruling class. Over time, many Chinese have married into Thai families and their descendants continue to integrate seamlessly into Thailand's ruling classes (Pisanbutra 2001). Brown et al. (1997) state that this is primarily because, unlike other countries in South-East Asia, in Thailand, the political system has a long history as a strongly centralised state. State power was further consolidated during the colonial era to survive against external pressures. With this strong centralised power, the Chinese could rely on the Thai state structure for protection against the Thai majority. The local population looked at the Chinese as part of the indigenous system, as they worked not with the European colonisers but with the Thai feudal ruling class. Local sentiment was not directed against the Chinese minority, unlike in Malaysia, Indonesia and other countries. By the end of the 1970s, most Sino-Thais born in Thailand were Thai citizens. Ironically, this younger generation became part of the new, highly educated urban class that resulted in the student movement overthrowing the military regime and turning Thailand into a more liberal society in the 1980s (Pan 1999).

According to Skinner (1957), a Chinese family's level of assimilation was based on their ability to speak Thai as fluently as a native and the regularity of their association with Thai people in everyday life. This assimilation can be classified into three categories (Punyodyana 1971). The first category contains those who did not receive a formal Thai education. They are mostly first-generation migrants: the older generation and newly arrived modern Chinese migrants of the past few decades. The Chinese in this category have the strongest sense of Chinese identity, identifying more as Chinese than Thai. The second group contains those who received a formal education in Thailand but are not fully integrated into Thai society. This group contains mostly second and third-generation Sino-Thais, and most still identify as Chinese. They prefer to intermingle with other Chinese more than with Thais, especially when it comes to marriage. If there is to be an interracial (interethnic) marriage between Chinese and Thais, they prefer to marry into the upper echelons of Thai society to improve their family's social standing. The last group of Sino-Thais are Chinese people who are fully integrated into Thai society, intentionally or otherwise. They have been in Thailand for many generations or they have married into Thai families and lost their sense of Chinese identity, although some may still claim to have mixed Chinese ancestry (Dixon 1999). Many obtain jobs after college in the government sector, where it is preferable to hide their Chinese identity to advance their career.

Nevertheless, there has never been a clearcut line between these three groups of Sino-Thais. The Chearavanont clan is one of the many Chinese families that falls into both the second and the third categories. They are well integrated into Thai society, yet they retain a very strong sense of Chinese identity and links with their family in China. This has given the clan an extremely advantageous position in Thai society as they can effectively navigate its economic and political dimensions and influence the country's relationship with China.

Under the current Thai feudalistic social structure, the line between the military, the bureaucratic ruling class and the Sino-Thai business class has become blurred. According to Crispin (2019b), a long-time observer of Thai politics, the military junta that transformed into the democratic government at the 2019 election was supported by the most powerful

Sino-Thai families—also known as 'the Big Five': the Chearavanont clan, the Sirivadhanabhakdi clan, the Srivaddhanaprabha clan, the Bhirombhakdi clan and the Chirathivat clan. Most of the wealth in Thailand is still in the hands of Sino-Thai business families. The wealth gap between classes has never been greater and the ruling elite has little interest in changing the current system. Families such as the Chearavanonts, strongly entrenched in Thailand's political system, can dictate the direction of any government in the foreseeable future.

The rise of the CP Group and its political influence

Having examined the historically close relationship between the Sino-Thai population and the Thai Government, this section focuses on one of the most influential Sino-Thai families, the Chearavanonts. The Chearavanont clan's cultural identity and beliefs as part of the elite of Thai society are explored in depth to show how these helped forge the family's close economic and political relationship with the Thai state and, in turn, with China.

The Chai (Chearavanont) family moved to Thailand in 1921 and opened a small agricultural business in Bangkok that later became known as the CP Group. The clan maintained close connections with their relations in China, especially after the re-establishment of Thailand's relationship with mainland China in 1975. The CP Group was the first foreign investor in China and, in 1979, it became the first foreign company registered in China's special economic zone of Shenzhen in Guangdong Province. The family continued to expand its agricultural business, focusing on animal feed from the 1950s to the 1970s. Dhanin Chearavanont, the youngest son of the Chearavanont clan, adopted a Thai name like most other business families at that time and energetically sought to forge a good relationship with the ruling elites. By the 1990s, CP Group had expanded into telecommunications and become one of the largest telecom companies in Thailand (True Corp). The company continues to invest, both in China and globally (Pananond and Zeithaml 1998).

In May 2019, a few days after the coronation of Thai King Rama X, the CP Group and Chearavanont's head, Dhanin, held a public meeting to pay homage to the new king. This event sent an important message to the public: the clan is part of the ruling elite. Thus, the Chearavanont family successfully followed the lead of previous Sino-Thais by integrating into the ruling class to gain political power and secure social status in Thailand's feudal structure. For many decades the clan has supported both civilian and military ruling elites, unwavering in their support of national rulers, even through Thailand's volatile political cycles and multiple coups d'état.

Despite being political actors, the Chearavanont family never directly created its own political party, unlike other Sino-Thai clans. For example, Sino-Thai former prime minister Thaksin Shinawatra created Thai Rak Thai and later the Pheu Thai Party. Instead, the Chearavanont clan focused on reinforcing its standing within Thailand's political class by sending its members to participate in the ruling coalitions of many governments, regardless of political affiliations. For example, General Pram Tinsulanonda, a long-serving prime minister and the head of the Royal Privy Council, was an adviser to the CP Group. Later, under Prime Minister General Surayud Chulanont, the CP Group was represented in government by its lawyer and executive Prasit Kovilaikul, who became a minister responsible for the government's legal affairs. During the premiership of Thaksin Shinawatra, two sons-in-law of the clan, Veerachai Veeramethikul and Watana Muangsook, joined the government as ministers. When the opposition party formed a new government, the clan also had a connection to incoming prime minister Abhisit Vejjajiva through his father, who had likewise worked for the CP Group.

The political influence of the Chearavanont clan is not limited to Thailand because its business now spans the globe. In the United States, for example, the Chearavanont clan tried to establish its influence over the political elites during the administrations of George H.W. Bush and Bill Clinton. In 1994, to much fanfare and local press coverage, President Bush visited China and Thailand as the CP Group's guest to celebrate the opening of its licensing agreement for Dutch Boy paint factories in China. The clan's relations with the Bush family were aimed at boosting its business in Asia, and they continue into the present. Neil Bush later established Interlink Management Corporation to forge business opportunities for US companies in China through his close relationship with the CP Group network (Corn and Moldea 2000). On 18 June 1996, clan leader Dhanin Chearavanont and other CP Group executives attended a White House meeting with President Clinton. The meeting was organised by Pauline Kanchanalak, a lobbyist later arrested for making illegal contributions to the Democratic Party. This event became one of the most infamous cases of foreign attempts to influence US politics during the 1990s (Chicago Tribune 1998).

The Chearavanont clan's attempts to influence American politicians and persuade the US Government to expand its business interests into China demonstrate that its Sino-Thai cultural and political identities go beyond the typical operations of a multinational company that generally aims to increase its financial profit and nothing more. It seems that the CP Group's interests include the improvement of China's foreign relations with other states. The role of the CP Group as a multinational company goes hand in hand with the goal of the Chinese Government to use business to further China's influence internationally.

The connections between the CP Group and China are extremely significant. Many CP Group family members retain Chinese citizenship and manage the family businesses in China from Hong Kong. For example, Tse Ping, one of the richest people in China, is a senior vice-chairman of the CP Group and manages Sino Biopharmaceutical Company and many others in China under the Zheng Da Group. There are also many CP Group businesses tied in with Chinese companies such as Huawei, Alibaba and China CITIC Bank International; by the 1990s, CP Group had more than 200 subsidiaries in China (Weidenbaum 1996). According to a company report, in 2013, the CP Group bought a majority of shares in one of the world's and China's largest insurance companies, Ping An Insurance. This made the CP Group one of the largest corporations in Asia. Today, it has RMB120 billion in investments and more than 400 businesses in China, more than 80,000 Chinese employees (of 300,000 employees worldwide) and more than RMB130 billion in annual sales—approximately 29 per cent of the CP Group's 2017 total revenue.

The CP Group is by far the most important link that brings Chinese businesses to Thailand. In 2014, the company signed an agreement with Greenland Group to develop real estate in Thailand and China Mobile invested in CP's True Corporation (one of the largest telecommunications companies in Thailand). In 2016, True Corporation partnered with Huawei to develop a 4.5G network in Thailand and later launched Thailand's 5G network. In 2016, the CP Group signed up with Ant Financial, led by Jack Ma, to develop e-payments in Thailand through CP's 7-Eleven network. According to a Bloomberg report (Schmidt and Chuwiruch 2019), the CP Group's involvement in China means it is becoming ever wealthier. The CP Group is important to China's key projects in Thailand, especially its plan to connect the BRI with Thailand's own mega-project, the EEC. The military-led government of General Prayut Chan-o-cha was extremely friendly with China and was working with Thailand's most important company to coax

China into helping develop the EEC; the generals believe China can provide the high-tech materials and expertise that Thailand needs to improve its outdated, low-cost industries.

The CP Group's business empire is pervasive in Thailand's economy. Projects such as the EEC could help the CP Group to expand its business even further. In 2014, the CP Group established a joint venture with China's SAIC Motor Corporation to build a new car plant as part of the EEC, to be opened in 2017. Later, the CP Group entered a joint venture with Guangxi Construction Engineering Group to develop a large industrial estate (490 hectares) catering to Chinese investors. And, in 2019, the CP Group won a contract to bring Chinese HSR technology to Thailand. This sparked much controversy among the Thai media, which was already wary about corruption. The CP Group's dual identity as a Sino-Thai business—half-Chinese, half-Thai—has seen it take an active role in bringing Thailand's political establishment further into China's economic and political embrace. This has advanced China's interests in Thailand and helped develop its BRI projects in the country.

The Chearavanont clan's role in Thailand's government and economy demonstrates that domestic actors could hold the key to understanding Thailand's intertwined international policy and domestic politics. The CP Group's dual identity has helped the two countries forge a close relationship and its substantial interests in China will continue to motivate the CP Group to move Thailand ever closer to China's sphere of influence.

The BRI, the EEC and the CP Group

The CP Group has become the economic tool of choice for China because it has maintained connections with every Thai Government in recent history, furthering its influence over the Thai political establishment. The CP Group's domination of business in Thailand, backed by its political connections, has provided an important means for China to combine its ambitious BRI with Thailand's most important project, the EEC. According to Dr Kanit Sangsubhan, secretary general of the Eastern Special Development Zone Policy Office under the Office of the Prime Minister, Thailand must rely on China and Japan to provide the high-level technology needed to improve its economy, as he explained at the China–Japan Cooperation on the EEC of Thailand seminar in Bangkok (Embassy of China 2018).

The EEC project encompasses a special economic zone across three provinces—Chachoengsao, Chonburi and Rayong—in eastern Thailand. It is the largest project ever created by the military junta. Thailand's former industry minister Uttama Savanayana stated that the EEC was a flagship project designed to upgrade Thai industrialisation to the next level of advanced economic development by inviting the private sector to invest in 80 per cent of the project and emphasised that the EEC must combine with China's BRI for mutual economic benefit (Bloomberg Markets: Asia 2017). Legislation on the EEC was formally approved in January 2017 and became effective on 15 May, when the EEC was recognised as the most important project for driving Thailand's economic development forward. The EEC lies in the industrial heart of the Eastern Gulf of Thailand, which has been progressively developed since the 1980s. The Eastern Seaboard Development Program was established between 1982 and 1986 under the Fifth Economic and Social Development Plan of Thailand (NESDC 1981). Thailand rapidly achieved one of the fastest growth rates in the world. By the 1990s, the Eastern Seaboard Development Program had propelled Thailand's transformation from an agricultural economy into a newly industrialised economy (Mieno 2013)

The current EEC proposal includes various important projects such as the expansion of the existing U-Tapao airport in Rayong Province and the improvement of the deep-sea ports of Laem Chabang, Map Ta Phut and Sattahip. Land connectivity will be achieved through the expansion and upgrade of existing motorways—most importantly through the development of a HSR connecting the EEC economic zone to Bangkok and its international airports. Many Sino-Thai businesses with strong links to China, especially the CP Group, made concerted efforts to convince the Thai Government that China was the most important source of investment for this project.

On 11 June 2019, the Chinese Chamber of Commerce in Thailand, in cooperation with the government of China's Guangdong Province and the Thai Government, organised a conference to which it invited more than 100 Chinese businesses seeking investment opportunities in the EEC project (EECO n.d.[a]). Li Xi, a member of the Political Bureau of the CPC Central Committee, met with then Thai prime minister Prayut Chan-o-cha, then deputy prime minister Somkid Jatusripitak and representatives of the overseas Chinese in Thailand. Li later visited Huawei Technologies (Thailand) Company Limited. The Thai Government proposed connecting the Guangdong Greater Bay Area with the EEC project in Thailand. Somkid

Jatusripitak stated that Thailand, as the chair of ASEAN in 2019, would act as a bridge to connect China's Guangdong Greater Bay Area with Thailand, Cambodia, Laos, Myanmar and Vietnam. CP Group Chief Executive Officer Suphachai Chearavanont, the youngest son of the family patriarch, stated that the EEC project would help Thailand become a connectivity hub for the whole region—from China to Singapore.

Eventually, a consortium led by the CP Group that included the China Railway Construction Corporation, won a THB225 billion contract to build a 200-kilometre rail network linking Bangkok's three international airports with many industrial zones on the east coast, creating significant economic corridors from Bangkok to Rayong. The CP Group plans to provide 70 per cent of the project's total capital investment and China Railway Construction Corporation will invest 10 per cent. The CP Group also won the bidding to build the U-Tapao airport in Rayong Province. These developments are controversial, as the CP Group does not have previous experience in large public transportation projects. However, with its political clout, sheer corporate size and strong connections with Chinese companies (a precondition for EEC participants), the CP group pushed its way into the project with ease.

By the end of 2019, there were 506 EEC projects, representing 59 per cent of total investment (THB440 billion of THB756 billion) in Thailand (EECO n.d.[b]). Among these projects, the CP Group's involvement in the HSR is among the biggest in terms of investment (THB224 billion), along with the development of U-Tapao International Airport and the new 'Aviation City' (THB290 billion), which are under different Sino-Thai family consortiums (Prachachat 2019). There are also many other projects involving the CP Group and joint projects with Chinese firms, such as the more than 600 hectares of industrial park in Rayong Province (DotProperty 2018). In 2019, the total foreign direct investment in Thailand by China surpassed Japanese investment for the first time, mainly attributable to investment in the HSR project, worth THB100 billion (Post Today 2020).

The CP Group is therefore a key facilitator of Chinese investment in Thailand. Its influence brings Thailand closer to China both strategically and economically; the CP Group's dual identity as a Sino-Thai business conglomerate naturally draws the two countries together. The recent rise in economic partnering between China and Thailand is directly linked to the rise of the CP Group business empire. The Thai Government's ambition to turn its eastern seaboard into a technology hub with bullet trains, high-tech factories and 5G network communications has attracted Chinese investment. The military-linked Government of Thailand will continue to rely on Chinese investment, despite growing public criticism. If, however, this criticism develops into a mainstream issue, there could be political unrest in Thailand. As concluded by Somnuck Jongmeewasin, a lecturer at Silpakorn University's International College who studies the EEC: 'Locals would be downgraded to second-class citizens … A colonial era is emerging in the EEC area through Thai–Chinese investment policies' (Schmidt and Chuwiruch 2019).

The political backlash against Thailand's ruling elites and China

Within the constructivist framework, the behaviour of states is often dictated not only by elite beliefs and cultural identities, but also by ever-changing social norms. Thailand is no exception. The ideological schism between different Thai generations is demonstrated by the political protests by high school and university students against the retirement-age ruling generals. These protests became a fight between two ideologies: liberalism and authoritarianism. Younger generations of Thais are sceptical about earlier generations' social traditions and the feudal system. In particular, since the death of the long-reigning monarch King Rama IX, many young people have become disillusioned with the monarchy. Social media has exposed as threadbare the long-running state narrative of the untouchable and infallible monarchical institution. Younger Thais believe that the ruling political elites of bureaucrats and military officers, together with the royal family and the Sino-Thai business class, have long been colluding to oppress the Thai people.

The close relationship between Sino-Thai family businesses, the Government of China and Chinese businesses has gradually become a major topic in political debates. The CP Group has demonstrated its commitment to China's power in a way very similar to that of many Chinese business elites in mainland China, such as Li Ka-shing and Gordon Wu. During the political struggle for democracy and freedom in Hong Kong in 2019, the CP Group bought advertising space in multiple Chinese news outlets. The clan head, Dhanin Chearavanont, used his Chinese name, Chia Kok Min or Xie Guomin (*guomin* means 'national' or 'citizen' in Chinese), to demonstrate his patriotic Chinese identity in ads on the front page of *Oriental Daily*

News, *Sing Tao Daily* and *Ming Pao*, calling for the Hong Kong Government to end the protests and restore law and order (Yiu 2019). This showed the CP Group's support for and alignment with the Chinese Government. It also made the strong political statement that the CP Group—and the Chearavanont family—did not support Thailand's youth and young adults demonstrating against the country's authoritarian ruling regime, which they perceived as conspiring with the business elites. The new generation of Thai political opposition leaders also tried to use the political unrest in Hong Kong to galvanise their own movements in Thailand.

Thanathorn Juangroongruangkit, for example, the former leader of the main opposition Future Forward Party (FFP), accused the government of supporting the monopolistic/oligarchic structure of the economy and providing certain businesses with enormous economic opportunities in recent years. Thanathorn stated that these business families had allied with an undemocratic government to create laws and regulations that protect them from competition with smaller businesses (Crispin 2019a). However, Thanathorn is himself a billionaire from the Thai Summit Group, which runs an automobile parts business with long and deep political connections to the previous government of Thaksin Shinawatra. The FFP—well-known as a party for young people and the foremost anti-ultraconservative and anti-royalist party, came second in the 2019 Thai election (in terms of votes, giving it 81 members of parliament [MPs]), based on an election campaign that attacked the large family oligarchies. In February 2020, political resistance to the current government was growing fast, especially after the FFP was ordered by a court ruling to dissolve (BBC News Thai 2020). The FFP transformed itself into a new political party under the name Kao Klai Party (KKP; 'Leap Forward Party'), represented by the remaining 55 FFP MPs led by Thanathorn's lieutenant, Pita Limjaroenrat (many of the other MPs having swapped sides to join the government parties) (Bangkok Post 2020). Opposition parties started harnessing the growing concerns among young people about the rise in power of Sino-Thai businesses and increasing social inequality, using them as political tools to galvanise opposition to the military-linked government.

Consequently, in February 2020, the FFP's MPs in the Thai parliament tabled a motion of no-confidence against six government ministers, including the prime minister, using as justification the issue of social inequality and concerns about the role of big business in shaping foreign policy towards China.[1] During the parliamentary debate, a member of the main opposition party, the Pheu Thai Party, Saratsanun Unnopporn, stated:

> The Retired Army General [that is, the Thai Prime Minister] has no understanding of economics management and policy … [He] just started to use Google and is trying to understand the digital economy … [and] could not be qualified to be Prime Minister … The leader of the country has no potential to develop the country's technology … Small and medium businesses could not compete with the large businesses that could access investment capital with lower interest rates … [He] only favours large businesses … especially foreign businesses, and claims that they will help Thailand to develop the country … In fact, the Prime Minister and the Cabinet are bringing conflict into the country.[2]

She concluded by discussing how the Chinese company Alibaba wanted to access Thai consumers' data for its own interests. The government's policy of courting Alibaba may not help Thai small businesses, but it could give the e-commerce market to existing large companies. Chinese businesses may be able to take advantage of opportunities in the Thai economy and many Thai businesses might be unable to compete because the government only protects Sino-Thai businesses. In the meantime, the government is focused on buying military equipment (submarines and tanks) from China, although it is suspected that these deals are corrupt. On X (formerly Twitter), Saratsanun Unnopporn argued that '4–5 Sino-Thai clans, especially the one that donated money to support the Junta-linked political parties, have all flourished during the past 5–6 years of Junta rule in Thailand'.[3]

If the current political opposition could change the status quo of the ruling powers, there might be a chance for Thailand to take steps to distance itself from authoritarian foreign regimes such as China. China's lack of a liberal culture also weakens its future standing with younger Thai people. However,

---

1   Several politicians from different parties similarly expressed their disapproval of the government during the debate, which can be viewed in full on the *Voice TV* channel, owned by the family of former Thai prime minister Thaksin Shinawatra: www.voicetv.co.th/read/6A-EFexTN.

2   ibid.

3   MP Saratsanun Unnopporn (Twitter [X] post, February 2020). However, it should be noted that this chapter's author was unable to access the post in August 2020. Saratsanun Unnopporn posted many more comments with further detail on her personal Twitter account (สรัสนันท์ อรรณพพร twitter.com/fangbulous13), which no longer exists. At the time of writing this piece (August 2020), the youth moment with an anti-ultraconservative royalist government agenda had gained significant momentum because of the February parliamentary no-confidence debate. Protests were spreading to many parts of the country, with unprecedented anti-monarchical undertones.

China's willingness to support the ruling elites in Thailand demonstrates that it wishes to maintain the status quo. Further, the symbolic linkage between demonstrators in Thailand and those in Hong Kong led to some cooperation between Thai conservatives and the Chinese Government. Former Thai Army chief Apirat Kongsompong, who is a hardline royalist, alleged that the FFP under Thanathorn's leadership conspired with Hong Kong democracy activist Joshua Wong to instigate the uprising against the Thai royal family. At the same time, the Chinese Embassy in Bangkok severely criticised Thanathorn for supporting separatism and harming Sino-Thai relations (BenarNews 2019).

The Chinese Government and Apirat appear unaware that young people in both Thailand and Hong Kong aspire to overcome the perceived oppression in their respective societies, and that young people wish to inspire and support each other in a time of struggle. China's influence and power are not unlimited; they could potentially backfire if splits appear in the fast-changing social norms in other countries (Buchanan 2020). This could lead to a change in Thai people's perception of and relationship with China in the future.

Conclusion

This chapter has discussed the role of the Thai-Chinese business class in facilitating Chinese influence in Thailand. The existence of this class, with its historical connections to China, is one of the most significant reasons China has been able to establish a strong and productive relationship with Thailand. The symbiotic relationship between Thailand's political and military ruling class and the Sino-Thai business class has helped the Chearavanont clan's CP Group rise to paramount power in Thailand. The company's considerable interests in China and its dual Chinese and Thai identities are the key reasons for its success, and enable it to seek out every opportunity to strengthen the relationship between Thailand and China. Although Thailand still seeks to hedge against the risks posed by the great-power rivalry in the region, China seems to be the most convenient choice for the ruling elites to cooperate with.

The BRI and EEC projects in Thailand are expected to continue to develop, meaning China's influence in Thailand will keep growing, despite increasing criticism by the Thai public. Even though Thailand's opposition parties have exploited the negative impacts of Chinese influence in Thailand to win the support of the people, domestic issues related to the dominant social class and the wealth gap remain at the forefront of Thai politics. Young people, who now largely espouse a more liberal political ideology, strongly resent the Sino-Thai business class because it represents an unelected group of ultra-wealthy, ubiquitously connected, diversely powerful rulers—just as it has for centuries. There are growing accusations from academics, journalists and opposition politicians against China, but most still criticise the Thai military regime and the role of Thailand's monarchical institutions rather than China or the BRI. Given the importance of the Sino-Thai business class in maintaining the status quo in Thailand, the strength of Sino-Thai relations features prominently in Thailand's domestic politics and is high on the opposition's agenda for change.

If there were to be a regime change to a more liberal and democratic government—the probability of which is very small—Thailand's policy stance could shift from being pro-China to being anti-China. Such a pivot away from China would be congruent with the people's expressed desire to escape from the dominance of the current ultraconservative royalist regime. In so doing, they would rid themselves of the dominance of the Sino-Thai mega-capitalist businesses that they perceive as exploiting Thailand in concert with foreign Chinese autocratic entities. This could lead to the fall of China's star in Thailand, regardless of China's own plans.

A far more likely scenario, however, is that Thailand will continue to be dominated by the military-backed regime that has governed Thailand for the past decade. The political and economic influence of China will continue to expand under the direction of its domestic agents, working closely with Thailand's political elite and the Sino-Thai business class, as represented by the CP Group.

References

Bangkok Post. 2020. 'Ex-FFP MPs Likely to "Take Over" Little-Known Party.' *Bangkok Post*, 7 March. www.bangkokpost.com/thailand/politics/1873744/ex-ffp-mps-likely-to-take-over-little-known-party.

BBC News Thai. 2020. 'Anakotmai: Mati san rathatamanoon sung youp pak anakotmai tud sid ko.ko. bo.ho. 10 pee [Future Forward: The Constitutional Court Orders the Dissolution of the Future Forward Party, Depriving Its Directing Committees of Political Activities for 10 Years].' *BBC News Thai*, 21 February. www.bbc.com/thai/thailand-51582581.

BenarNews. 2019. 'China's Bangkok Mission Criticizes Thai Politician for Contacting Hong Kong Activist.' *Radio Free Asia*, 10 October. www.rfa.org/english/news/china/politician-10102019163100.html.

Bloomberg Markets: Asia. 2017. 'Thai Industry Minister Says EEC Project is Game Changer.' *Bloomberg Television*, 21 June. www.youtube.com/watch?v=_597ui E5UlI.

Brown, Michael E., Owen R. Coté, jr, Sean M. Lynn-Jones, and Steven E. Miller. 1997. *Nationalism and Ethnic Conflict*. Cambridge: MIT Press.

Buchanan, James. 2020. 'How a Photo Sparked a Twitter War between Chinese Nationalist Trolls and Young Thais.' *VICE News*, 14 April. www.vice.com/en/article/twitter-war-thailand-china-nationalism-trolls-memes/.

Chachavalpongpun, Pavin. 2010. *Reinventing Thailand: Thaksin and His Foreign Policy*. Singapore: Institute of Southeast Asian Studies. doi.org/10.1355/9789814279208.

Chicago Tribune. 1998. '2 Indicted for Alleged Illegal Foreign Donations to Democrats.' *Chicago Tribune*, 14 July. www.chicagotribune.com/1998/07/14/2-indicted-for-alleged-illegal-foreign-donations-to-democrats/.

Corn, David, and Dan Moldea. 2000. 'Influence Peddling, Bush Style.' *The Nation*, 5 October. www.thenation.com/article/archive/influence-peddling-bush-style.

Crispin, Shawn W. 2019a. 'Thanathorn Speaks Inconvenient Truths in Thailand.' *Asia Times*, 15 November. asiatimes.com/2019/11/thanathorn-speaks-inconvenient-truths-in-thailand.

Crispin, Shawn W. 2019b. 'Thailand's "Five Families" Prop and Imperil Prayut.' *Asia Times*, 13 December. www.asiatimes.com/2019/12/article/thailands-five-families-prop-and-imperil-prayut.

Deng, Yong. 1992. 'Sino-Thai Relations: From Strategic Co-Operation to Economic Diplomacy.' *Contemporary Southeast Asia* 13, no. 4: 360–74. www.jstor.org/stable/25798124?seq=1.

Dixon, Chris J. 1999. *The Thai Economy: Uneven Development and Internationalisation*. London: Routledge.

DotProperty. 2018. 'CP. judtup truamsang nikomusahakum nai EEC bon teeden pen yai kwa 3000 Rai Na Jo. rayong [CP Prepared to Invest in Large Plot of Land Over 1500 Acres, in Rayong Province].' *DotProperty*, 23 November. www.dotproperty.co.th/blog/ซี-พี-จัดทัพเตรียมสร้าง-นิคมอุตสาหกรรมใน-eec.

Dunseith, Bradley. 2018. 'Thailand's Eastern Economic Corridor—What You Need to Know.' *ASEAN Briefing*, 29 June. Hong Kong: Dezan Shira & Associates. www.aseanbriefing.com/news/thailand-eastern-economic-corridor.

Eastern Economic Corridor Office (EECO). n.d.(a). 'Guangdong Investors.' [Online]. Bangkok: EECO. www.eeco.or.th/pr/news/GuangdongInvestors ConncetGBABRIEEC [page discontinued].

Eastern Economic Corridor Office (EEC). n.d.(b). 'Investments EEC.' [Online]. Bangkok: EECO. www.eeco.or.th/pr/news/Investment-Application-EEC-BOI-2019 [page discontinued].

Economist. 2020. 'South-East Asian Tycoons' High-Wire Act.' *The Economist*, 28 May. www.economist.com/business/2020/05/28/south-east-asian-tycoons-high-wire-act.

Embassy of China. 2018. 'Seminar on China–Japan Cooperation on Eastern Economic Corridor of Thailand.' 6 June. Bangkok: Embassy of the People's Republic of China in the Kingdom of Thailand.

Farnham, Barbara. 2004. 'Impact of the Political Context on Foreign Policy Decision-Making.' *Political Psychology* 25, no. 3: 441–63. doi.org/10.1111/j.1467-9221. 2004.00379.x.

Lim, Linda Y.C., and Peter L.A. Gosling. 1983. *The Chinese in Southeast Asia. Volume 1*. Singapore: Maruzen Asia.

Luangthongkum, Theraphan. 2007. 'The Position of Non-Thai Languages in Thailand.' In *Language, Nation and Development in Southeast Asia*, edited by Hock Guan Lee and Leo Suryadinata, 181–94. Singapore: ISEAS–Yusof Ishak Institute. doi.org/10.1355/9789812304834-012.

Mieno, Fumiharu. 2013. 'The Eastern Seaboard Development Plan and Industrial Cluster in Thailand: A Quantitative Overview.' In *Aid as Handmaiden for the Development of Institutions*, edited by Machiko Nissanke and Yasutami Shimomura, 81–105. London: Palgrave Macmillan. doi.org/10.1057/9781 137023483_3.

National Economic and Social Development Council (NESDC). 1981. *The Fifth National Economic and Social Development Plan (1982–1986)*. Bangkok: Government of Thailand. www.nesdc.go.th/nesdb_en/ewt_dl_link.php?nid=3780.

Neack, Laura. 2008. *The New Foreign Policy: Power Seeking in a Globalized Era*. 2nd edn. Lanham: Rowman & Littlefield.

Pan, Lynn. 1999. *The Encyclopedia of the Chinese Overseas*. Cambridge: Harvard University Press.

Pananond, Pavida, and Carl P. Zeithaml. 1998. 'The International Expansion Process of MNEs from Developing Countries: A Case Study of Thailand's CP Group.' *Asia Pacific Journal of Management* 15: 163–84. doi.org/10.1023/A:1015485413835.

Pisanbutra, Pimprapai. 2001. *Sampoa sayam: Tamnan jek Bangkok* [*The Chinese Junk of Siam: Legend of Bangkok Chinese*]. Bangkok: Nanmeebooks.

Post Today. 2020. 'EEC longtun kugkak pee 62 talue 4.4 sanlan jin kwa longtun sungsud sang kaprajum yeepun [Investment in EEC Is Booming in 2019, over 40 billion Baht. China Invested More than Japan for the First Time].' *Post Today*, 13 January. www.posttoday.com/economy/news/611545#cxrecs_s.

Prachachat. 2019. 'CP. po Toe Toe yued longtun EEC bangkeg 4 project yak [CP and PTT Dominated in Investment of the 4 Mega Projects in EEC].' *Prachachat*, 27 April. www.prachachat.net/property/news-318701.

Punyodyana, Boonsanong. 1971. *Chinese–Thai Differential Assimilation in Bangkok: An Exploratory Study*. Cornell Thailand Project: Interim Report Series No. 13, Data Paper No. 79. Ithaca: Southeast Asia Program, Department of Far Eastern Studies, Cornell University. hdl.handle.net/1813/57547.

Purcell, Victor. 1965. *The Chinese in Southeast Asia*. Oxford: Oxford University Press.

Schmidt, Blake, and Prim Chuwiruch. 2019. 'Richest Family in Thailand Gets Richer by Helping China.' *Bloomberg*, 24 April. www.bloomberg.com/news/articles/2019-04-23/richest-family-in-thailand-is-getting-richer-by-helping-china.

Skinner, George W. 1957. 'Chinese Assimilation and Thai Politics.' *Journal of Asian Studies* 16, no. 2: 237–50. www.jstor.org/stable/pdf/2941381.pdf?seq=1. doi.org/10.2307/2941381.

Skinner, George W. 1965. '*The Chinese in Southeast Asia*. By Victor Purcell. Second edition. [London: Oxford University Press, 1965. 623 pp. 84s.].' [Book review]. *The China Quarterly* 24: 181–83. doi.org/10.1017/S0305741000010250.

Stuart-Fox, Martin. 2003. *A Short History of China and Southeast Asia: Tribute, Trade and Influence*. Sydney: Allen & Unwin.

Weidenbaum, Murray. 1996. 'The Chinese Family Business Enterprise.' *California Management Review* 38, no. 4: 141–56. doi.org/10.2307/41165857.

Wendt, Alexander. 1999. *Social Theory of International Politics*. Cambridge: Cambridge University Press.

Yiu, Enoch. 2019. 'Thailand's Richest Man Calls for Peace and Order in Hong Kong, Adding His Voice to the Chorus of Condemnation against Violence.' *South China Morning Post*, 27 August. www.scmp.com/business/companies/article/3024499/thailands-richest-man-calls-peace-and-order-hong-kong-adding-his.

Zhang, Zhexin. 2018. 'The Belt and Road Initiative: China's New Geopolitical Strategy?' *China Quarterly of International Strategic Studies* 4, no. 3: 327–43. doi.org/10.1142/S2377740018500240.

Zhu, Guohong. 1991. 'A Historical Demography of Chinese Migration.' *Social Science in China* 12, no. 4: 57–84.

7

The Jakarta–Bandung high-speed railway and Indonesia's domestic 'alliance'

Trissia Wijaya[1]

Introduction

High-speed railway (HSR) has become the cornerstone of China's infrastructure diplomacy under the Belt and Road Initiative (BRI). Chinese leaders, companies and pundits endeavour to promote HSR as a new cooperation mechanism for China to work with South-East Asian countries, portraying China as a fellow developing country that uses HSR to generate more 'concrete' development outcomes and boost connectivity (Lawrence et al. 2019; Pavlićević and Kratz 2018). In this regard, Indonesia has been one of the frontrunners in cooperating with China, if not 'the first country in Southeast Asia to join the bullet train club' (Li 2019). After close competition between China and Japan during the bidding process, on 29 September 2015, the Indonesian Government announced that China had won the rights to build the USD5.5-billion Jakarta–Bandung HSR line, while attempting to mitigate the Japanese Government's disappointment by offering it other infrastructure projects (Harding et al. 2015).

---

1 The major parts of the chapter were written in 2021. For the most updated information, see Wijaya (2024).

In an apparent effort to justify the decision, then president Joko Widodo (popularly known as 'Jokowi') claimed that Indonesia would proceed with the project because China offered the HSR through a business-to-business (B-to-B) scheme (meaning the project would not require an Indonesian state guarantee), rather than through government-to-government cooperation (Negara and Suryadinata 2018). For the Chinese Government, the project was considered the most successful and exemplary case of HSR export, in which for the first time the Chinese railway sector exported an entire Chinese HSR industry chain to a foreign country. The Chinese Government emphasises that the project created a win-win opportunity for the two countries, including but not limited to supporting Jokowi's Global Maritime Fulcrum strategy. Meanwhile, for the Indonesian Government, China's involvement in the construction of the HSR line brought about technological transfer without placing a financial burden on the Indonesian state and helped stimulate economic growth (Xiao 2018, 2019).

Scholars and policymakers have since been intrigued by Jokowi's decision to choose China over Japan and have devoted a good deal of attention to the puzzle. As a result, there has been a stream of literature focusing on the Jakarta–Bandung HSR, as well as competition between China and Japan over infrastructure projects more generally. Neo-institutionalist explanations have been particularly prolific in the literature on the political economy of large-scale infrastructure schemes. Researchers from this camp usually devote their efforts to constructing typologies of ideal HSR projects and ideal institutions for shaping them (such as a regulatory framework and system of good governance) in line with the standards of the OECD (Kratz and Pavlićević 2019; Liao and Katada 2020; Oh 2018; Zhao 2019).

Unsurprisingly, critiques of China from this perspective have been generally negative. The prevailing perception is that the absence or poor functioning of infrastructure governance systems leaves the associated financial and political risk unchecked, making HSR extremely appealing to the host government. For example, Liao and Katada (2020) argue that loans for HSR that are normally deemed unfeasible and high risk have been triggered by 'pull factors', which in this context refer to local Indonesian politicians who chase after easy money—that is, soft loans, which have either zero interest or a below-market rate of interest—for political gain. This also reaffirms Kratz and Pavlićević's study (2019), which shows that significant financial support came at a time when Jokowi's government was struggling to finance its massive infrastructure projects. Soft loans from the China Development

Bank (CDB) and long grace periods thus appealed to the government, which did not have enough resources or fiscal capacity to invest in such a risky project itself (Oh 2018: 539).

The main defect of such mainstream analyses is twofold. First, they do not adequately foreground the politics of the BRI. We often lose sight of the fact that while the BRI is in one sense a global and market-based challenge, it is also a political phenomenon played out at a domestic level, involving multiple actors and interests in the host countries. Second, these analyses do not have sufficient analytical power to lay bare the post-agreement dynamics of Indonesia's HSR, which include the negotiations over land use, the environmental impact assessment and the equity management among stakeholders—none of which was properly handled before the signing of the project in September 2015. Therefore, to fill in the analytical gap, this chapter unpacks three essential questions: How could such a high-risk and controversial project begin in the first place? Whose interests prevailed? How has the cooptation of actors originally opposed to the project unfolded? Essentially, infrastructure projects always represent a complex political calculation and the governing institutions cannot simply be reformed to produce 'win-win' solutions. Rather, infrastructure as part of a development strategy has distributional consequences, generating conflicts and compromises in which different levels of power and interests are contested (see Robison 2009).

Recent literature has inquired into how the domestic conditions in Indonesia, including elite politics and coalitions among financiers, have influenced the development of the HSR. For example, Kim (2016) posits that a Chinese coalition, backed by the then influential Indonesian minister for state-owned enterprises (SOEs) Rini Soemarno was able to balance the opposition led by then transport minister Ignasius Jonan, who reportedly preferred Japan over China (see also Aiyara 2019). Using Putnam's two-level game theory, Camba (2020) extends the analysis. At the first level, Chinese and Indonesian companies and officials formed a financing coalition to combine and wield resources to build the project. At the second level, the financing coalition encountered opposition at subnational levels, including but not limited to regional elites and competing enterprises both upstream and downstream in the Indonesian supply chain.

Following this approach, continuity for the HSR project was thus contingent on the extent to which the financing coalition could incorporate the interests of the opposition within the project. A recent publication on the role of domestic politics in Indonesia and Malaysia by Lim et al. (2021) narrows the scope of analysis, focusing on the interplay between Indonesia's central and provincial governments and how this caused a delay with the HSR project. Although it is relevant, this emerging stream of research has become somewhat trapped within dualistic terms of contention (such as the Japan coalition versus the China coalition, or the financing coalition versus the opposing coalition) and static views of political coalitions and of the conflict associated with the project. The last is reduced to elite-centred explanations and thus neglects the influence of non-elite social forces.

To provide a more fine-grained analysis, in this chapter, I apply social conflict theory combined with the concept of the politics of scale to unpack the domestic governance process that made the continuation of the project possible, despite some delays. This does not deny the existence of strategic interests and geopolitical competition, but it offers a more realistic picture of the conflicts and compromises between actors and interests at different levels that have shaped the HSR project and the BRI in a wider sense. To elaborate, three arguments are employed. First, since Indonesian state functions are unevenly distributed across scales, state actors and businesses at different levels constitute separate social forces that dispute and debate the risks associated with the HSR project. Second, actors and interests at different scales tend to dominate the bargaining over vital resources for railway development, including capital and land. The material form of the project—that is, the financial benefits and sociopolitical (dis)advantages that the project represents—requires a political settlement that reflects the balance of power between different social forces (elites, political factions, economic groups and social classes). Third, conflicts associated with the project tend to fragment and weaken the opposition (including both elite and non-elite forces), whose interests can thus be easily coopted by a resource distribution system, leading to compromise even as they struggle against the project.

The analysis begins by explaining social conflict theory and the concept of the politics of scale. The point here is not simply to elaborate the concept but also to articulate a framework that enables consideration of the complex politics of BRI-tagged projects. This is followed by three empirical sections that examine how the cooptation and compromise of actors and groups who might otherwise have been critical of the project was achieved. Specifically, the empirical sections elucidate how a politics of scale was involved in the development of the HSR and illuminate how multiple conflicts evolved (between Indonesian SOEs, between local governments and between elites and non-elites), which were subsequently contained across different scales. The chapter concludes with a summary of the main arguments and puts forward some potential areas for future BRI-related research.

BRI, social conflict theory and the politics of scale

As has been discussed, it is essential to analyse the post-agreement dynamics of the HSR scheme beyond elite-based explanations. This requires adopting a framework free of the binds of heavily 'state-as-black-box' approaches, as is common within neo-institutionalism, to delve deeper into the political machinations that thread through the tapestry of relationships among actors and interests at different levels, shaping the system of governance. For this purpose, the analysis applies 'social conflict theory', through which critical political economy scholars have explored various social forces and alliances that have shaped institutional arrangements and the outcomes of transnational projects (Carroll 2010; Hameiri and Jones 2020; Hutchison et al. 2014; Jayasuriya and Rodan 2007). The merit of this approach is its focus on alliances and social forces and the ontological implications for how the state and institutions are conceptualised by social forces and alliances.

Drawing on Gramscian state theory, further developed by Poulantzas (1978) and Jessop (1990, 2008), institutions are understood as both the outcomes of and the terrain for political and social conflict, reflecting the interests, ideologies and strategies of various forces (Hameiri and Jones 2020: 18–20; Rodan 2018: 81). This perspective provides a rebuke to the use of static dichotomies in which, for example, a host country's governing institutions are regarded as being either 'weak' or 'strong' in facilitating or constraining a particular project. Instead, applying social conflict theory conceives of governance as a process contested by interests—in particular, those of political forces within the state and forces of capital (both domestic and foreign). In this sense, as international actors (for example, China) become embedded in multiple, overlapping and complex social relations, they are not counted as merely external variables, but rather increasingly become part of the domestic power struggles in the host country (Carroll 2020; Hameiri and Scarpello 2018).

In addition to adopting social conflict theory, the approach deployed here has some synergy with the literature on the politics of scale emerging out of critical political geography (Brenner 2004; Brenner and Theodore 2002; Young 2002). In political geography, 'scale' basically stands for a territorial space in which social, political and economic relations are contested and may reflect existing political tiers within a state (regional, urban, provincial or national, for example) or cut across them, such as transgovernmental or global networks (Hameiri and Jones 2017: 454). This literature challenges the inadequacy of a 'purely territorialist, nationally focused' analytical model for understanding the politically contested shift and interrelated nature of various scale relations (that is, national and subnational governments) and the interests and actors associated with each project (Carroll and Sovacool 2010: 626–7). For this scholarship, state powers often no longer rest with the national government but are spread across authorities in multiple geographical spaces (provincial, city, regional). Power and resources are reallocated across different scales—for example, decentralising power to subnational or state-based agencies to issue licences and control land use—implying that no single scale prevails as the dominant scale of decision-making (Brenner 2004: 1–7; Jessop 2002). Therefore, as with the resources and opportunities that are located at different scales, conflicts between sociopolitical forces may be located at different scales and involve complex, tactical and multiscalar alliances. These alliances strategically reinforce or even challenge prevailing scalar configurations of power to promote their respective aspirations and interests (Jessop 2002: 195).

What does it mean for HSR governance to be contested, rescaled and compromised? First, HSR is explained as a product of conflict and compromise between multiple actors across varying scales. As different opportunities, alliances and resources are available at any given scale, actors may attempt to contest issues at a particular scale or across multiple scales that are most beneficial to their interests (Hameiri and Jones 2017: 456). It is worth noting that whether actors at the subnational level choose to support Chinese-led alliances is not determined simply by their physical location (regional, provincial, national). Rather, they are highly heterogeneous and dynamic and thus have different stances vis-a-vis the project, generating complex, multiscalar alliances. For example, ethnic community leaders and some civil society actors may favour a provincial government's moves to facilitate the project within one scale, yet other groups located at the same scale may resist this and find alliances at another scale, such as government ministries. Put simply, HSR is not a static phenomenon, but a dynamic and frequently contested and reproduced political space.

Second, the institutional outcome related to the HSR's development is contingent on conflict and compromise over how power, resources and authority should be allocated to prospective and/or existing institutions at different territorial levels. Before Indonesia's democratisation, provincial and local governments were mere branches of the central government, with direct control over their budgets and resource allocation. As decentralisation unfolds, however, the central government has devolved additional powers and responsibilities to subnational governments. Consequently, subnational governments can manipulate local issues to bargain for their own interests (Karim 2019; Lane 2014). A case in point is when provincial governments open contestation and compromise over broader issues around resource allocation for infrastructure projects, such as building licences, environmental permits and land use. They can also either help coopt the interests of non-elite forces or provoke their opposition.

Existing institutional arrangements: The case of PT Kereta Cepat Indonesia–China

After a series of negotiations over the Jakarta–Bandung HSR, during which Japan insisted that the project required viability-gap funding from the Indonesian Government, China eventually won because the government preferred not to allocate any state funds to the project. In September 2015, the Indonesian Ministry of State-Owned Enterprises quickly set up a fast-train consortium called PT Kereta Cepat Indonesia–China (KCIC; 'Indonesia–China Fast Train'), between Indonesian and Chinese SOEs. Indonesia is represented by PT Pilar Sinergi BUMN Indonesia, comprising four Indonesian SOEs: PT Wijaya Karya (construction, 38 per cent stake), PT Jasa Marga (toll road builder, 12 per cent), PT Kereta Api Indonesia (railway, 25 per cent) and PT Perkebunan Nusantara VIII (plantations, 25 per cent). Meanwhile, the Chinese side is represented by China Railway Construction Corporation (CRCC).[2]

The initial deal included lending from the CDB, comprising 75 per cent of the total USD6-billion cost, lent with a 10-year grace period and a 2 per cent interest rate for the dollar-denominated loan (Salim and Negara 2016: 8). Meanwhile, the remaining 25 per cent of the project cost was

---

2   The Chinese consortium comprises: CRCC, China Railway Group Limited, China Railway International Group, Sinohydro and China Railway Signal & Communication Corporation.

funded by equity provided by the consortium. While the problems of equity financing were yet to be resolved, on 21 January 2016, the groundbreaking ceremony of the Jakarta–Bandung HSR was held in Walini, West Java Province, and attended by president Jokowi. A high-level Chinese delegation headed by Chinese state councillor Wang Yong and CRCC's general manager Sheng Guangzu also attended the much-publicised event, celebrating the historic occasion of China's HSR 'Going Global' (Deng 2016).

Among the conspiracy theories finding a firm foothold in public discussion is that the KCIC was backed by the then influential Indonesian minister for SOEs Rini Soemarno, who sought to hold Indonesia captive to the BRI (see Sulistyowati et al. 2018). Ideally, cooperation through the B-to-B mechanism meant that the project could adopt Chinese technical railway standards that would subsequently lead to technology transfer and staff training, while KCIC would serve as the entity receiving credit from the CDB. Clearly, had the project's financial arrangements and civil works followed through, combined with the low-interest credit from the CDB, Chinese enterprises and Indonesian SOEs would emerge as the immediate beneficiaries, while the success of the project would help Jokowi build his political legitimacy. However, what was at work here was in fact far more complex.

At the initial stage, there was intense strife between the Indonesian SOEs about their involvement in such a high-risk project. With a 60 per cent share in the joint venture, the Indonesian consortium was responsible for contributing 25 per cent of the equity investment, as the remaining 75 per cent of the total financing would be provided by the loan from the CDB (Heriyanto 2016). However, these Indonesian SOEs were debt-heavy entities and, before the inception of KCIC, they were already struggling to meet their repayment obligations. Thus, they would never be able to meet this equity requirement, which was one of the key conditions for upholding banking prudence (Suzuki and Maulia 2016a). Moreover, even as Jasa Marga, Kereta Api Indonesia and Perkebunan Nusantara VIII struggled to fulfil their equity provision commitments, there was no guarantee that the project would generate a quick return. For these companies, the HSR would generate benefits only for the key shareholder in the consortium, Wijaya Karya (WIKA), which would harvest a steady profit by implementing the construction. Due to their poor financial performance and uneven profit distribution, the SOEs were in fact reluctant to be involved in the high-risk project.

One Indonesian official told me in an interview that the Indonesian SOEs first assumed that they could have achieved a firmer position by readjusting the ratio between cash capital and land assets if CDB agreed to accept more of the latter from the Indonesian SOEs.[3] Therefore, in KCIC's early inception, it was planned that the land owned by the respective SOEs would become the main asset they could hold and they could trade it to push the project forward. Although this approach seems purely technical, it exemplifies the infrastructure politics in the interplay between Chinese companies and Indonesian SOEs. One result can be identified in the earlier decision about where to locate the four main stations along the route: Halim (East Jakarta), Karawang (West Java), Walini (West Java) and Tegalluar (West Java). The final positions, however, were different from the original route proposed by the Chinese delegation before the inception of KCIC.[4]

Indonesian SOEs expect to be compensated for their short-term loss by developing their valuable land assets along the HSR route, which is expected to generate long-term profits once the project and township development surrounding it are finished. The assets include land in Walini that is managed by the state plantation firm Perkebunan Nusantara VIII and land in Karawang that is owned by WIKA. The former has an ambition to develop Walini to be a new tourism hub in West Java (Mufti 2019). Covering 1,270 hectares, Walini has been promoted as the largest transit-oriented development project, where a new township will be constructed. KCIC also set up Walini, which is known for its tea plantations and production, to become an agro-tourism and education centre where medium-rise residential and office blocks, a university and an integrated healthcare facility will be developed. Put simply, with the use of state assets such as land, if the project succeeds, SOEs will enjoy windfall profits from the land use, especially for township developments around at least two of the four stops between Jakarta and Bandung (Tempo Publishing 2020). Specifically, WIKA expects to gain orders worth IDR17 trillion from the first phase alone[5] (Suzuki and Maulia 2016b).

---

3   Interview with Indonesian government officials, Jakarta, April 2019.
4   Interview with Jakarta-based consultants, April 2019.
5   KCIC granted a USD4.3-billion construction and engineering procurement contract to PT Wijaya Karya in December 2016, together with the Chinese state-owned companies China Railway International Group, China Railway Group Limited, Sinohydro, CRCC Qingdao Sifang, China Railway Signal & Communication Corporation Limited and the Third Railway Survey and Design Institute Group Corporation.

While Rini Soemarno might have exerted influence over the initial process of HSR development, KCIC would not be able to maintain a solid position without a strong alliance among the Indonesian SOEs and the structural power SOEs have in the country. KCIC, established as one of the institutional pillars of the BRI in Indonesia, reconsolidated the state-owned enterprises' material interests and thus appeared to be one of the key social forces able to push forward the BRI in Indonesia. As can already be seen, the pre-Covid decision about where to position the railway stations— Halim in East Jakarta, Karawang, Walini and Tegalluar in West Java—was the result of compromise among these forces of capital, which has indirectly created an enabling environment for the BRI. It is beyond the scope of this chapter to elaborate on the final outcome of the HSR, and a more detailed explanation of the politics of HSR can be found elsewhere (see Wijaya 2024). While the compromise among these forces of capital has indirectly sustained the HSR development, the impact of Covid-19 and Indonesian SOE's plunging financial situation have resulted in KCIC's financial restructuring, which features significant capital injection from the Indonesian Government. However, what is discernible here is that the consensual politics among SOEs has shaped, if not sustained, the BRI's progress in Indonesia. Moreover, KCIC's interactions with decentralised authorities and the politics of scale embedded within the process, which began in 2016, add nuance to the consensual politics. During this process, state actors at different scales, such as provincial and local governments, tapped into the reshaping of governance systems and plans for the HSR. It is to this that we now turn.

Rescaling conflict and compromise: Subnational government and capital as social forces

While it is important to understand the consensual politics taking shape within institutional arrangements like the KCIC, real control of the B-to-B scheme sat not with KCIC alone, but with a wide range of actors and national and local governments who maintained control over the land. These actors could either boost or constrain the permissive conditions for the HSR. In short, the reshaping of institutional arrangements for the HSR evolved into a politics of scale in which actors across multiple scales of government bargained over the railway's alignment and station siting for the benefit of their own interests, while Chinese sources of capital were internalised within KCIC and implicitly became part of the domestic struggle in Indonesia.

In October 2023, Jokowi inaugurated the HSR and, in his remarks, named the project 'Whoosh'—an abbreviation for *Waktu Hemat, Operasi Optimal, Sistem Handal*[6] ('timesaving, optimal operation, reliable system') (Business Indonesia, 2023). However, unlike its name, in the past few years, the development of the Whoosh has been contingent on conflict and compromise between different levels of subnational government. On the one hand, these bodies have aligned their ideological and material interests with KCIC and managed to harness the existing regulatory framework to pave the way for the project. On the other hand, the enmeshing of subnational government and infrastructure politics has made it difficult to separate the interests of these groups from their material interests, which poses a challenge for KCIC (see Lim et al. 2021). They can even manipulate local issues to bargain for their own interests, leveraging the accessibility and benefits associated with station development where development zones and new towns are being constructed. This kind of political dynamic is apparent in the subnational governments' entanglement with the politics of key station development for the HSR.

Part of the justification for the HSR project derives from the idea that it is smoothly transferable as a 'reproducible, repeatable formula'. Since its introduction, the Beijing–Tianjin HSR—China's flagship development project—has been promoted as a model for Jakarta–Bandung that would create a new growth pole and promote connectivity and the development of a green smart city (Zhang 2019). Indeed, Indonesia's regional governments have expressed similar optimism, although it is highly contested whether the Jakarta–Bandung HSR will really bring about a new growth pole in the same way as the Beijing–Tianjin HSR.

Among the regional governments in Indonesia, the government of Karawang Regency has been at the forefront in defending the HSR since 2016. Soon after the groundbreaking ceremony, Karawang quickly revised the Regional Government Spatial Planning 2011–2031 directive to include the HSR (Winarshi 2017). As a strong defender of the project, the regent of Karawang, Cellica Nurrachadiana, frequently dispatched representatives

---

6   For an in-depth analysis of the HSR development, see Wijaya (2024).

to China for coordination. She even repositioned Karawang as 'the heart of the Jakarta–Bandung economic corridor' and a preferred location for manufacturers, served by major transport nodes including the HSR.

Likewise, then governor of West Java Ridwan Kamil shared the KCIC's optimism. His public statements were noted for their high hopes that the HSR would promote the economic integration of cities in West Java and that the new railway would meet the growing demand for intercity travel. In several media interviews, Ridwan Kamil expressed his support for the project and reiterated the belief that it represented a 'reproducible, repeatable formula'. He claimed:

> Operation of the Jakarta–Bandung HSR train would set a new city development standard that strongly emphasises advanced connectivity. We hope that it would also link the newly developed cities with strategic and essential places to further boost the economy. (cited in Mu 2019)

The governor not only was keen to host the HSR but also introduced a set of incentives including a tax holiday and discount scheme to rent the state's landholdings to investors willing to be involved in the project, particularly in its township development. He has also actively publicised and marketed the HSR along with its green smart city plans, heavily promoting his own image as a 'visionary leader' who furthered the development of a 'dream city' and modern infrastructure such as the HSR. The wide circulation of hyper-modern images taken from the green smart city master plan also helped disseminate the idea of a futuristic 'world city', modelled on Tianjin, which is supposed to rise out of this agrarian landscape in Walini (Widowati 2019).

More interestingly, these regional governments have also built alliances with civil society actors and other forces of capital that would like to benefit from the HSR project. For example, one of Indonesia's largest traditional Islamic organisations, Nahdlatul Ulama (NU), has been a key supporter of the project. Its West Java branch frequently claims that Indonesia will not lose out from the fruits of HSR development, as the project will help create jobs (Safaat 2015). Further empirical investigation is required to understand the terms and conditions under which NU allied itself with KCIC. What does become clear, however, is that this alliance-building conflicts with the portrayal in the mainstream scholarship of Islamic forces in Indonesia as key agents driving opposition to Chinese investment in the country.

Furthermore, and particularly in Karawang, numerous Chinese capitalists have joined Indonesian SOEs and private sector businesses in backing the HSR within their industrial plans. These new alliances constitute a cluster of industrial and property businesses that has expanded within the Jakarta–Bandung region on the back of massive global financial inflows. For example, Indonesia's Lippo Group (owned by the politically connected Mochtar Riady, who also has strong links to China) has been developing a USD20-billion mega-project known as Meikarta on the eastern fringes of Jakarta and a satellite city that would be the nerve centre of the Jakarta–Bandung corridor connected by the HSR (Wijaya 2018).

Meanwhile, China Fortune Land Development, through its Singapore office, has developed Karawang New Industry City at a cost of USD100 million. The industrial estate is depicted as a standard demonstration zone for the BRI in Indonesia to complement the HSR development, promising an integrated production and service base in the region (China Daily 2019). These forces of capital sought support from the Indonesian Government to proceed with the HSR plan, given that the success of their projects was contingent on the HSR's sustainability. The material interests of these forces of capital are also entwined with the interests of the regional government, encouraging it to take on the development mandate and cement its political legitimacy through the HSR project.

Nonetheless, as I argue here, compromises between different scales of government are accompanied by political contestation at another scale, since no single scale is dominant in decision-making (see the earlier section on social conflict and the politics of scale). Provincial governments, along with various other actors and interests, always open debates and compromises over broader issues focusing on resources associated with the project. The following section will discuss this dynamic.

Weakening the opposition and setting the boundaries of permissible conflict

At the local scale, Aa Umbara Sutisna, former regent of West Bandung, was one of the staunchest opponents of the HSR and attempted to challenge the project's progress. In June 2019, Aa Umbara was still withholding a permit for railway construction, questioning the commitment of KCIC to improve the local infrastructure surrounding the project (including roads) or to boost the local economy. He highlighted the roads connecting Cikalongwetan to the districts of Cisarua and Cipeunduey, which were intended to connect the region with 10 tourist cities the regent had been planning. He asserted that the 'Jakarta–Bandung HSR must bring positive impacts for the West Bandung community' (Jakarta Post 2019b).

KCIC instead adopted a path-breaking corporate social responsibility (CSR) approach to contain the conflict emerging at this local scale. In October 2019, Aa Umbara reached a compromise with two of the SOEs in the consortium, WIKA and Perkebunan Nusantara VIII, and with KCIC, signing an MoU to accelerate development of the 'Walini Raya Zone' in Cikalongwetan. Under the terms of the MoU and using its CSR fund, KCIC committed to improving the quality of road infrastructure in West Bandung—specifically: 21.9 kilometres of the road between Cisarua and Tugu Nanas, 10.7 kilometres of the road between Cipada and Wadon and 13.2 kilometres of the Nanggeleng–Sirnaraja–Mandalamukti road, while existing roads would also be widened from 3–5 to 10 metres. In return, Aa Umbara agreed to issue a building permit for the development of the HSR in Walini covering 6,832 hectares, including 1,270 hectares for transit-oriented development provided to KCIC (KCIC 2019b). Aa Umbara lauded KCIC for its 'clear commitment and management to bring about multiplier effects for surrounding communities that is inherently part of CSR', noting how 'the road improvement will bring access to agriculture and tourism in West Bandung' (cited in Kamaludin 2019). KCIC reiterated that its CSR program was the result of input from and collaboration with stakeholders and local authorities to give as much positive impact as possible to the public (KCIC 2019b). However, this was certainly not the outcome of simple corporate ethics. The infrastructure politics here mean that KCIC and its allies changed the narrative from conflict over land use to compromise over the distribution of benefits at the local scale, dodging the bullet of public protest through its CSR program.

Apart from conflicts emerging at the regional level, the HSR project generated resistance from social groups at many different scales. Since the project's inception in late 2015, news stories by numerous media sources dropped hints about the severe impact of the Jakarta–Bandung HSR on the environment, community land dispossession and the debt burden on Indonesian SOEs. In early 2016, numerous short articles highlighted the Indonesian Trade Union Confederation's critique, which cited the HSR decision as one of the key factors leading to the closure of Japan's Panasonic and Toshiba factory in West Java in February 2016, in retaliation against the

Indonesian Government over the outcome of the bidding process. It had been hoped that KCIC would boost employment in the region by inviting bids for work on the project to compensate for the unemployment caused by the factory closure (Alvionitasari and Wisnu 2016; Hendra 2016).

Meanwhile, activists in Indonesia led by the Indonesian Forum for the Environment (Walhi) staged a series of protests demanding that the Indonesian Government reassess the project's feasibility. They argued that rushing to develop the HSR without designing adequate control and management mechanisms, a master plan or an environmental assessment had led to several negative outcomes (Jong and Susanty 2016). As discussed elsewhere, this argument was shared by academics and environmentalists (see Wijaya 2024). Walhi, supported by some officials from the Indonesian Ministry of Public Works and politicians from Jokowi's own Indonesian Democratic Party of Struggle, questioned the environmental impact assessment submitted by KCIC in early 2016, which took only 10 days to complete and was approved in a single day, even though the process should take at least 100 days (see Weng et al. 2021: 5–6).

Opposition also came from the Dewan Perwakilan Rakyat (DPR; House of People's Representatives). Throughout 2016, Rini Soemarno faced criticism in the DPR for what was seen as an intrusion on the authority of the transport minister. Some DPR members called on the government to halt the project amid concerns about the state budget and other irregularities. Among others, Achmad Hafisz Tohir of the House Commission VI (overseeing state enterprises) expressed his concerns about the use of state assets, which could be seized to guarantee the consortium's debts, should the project fail (Riana 2016). Of greater political impact was the fact that Prabowo Subianto, a challenger to Jokowi's presidency during the 2019 general election and now president-elect, built his campaign on the claim that Indonesia's economic shortfalls were due to Chinese exploitation, and he also staged a counter-mobilisation against the Jakarta–Bandung HSR. As part of that campaign, Prabowo's team promised to renegotiate—if not cancel—the project, claiming that Indonesia 'must get a better deal', given that Chinese investment had eroded national interests (Salna and Aditya 2019).

Many predicted that the rise of this opposition combined with Prabowo's counter-mobilisation would imperil the whole development. However, in the end, the opposition campaign did not lead to further mobilisation. This was not merely because Prabowo did not win the 2019 presidential election, but also because, to some extent, the involvement of several powerful figures in ensuring the success of the project limited the scope for the opposition to influence decisions further. As Honna (2018) notes, military interests, backed by Jokowi's right-hand men, including Coordinating Minister of Maritime and Investment Affairs Luhut Binsar Pandjaitan, served as a bulwark against opposition groups which tried to challenge Chinese-sponsored projects in Indonesia. Just as in other South-East Asian countries, in Indonesia, elite-level support provided an important driving force for Chinese investment.[7] Yet, this is only half the story.

It is important to examine the relationship between elites and non-elites when looking at infrastructure politics, and such relationships can be observed in three contexts. First, as explained in the previous section, the ability of KCIC to form interscale coalitions at the provincial and local government levels as well as within social groups in Indonesia drove a wedge between any prospective alliances among different groups (including environmentalists, academics and some political factions) who would otherwise have opposed the project's development. They tried to justify the BRI-tagged project by fostering alliances with nonstate actors who would campaign for the HSR. Even if Prabowo had won the 2019 presidential election, any attempt to cancel the project would also have had to overcome contestation emerging from various state actors in West Java, since their material interests were already closely entwined with the project's continuation.

Second, nonstate actors, including NGOs critical of the project such as Walhi, unwittingly promoted KCIC's own framing of the negative impacts. While Walhi released a statement in favour of delaying the HSR until a proper feasibility study could be carried out and the land acquisition mechanism determined, it could not expand its coalition base to advocate for full cancellation. Clearly, there is no evidence that the NGO intentionally constrained or supported the project. However, Walhi's reframing of the HSR's impacts, such as environmental concerns in some areas along the rail route and land dispossession, indirectly helped KCIC to externalise the social and environmental costs around those issues (Jakarta Post 2019a).

There is an observable tendency for companies to continue working on a project as long as they can deal with the externalised problems. For example, in October 2019, a construction mishap by KCIC triggered Indonesia's

---

7   The propensity of the host state to form alliances with private sector developers, including Chinese enterprises of dubious reputation, remains all too common. The literature on Chinese-funded hydropower projects in the Mekong region often extrapolates such a dynamic (for more details, see Middleton and Aung 2016).

state-owned Pertamina oil pipeline to erupt in flames, which sparked public suspicion about the project's technical assessment. Furthermore, in March 2020, the Indonesian Ministry of Public Works decided to temporarily halt the project when it caused flooding around the Jakarta–Cikampek toll road (Rachman and Lamboge 2020). However, work on the HSR resumed the next month. KCIC claimed that new measures had been implemented to protect surrounding communities and that participation between all parties was stepped up, including in the process of land acquisition (see KCIC 2020). This left no room for Walhi to counter-argue because KCIC had nominally addressed the issue as reframed by Walhi (although implementation remained questionable). In other words, the boundaries of conflict associated with the project were reset around the issues of feasibility and land acquisition, meaning that KCIC could easily claim it had resolved or improved the problem.

Third, the B-to-B scheme generated significant opportunity-infusing aspirations among state actors, both to build intrascale and interscale alliances and to insulate some institutions and actors against 'undesirable' forms of conflict. Political parties and members of parliament critical of the project were neutralised through the narrative that B-to-B would bring about a 'steady' state. In the face of growing opposition from state actors, KCIC and its allies, including provincial and local governments, justified the project's legitimacy by expounding the merits of B-to-B, affirming that such mechanisms would steer Indonesian SOEs and Chinese companies away from the purview of the Indonesian state, so the HSR would not be a drain on the state budget (Negara and Suryadinata 2018; Parlina and Susanty 2016).

In a nutshell, irrespective of who holds the position of minister for SOEs, this ministry has been the guardian of the 'steady' state narrative and played a key role in preventing the opposition from contesting the 'debt trap' issue. As SOE minister, Rini Soemarno repeatedly claimed that the government only intended to provide legal certainty for the high-profile project. She claimed that the consortium had never requested a financial guarantee, adding that KCIC only asked for the issuance of a legal basis for the long-term operation of the HSR (Tempo Publishing 2020). Likewise, Erick Thohir, the current SOE minister, reaffirmed that the HSR was one of the national strategic projects being carried out by Indonesian SOEs to uphold their development mandate without creating debt liability for the state. The minister also restarted the project after it was halted by the Ministry of Public Works in March 2020, claiming the HSR would kickstart the national economy and create new jobs during (and after) the Covid-19 crisis (Dahono 2020).

In sum, HSR remains a political space in which conflict and compromise around power, resources and authority take shape. Nonetheless, the opposition generally remains marginalised and has instead helped compound the political fragmentation, meaning that it can easily be coopted through a resource distribution system shaped by HSR alliances.

Conclusion

The politics of the post-agreement dynamics that unfolded within the Jakarta–Bandung HSR project has been largely ignored in favour of overheated discussions focusing on elite-based explanations and static dichotomies such as pull–push factors or good versus bad governance. Using the dual lenses of the politics of scale and social conflict theory, this chapter has demonstrated how the infrastructure politics of HSR revolved around struggles and compromises across multiple scales of actors and interests, explicating why a project of this nature did not seem to generate greater resistance. It has also shown that the resultant institutional outcome related to HSR, amid the pressure of a largely decentralised Indonesian state, evolved from being a centralised pursuit at the national level to a negotiation process involving both state and nonstate actors at multiple scales.

Mainstream scholarship tends to view Chinese infrastructure modalities as the antithesis of the standards imposed by the OECD, which refer to self-development as having no political conditions. The BRI offers equality and 'win-win' solutions that appeal to host governments, which subsequently facilitate an 'enabling environment' for Chinese companies (see Rosser and Tubilewicz 2016; Shimomura and Wang 2012). As this case study has shown, this is a purely nominal approach, given that the Chinese-sponsored infrastructure project invariably opens political spaces for conflict and compromise, meaning that such a win-win solution becomes impossible. The political context involved efforts by KCIC to set the permissible boundaries of conflict, build intrascale and interscale coalitions and shape the system of governance to suit its own interests. One visible outcome of this apparently consensual politics relates to the siting of four railway stations, which was by no means a random or solely technical-rational decision. Instead, it reflects something decidedly political: consensus politics among SOEs accompanied by their interactions in a generally decentralising authority. During this process, which began in 2016, state agents and nonstate actors across different scales (national, provincial, local) entered a reshaping of HSR plans that ultimately also helped shape the BRI.

In sum, the BRI sends a strong geopolitical message to the region. The emerging literature on Japanese infrastructure aid and investments in South-East Asia hints at Sino-Japanese competition that would diversify host countries' financing options and give them significant latitude in maintaining policy autonomy and negotiating economic costs, such as offering Japanese companies another mega-project to hedge the risk (see Yan 2021; Wang 2022). However, what we learned from the case of HSR is that this apparent competition does not necessarily lead to bifurcation—that is, there would be a similar division of labour between Japan and China. From the country perspective, the BRI, as well as Japanese investment programs such as the Partnership for Quality Infrastructure (PQI), are more about providing input and enabling actors and agencies at different levels to strengthen their role or undermine that of their counterparts.

Infrastructure, which is the core component of the BRI and the PQI, clearly has a role to play within notions of development, making these investment strategies contingent and contextual. What matters most are the everyday spaces and practices where different levels of power and interests are contested and enacted. Ultimately, this study leaves considerable scope for further scholarship to recontextualise infrastructure as a product constituted by a complex web of political relations and social dynamics. When it comes to China–Japan infrastructure competition, it is not solely the BRI or the PQI that shapes the synergy between infrastructure players; rather, it is the latter that helps shape them and reproduce them in different scenarios.

References

Aiyara, Trin. 2019. 'The Rise of China and High-Speed Politics in Southeast Asia: Thailand's Railway Development in Comparative Perspective.' PhD diss., National Graduate Institute for Policy Studies, Tokyo. doi.org/10.24545/00001706.

Alvionitasari, Rezki, and Arkhelaus Wisnu. 2016. 'Minister Comments on the Shutdown of Panasonic, Toshiba Factory.' *Tempo English*, 3 February. en.tempo.co/read/741875/minister-comments-on-the-shutdown-of-panasonic-toshiba-factory.

Brenner, Neil. 2004. *New State Spaces: Urban Governance and the Rescaling of Statehood*. New York: Oxford University Press.

Brenner, Neil, and Nik Theodore. 2002. 'Cities and the Geographies of "Actually Existing Neoliberalism".' *Antipode* 34, no 3: 349–79. doi.org/10.1111/1467-8330.00246.

Camba, Alvin. 2020. *Derailing Development: China's Railway Projects and Financing Coalitions in Indonesia, Malaysia, and the Philippines*. GCI Working Paper 8, January. Boston: Global China Initiative, Global Development Policy Center, Boston University. www.bu.edu/gdp/files/2020/02/WP8-Camba-Derailing-Development.pdf.

Carroll, Toby. 2010. *Delusions of Development: The World Bank and the Post–Washington Consensus in Southeast Asia*. London: Palgrave Macmillan. doi.org/10.1057/9780230289758.

Carroll, Toby. 2020. 'The Political Economy of Southeast Asia's Development from Independence to Hyperglobalisation.' In *The Political Economy of Southeast Asia: Politics and Uneven Development under Hyperglobalisation*, edited by Toby Carroll, Shahar Hameiri, and Lee Jones, 35–84. London: Palgrave Macmillan. doi.org/10.1007/978-3-030-28255-4_2.

Carroll, Toby, and Benjamin Sovacool. 2010. 'Pipelines, Crisis and Capital: Understanding the Contested Regionalism of Southeast Asia.' *Pacific Review* 23, no. 5: 625–47. doi.org/10.1080/09512748.2010.522248.

China Daily. 2019. 'CFLD International Marks Further Progress at Latest Indonesia Project.' *China Daily*, 21 June. www.chinadaily.com.cn/a/201906/21/WS5d0c411ba3103dbf143297ff.html.

Dahono, Yudo. 2020. 'Labor Union Tells Gov't to Hire More Local Workers for Bullet Train Project.' *Jakarta Globe*, 11 June. jakartaglobe.id/news/labor-union-tells-govt-to-hire-more-local-workers-for-bullet-train-project.

Deng, Qiang. 2016. 'Indonesia's Jakarta–Bandung High-Speed Railway Project Jointly Built by CRSC Is Launched.' News release, 25 January. Beijing: China Railway Signal & Communication Corporation Limited. www.crsc.cn/news/tsi_3195_6857_17626.html.

Hameiri, Shahar, and Lee Jones. 2015. 'The Political Economy of Non-Traditional Security: Explaining the Governance of Avian Influenza in Indonesia.' *International Politics* 52, no. 4: 445–65. doi.org/10.1057/ip.2015.6.

Hameiri, Shahar, and Lee Jones. 2017. 'Beyond Hybridity to the Politics of Scale: International Intervention and "Local" Politics.' *Development and Change* 48, no. 1: 54–77. doi.org/10.1111/dech.12287.

Hameiri, Shahar, and Lee Jones. 2020. 'Theorising Political Economy in Southeast Asia.' In *The Political Economy of Southeast Asia: Politics and Uneven Development under Hyperglobalisation*, edited by Toby Carroll, Shahar Hameiri, and Lee Jones, 3–34. London: Palgrave Macmillan. doi.org/10.1007/978-3-030-28255-4_1.

Hameiri, Shahar, and Fabio Scarpello. 2018. 'International Development Aid and the Politics of Scale.' *Review of International Political Economy* 25, no. 2: 145–68. doi.org/10.1080/09692290.2018.1431560.

Harding, Robin, Avantika Chilkoti, and Tom Mitchell. 2015. 'Japan Cries Foul after Indonesia Awards Rail Contract to China.' *Financial Times*, 1 October. www.ft.com/content/eca4af84-67fa-11e5-97d0-1456a776a4f5.

Hendra, Lukas T.M. 2016. 'Relokasi pabrik panasonic: Pramono bantah terkait kegagalan jepang di proyek kereta cepat [Panasonic Factory Relocation: Pramono Denies Link with Japan's Loss in Bidding for High-Speed Railway].' *Bisnis*, 4 February. ekonomi.bisnis.com/read/20160204/257/516156/relokasi-pabrik-panasonic-pramono-bantah-terkait-kegagalan-jepang-di-proyek-kereta-cepat.

Heriyanto, Devina. 2016. 'Q&A: High-Speed Railway Tug of War—Japan vs. China.' *The Jakarta Post*, 11 April. www.thejakartapost.com/academia/2016/04/11/qa-high-speed-railway-tug-of-war-japan-vs-china.html.

Honna, Jun. 2018. 'Civil–Military Relations in an Emerging State: A Perspective from Indonesia's Democratic Consolidation.' In *Emerging States at Crossroads*, edited by Keiichi Tsunekawa and Yasuyuki Todo, 255–70. Singapore: Springer. doi.org/10.1007/978-981-13-2859-6_12.

Hutchison, Jane, Wil Hout, Caroline Hughes, and Richard Robinson. 2014. *Political Economy and the Aid Industry in Asia*. London: Palgrave Macmillan. doi.org/10.1057/9781137303615.

Jakarta Post. 2019a. 'Land Acquisition Process for Jakarta–Bandung High-Speed Train to Conclude in April.' *The Jakarta Post*, 20 March. www.thejakartapost.com/news/2019/03/20/land-acquisition-process-for-jakarta-bandung-high-speed-train-to-conclude-in-april.html.

Jakarta Post. 2019b. 'West Bandung Regent Withholds Permit for Railway Construction.' *The Jakarta Post*, 28 June. www.thejakartapost.com/news/2019/06/28/west-bandung-regent-withholds-permit-for-railway-construction.html.

Jayasuriya, Kanishka, and Garry Rodan. 2007. 'Beyond Hybrid Regimes: More Participation, Less Contestation in Southeast Asia.' *Democratization* 14, no. 5: 773–94. doi.org/10.1080/13510340701635647.

Jessop, Bob. 1990. *State Theory: Putting the Capitalist State in its Place*. Cambridge: Polity Press.

Jessop, Bob. 2002. *The Future of the Capitalist State*. Cambridge: Polity Press.

Jessop, Bob. 2008. *State Power: A Strategic-Relational Approach*. Cambridge: Polity Press.

Jong, Hans Nicholas, and Farida Susanty. 2016. 'Walhi to Launch Moves against Jakarta–Bandung High-Speed Rail.' *The Jakarta Post*, 6 April. www.thejakarta post.com/news/2016/04/06/walhi-launch-moves-against-jakarta-bandung-high-speed-rail.html.

Kamaludin, Hilman. 2019. 'Wawancara bupati bandung barat terkait kawasan walini raya, ingin KBB dikenal dunia [Interview with the Regent of West Bandung Regarding Walini Raya Zone: Expectations for West to Gain Global Recognition].' *Tribun Jabar* [*West Java Tribune*], 11 November. jabar.tribunnews.com/2019/11/11/wawancara-bupati-bandung-barat-terkait-kawasan-walini-raya-ingin-kbb-dikenal-dunia.

Karim, Moch F. 2019. 'State Transformation and Cross-Border Regionalism in Indonesia's Periphery: Contesting the Centre.' *Third World Quarterly* 40, no. 8: 1554–70. doi.org/10.1080/01436597.2019.1620598.

Kereta Cepat Indonesia–China (KCIC). 2019a. '8 Kabupaten telah serahkan hasil pengadaan tanah, proses pembebasan lahan kereta cepat mulai memasuki tahap sertifikasi [8 Regencies Have Submitted Land Acquisition Results: Now Entering the Land Certification Stage].' News release, September. Jakarta: KCIC. kcic.co.id/kcic-siaran-pers/8-kabupaten-telah-serahkan-hasil-pengadaan-tanah-proses-pembebasan-lahan-kereta-cepat-mulai-memasuki-tahap-sertifikasi/.

Kereta Cepat Indonesia–China (KCIC). 2019b. 'KCIC, PTPN VIII, Wika, pemda KBB tandatangani MoU bangun kawasan Walini Raya [KCIC, PTPN VIII, Wika and KBB Local Government Sign an MoU on Walini Raya Zone Development].' News release, 21 November. Jakarta: KCIC. kcic.co.id/sinergitas-pembangunan-kawasan-walini-raya-pt-kcic-ptpn-viii-wika-pemda-kab-bandung-barat-tandatangani-mou.

Kereta Cepat Indonesia–China (KCIC). 2020. 'Masuki masa new normal, kereta cepat Jakarta Bandung optimalkan progres di berbagai sisi [Entering the New Normal: Jakarta–Bandung High-Speed Railway Optimises Progress].' News release, 14 July. Jakarta: KCIC. kcic.co.id/kcic-siaran-pers/masuki-masa-new-normal-kereta-cepat-jakarta-bandung-optimalkan-progres-di-berbagai-sisi.

Kim, Kyunghoon. 2016. 'Institutional Challenges in Indonesia's State-Driven Development.' *East Asia Forum*, 6 December. www.eastasiaforum.org/2016/12/06/institutional-challenges-in-indonesias-state-driven-development/.

Kratz, Agatha, and Dragan Pavlićević. 2019. 'Norm-Making, Norm-Taking or Norm-Shifting? A Case Study of Sino–Japanese Competition in the Jakarta–Bandung High-Speed Rail Project.' *Third World Quarterly* 40, no. 6: 1107–26. doi.org/10.1080/01436597.2018.1523677.

Lane, Max. 2014. *Decentralization and its Discontents: An Essay on Class, Political Agency and National Perspective in Indonesian Politics.* Singapore: Institute of Southeast Asian Studies.

Lawrence, Martha, Richard Bullock, and Ziming Liu. 2019. *China's High-Speed Rail Development.* Washington, DC: World Bank Group. doi.org/10.1596/978-1-4648-1425-9.

Li, Quiaoyi. 2019. 'Indonesian High-Speed Rail Serves as BRI Enlightener.' *Global Times*, 25 July. www.globaltimes.cn/content/1159232.shtml.

Liao, Jessica C., and Saori N. Katada. 2020. 'Geoeconomics, Easy Money, and Political Opportunism: The Perils under China and Japan's High-Speed Rail Competition.' *Contemporary Politics* 27, no. 1: 1–22. doi.org/10.1080/13569 775.2020.1816626.

Lim, Guanie, Chen Li, and Emirza A. Syailendra. 2021. 'Why Is It So Hard to Push Chinese Railway Projects in Southeast Asia? The Role of Domestic Politics in Malaysia and Indonesia.' *World Development* 138. doi.org/10.1016/j.worlddev. 2020.105272.

Middleton, Carl, and Zaw Aung. 2016. 'Social Movement Resistance to Accumulation by Dispossession in Myanmar: A Case Study of the Ka Lone Htar Dam Near the Dawei Special Economic Zone.' In *Water Governance Dynamics in the Mekong Region*, edited by David J.H. Blake and Lisa Robins, 181–210. Petaling Jaya: Strategic Information and Research Development Centre.

Mu, Xuequan. 2019. 'Indonesia Settles 99 pct of Land Compensation for Jakarta–Bandung High-Speed Railway.' *Xinhua*, 12 November. www.xinhuanet.com/english/2019-11/12/c_138549889.htm.

Mufti, Riza Roidila. 2019. 'Jakarta–Bandung High-Speed Railway Township to Become Economic Hub.' *The Jakarta Post*, 4 May. www.thejakartapost.com/news/2019/05/03/jakarta-bandung-high-speed-railway-township-to-become-economic-hub.html.

Negara, Siwage Dharma, and Leo Suryadinata. 2018. 'Jakarta–Bandung High Speed Rail Project: Little Progress, Many Challenges.' *ISEAS Perspective* No. 2. Singapore: ISEAS–Yusof Ishak Institute. www.iseas.edu.sg/articles-commentaries/iseas-perspective/20182-jakartabandung-high-speed-rail-project-little-progress-many-challenges/.

Oh, Yoonah. 2018. 'Power Asymmetry and Threat Points: Negotiating China's Infrastructure Development in Southeast Asia.' *Review of International Political Economy* 25, no. 4: 530–52. doi.org/10.1080/09692290.2018.1447981.

Parlina, Ina, and Farida Susanty. 2016. 'Jokowi Gets Behind Rail Project.' *The Jakarta Post*, 30 January. www.thejakartapost.com/news/2016/01/30/jokowi-gets-behind-rail-project.html.

Pavlićević, Dragan, and Agatha Kratz. 2018. 'Testing the China Threat Paradigm: China's High-Speed Railway Diplomacy in Southeast Asia.' *Pacific Review* 31, no. 2: 151–68. doi.org/10.1080/09512748.2017.1341427.

Peck, Jamie. 2002. 'Political Economies of Scale: Fast Policy, Interscalar Relations, and Neoliberal Workfare.' *Economic Geography* 78, no. 3: 331–60. doi.org/10.1111/j.1944-8287.2002.tb00190.x.

Poulantzas, Nicos. 1978. *State, Power, Socialism*. New York: Verso.

Rachman, Arpan, and Andi A. Lamboge. 2020. 'Bungled Jakarta–Bandung High-Speed Rail Line Causes Chaos.' *Dialogue Earth*, 28 July. chinadialogue.net/en/transport/bungled-jakarta-bandung-high-speed-rail-line-causes-chaos.

Ramdan, Dadan. 2016. 'Environmental and Social Impacts of Proposed Jakarta–Bandung High Speed Rail.' Letter to China Development Bank, 15 August. Bandung, Indonesia: Walhi West Java—Friends of the Earth Indonesia. media.business-humanrights.org/media/documents/files/documents/High_Speed_Rail_Train_WALHI_west_java_complain_to_CDB.PDF.

Riana, Friski. 2016. 'House Member Urges Evaluation of High-Speed Train Project.' *Tempo English*, 2 February. en.tempo.co/read/741557/house-member-urges-evaluation-of-high-speed-train-project.

Robison, Richard. 2009. 'Strange Bedfellows: Political Alliances in the Making of Neo-Liberal Governance.' In *Governance and the Depoliticisation of Development*, edited by Wil Hout and Richard Robison, 20–37. London: Routledge.

Rodan, Garry. 2018. *Participation Without Democracy: Containing Conflict in Southeast Asia*. Ithaca: Cornell University Press. doi.org/10.7591/9781501720130.

Rosser, Andrew, and Czeslaw Tubilewicz. 2016. 'Emerging Donors and New Contests over Aid Policy in Pacific Asia.' *Pacific Review* 29, no. 1: 5–19. doi.org/10.1080/09512748.2015.1066413.

Safaat, Aat S. 2015. 'Ulama Jabar dukung rencana pembangunan kereta cepat [West Java Clerics Support High-Speed Railway].' *Antara News*, 18 October. www.antaranews.com/berita/524262/ulama-jabar-dukung-rencana-pemban gunan-kereta-cepat.

Salim, Wilmar, and Siwage Dharma Negara. 2016. 'Why Is the High-Speed Rail Project So Important to Indonesia.' *ISEAS Perspective* No. 16. Singapore: ISEAS–Yusof Ishak Institute. www.iseas.edu.sg/wp-content/uploads/pdfs/ISEAS_Perspective_2016_16.pdf.

Salna, Karlis, and Arys Aditya. 2019. 'Indonesia May Be Next Asian Country to Spurn China in Election.' *Bloomberg*, 31 March. www.bloomberg.com/news/articles/2019-03-31/indonesia-may-be-next-asian-country-to-spurn-china-in-election.

Shimomura, Yasutami, and Ping Wang. 2012. 'The Evolution of "Aid, Investment, Trade Synthesis" in China and Japan.' In *The Rise of Asian Donors: Japan's Impact on the Evolution of Emerging Donors*, edited by Sato Jin and Yasutami Shimomura, 114–32. London: Routledge.

Sulistyowati, Retno, Akbar Tri Kurniawan, Pingit Aria, and Khairul Anam. 2018. 'Rini Soemarno: It's an Instruction from the President.' *Tempo English*, 19 October. en.tempo.co/read/708951/rini-soemarno-its-an-instruction-from-the-president.

Suzuki, Wataru, and Erwida Maulia. 2016a. 'Indonesian Rail Project a Big Test for Wika's Survival.' *Nikkei Asia*, 30 January. asia.nikkei.com/Business/Indonesian-rail-project-a-big-test-for-Wika-s-survival.

Suzuki, Wataru, and Erwida Maulia. 2016b. 'Stakes Couldn't Be Higher for Indonesia's High-Speed Rail Contractor.' *Nikkei Asia*, 4 February. asia.nikkei.com/Business/Stakes-couldn-t-be-higher-for-Indonesia-s-high-speed-rail-contractor.

Tempo Publishing. 2020. *Menteri Rini Soemarno dan sepak terjang mengelola BUMN* [*Minister Rini Soemarno and Her Efforts in Managing BUMN*]. Jakarta: Tempo Publishing.

Wang, Liqin. 2022. 'China–Japan Competition in Infrastructure Investment in Southeast Asia: A Two-Level Analysis.' *Chinese Political Science Review* 8: 527–52. doi.org/10.1007/s41111-022-00231-7.

Weng, Lingfei, Lan Xue, Jeffrey Sayer, Rebecca A. Riggs, James D. Langston, and Agni K. Boedhihartono. 2021. 'Challenges Faced by Chinese Firms Implementing the "Belt and Road Initiative": Evidence from Three Railway Projects.' *Research in Globalization* 3: 100074. doi.org/10.1016/j.resglo.2021.100074.

Widowati, Hari. 2019. 'Walini, calon ibu kota baru Jabar yang diincar pengembang kakap [Walini, Candidate for New Capital City of West Java Targeted by Big Developers].' *Katadata*, 30 August. katadata.co.id/hariwidowati/berita/5e9a503 21b92b/walini-calon-ibu-kota-baru-jabar-yang-diincar-pengembang-kakap.

Wijaya, Trissia. 2018. 'China's Belt and Road Initiative: The Sum of Messy Parts.' *Asia Sentinel*, 17 October. www.asiasentinel.com/p/china-belt-and-road-initiative-messy-parts.

Wijaya, Trissia. 2024. '"Risk Is Not Measured, but Contested and Compromised": A Case Study of Jakarta–Bandung High-Speed Railway.' *Journal of Contemporary Asia* [Online first]. doi.org/10.1080/00472336.2024.2378856.

Winarshi, Ita N. 2017. 'Karawang tunggu action kereta cepat [Karawang Waiting for Fast Train Action].' *Republika*, 3 December. www.republika.co.id/berita/nasional/daerah/17/12/03/p0dkg7282-karawang-tunggu-action-kereta-cepat.

Xiao, Qian. 2018. 'Remarks by Ambassador Xiao Qian at Seminar on China–Indonesia Comprehensive Strategic Partnership.' 4 December. Jakarta: Embassy of the People's Republic of China in the Republic of Indonesia. id.china-embassy.gov.cn/eng/sgdt/201812/t20181204_2049028.htm.

Xiao, Qian. 2019. 'Belt and Road Benefits Indonesia, the World.' *The Jakarta Post*, 5 April. www.thejakartapost.com/academia/2019/04/05/belt-and-road-benefits-indonesia-the-world.html.

Yan, Karl. 2021. 'Navigating between China and Japan: Indonesia and Economic Hedging.' *The Pacific Review* 36, no. 4: 755–83. doi.org/10.1080/09512748.2021.2010795.

Young, Oran R. 2002. *The Institutional Dimensions of Environmental Change: Fit, Interplay, and Scale*. Cambridge: MIT Press. doi.org/10.7551/mitpress/3807.001.0001.

Zhang, Hongpei. 2019. 'Nation's High-Speed Rail to Go Intelligent.' *Global Times*, 25 October. www.globaltimes.cn/content/1167976.shtml.

Zhao, Hong. 2019. 'China–Japan Compete for Infrastructure Investment in Southeast Asia: Geopolitical Rivalry or Healthy Competition?' *Journal of Contemporary China* 28, no. 118: 558–74. doi.org/10.1080/10670564.2018.1557946.

8

The China–Myanmar Economic Corridor and the National League for Democracy government

Lwin Cho Latt

Introduction

In 2013, China and Myanmar developed a comprehensive strategic cooperative partnership in tandem with China's Belt and Road Initiative (BRI). China had attempted to boost its relationship with Myanmar since the National League for Democracy (NLD) took power in March 2016 (although it was removed from power by a military takeover in February 2021), probably to restore China's stalled infrastructure projects in the country and meet its global objectives under the BRI framework. Soon after China announced its One Belt, One Road project in 2013—now known as the BRI—a salient issue in Myanmar became whether, and how, to participate in this initiative. Although the development of physical infrastructure such as railways, roads and ports is mostly welcome, local communities have various concerns about BRI-related projects such as the China–Myanmar Economic Corridor (CMEC).

The core research question of this chapter is: why did the NLD government agree to implement the CMEC plan, given the high level of public criticism? To better understand Myanmar's foreign policy behaviour towards China's

BRI-related CMEC projects, this chapter examines Myanmar's domestic politics to evaluate the outcomes and challenges that emerged from policy inputs. The most important influence on domestic politics to consider is the peace process. During its five years in office, the NLD government achieved some tangible outcomes from its policy implementation, including bringing two more ethnic armed groups (EAGs) into the Nationwide Ceasefire Agreement (NCA). However, the more powerful armed wings of these groups, such as the United Wa State Army (UWSA) and the Kachin Independence Army (KIA), were reluctant to join the NCA. If the remaining EAGs were to become signatories of the agreement, this would be considered one of the greatest gains for the government.

Peace negotiations took place at the Union Peace Conference, also known as the Twenty-First-Century Panglong[1] (21CP) Conference, but they had not been without challenges. During the conference, two of the NCA signatories, the Karen National Union (KNU) and the Restoration Council of Shan State (RCSS), suspended participation in the political dialogue. In addition, seven non-signatory EAGs did not even join in the peacemaking process provided by the NLD, four of which have close relations with China: the UWSA, the Myanmar National Democratic Alliance Army (MNDAA), the National Democratic Alliance Army (NDAA) and the KIA.

Literature review

Since the BRI's inception, most studies have focused on the negative consequences of China's BRI-related cooperation with Myanmar on the country's political and socioeconomic concerns. Ramachandran (2018) observed that the Kyaukphyu Deep-Sea Port project within the BRI strategy has triggered major anxieties about Myanmar's sovereignty, China's political control and indebtedness to China, even though the CMEC is seen as an opportunity for Myanmar to modernise its infrastructure. Myanmar's

---

1   'Twenty-First Century Panglong' (21CP) was added by Aung San Suu Kyi to the label of the Union Peace Conference that had been initiated by the Union Solidarity and Development Party (USDP) government. However, the reference to 'Panglong' is controversial because of its historical significance. The original Panglong Conference was held in February 1947, at which Aung San Suu Kyi's father, General Aung San, made a political commitment to the main ethnic groups that has yet to be implemented. Therefore, when the series of Union Peace Conference (21CP) meetings began, the leaders of the different ethnic groups believed that the 1947 Panglong Conference's unfinished commitments would be followed up and implemented by the NLD government. This misunderstanding resulted in the peace negotiations being greatly prolonged.

development experts and economists have expressed their unease with the CMEC plan and particularly the question of whether Myanmar could become ensnared in China's 'debt trap', considering the experience of Sri Lanka. Myanmar has learned an important lesson from Sri Lanka's Chinese-backed Hambantota Port project, the control of which Sri Lanka handed over to China to pay off its debt on a 99-year lease. According to discussions on social media, the debt trap is the greatest issue of concern at the local level, even though the business class and government elites have committed to the CMEC as part of China's BRI strategy.

From a political perspective, Ramachandran (2018) adds that the CMEC has the potential to worsen Myanmar's interethnic conflicts. Kyee (2019) warns that the CMEC presents potential challenges, including the additional militarisation of active conflict zones and increased local grievances, which will impede Myanmar's peace process if the long-term consequences are disregarded in favour of short-term gains. Myint (2019b) sees the NLD government's actions in accepting the CMEC plan as a diplomatic concession to China over the dilemma of the Myitsone Dam. The Myitsone Dam project is dependent on Chinese capital, but it has generated a great deal of criticism over its potential environmental impact. The project was unilaterally suspended by the previous military-supported government of the Union Solidarity and Development Party (USDP) in September 2011, in response to domestic concerns about these issues and anti-China sentiment. However, Perlez and Moe (2016) predict that China will not abandon its interest in investing in Myanmar's public infrastructure and will aim to replace the controversial Myitsone Dam project with another ambitious project if work does not resume on the dam.

Due to substantial anti-Chinese sentiment connected to China's behaviour in the business sector, many Myanmar scholars seem reluctant to discuss the potential benefits of the CMEC plan. However, when it comes to Myanmar's position vis-a-vis the BRI and the associated CMEC, it is essential to analyse how the NLD was utilising China's economic corridor for regime legitimation. To gain a more comprehensive insight into the Myanmar–China relationship, there now follows an analysis of the fundamental reasons behind this need for regime legitimation, despite the challenges that will have to be overcome to achieve it.

Conceptual framework

This analysis draws on Kuik's argument that domestic politics shapes state behaviour, which it uses as its conceptual lens. Kuik (2008: 161) contends that 'the ruling elite evaluate—and then utilise—the opportunities and challenges of the rising power for their ultimate goal of consolidating their authority to govern at home', which he calls 'regime legitimation'. This contention helps us understand that a country's foreign policy behaviour is likely to be motivated by its domestic politics when this relates to regime legitimation.

Using this conceptual framework, we can establish the following hypothesis in the context of Myanmar and its foreign policy vis-a-vis China. If the domestic policies favoured by the NLD government resulted in either similar or equal benefits to those of its predecessor, it was not necessary to enhance cooperation with China when setting domestic and foreign policy. However, once the NLD government perceived a possibility of policy failure that could threaten its regime legitimation, it looked to China to support it in the peace negotiations and thus enhance the government's legitimation among its domestic constituency.

Consequently, the NLD government considered the CMEC helpful in strengthening its legitimacy thanks to the prospect of wealth creation, which would be dependent on the successful implementation of the ceasefire agreement. Therefore, this chapter argues that the NLD government perceived the CMEC as a harbinger of internal peace, which would bring about the country's economic prosperity. Hence, the BRI was extremely important for the NLD government in its quest for stability as it attempted to establish a ceasefire and generate economic development in Myanmar.[2]

To develop this argument, the following analysis is divided into two sections. The first considers the NLD government's legitimation, focusing on its policy priorities and challenges in the domestic sphere. The second rethinks the China factor in relation to Myanmar's domestic politics and how it

2   This chapter was written before the 2021 military takeover of the country. The argument here is empirically constructed on the analysis of regime legitimation, through which the government sought internal legitimation through China's role in the peacemaking process and the CMEC agreement. Given that achieving peace is also one of the main political goals of the military regime's State Administration Council, it is likely that the military leaders will follow the same path of looking to China for regime stability.

enabled the NLD government to achieve its policy goals—not least the significance of the CMEC for achieving a ceasefire and providing economic development to guarantee regime legitimation.

The NLD government's priorities and challenges in domestic politics

When Myanmar's lengthy military regime came to an end in 2011, the incoming USDP government (2011–16) began significant democratic reforms and established its legitimacy by inviting the different EAGs to attend peace talks, in August 2011. However, only eight EAGs signed the NCA on 15 October 2015, which left several powerful armed groups outside the agreement (see Table 8.1).

In 2016, power moved to the NLD. Building a democratic federal union in Myanmar had always been central to the NLD's political goals, so to implement its 'federal' dream, the government decided to follow up on the unfinished NCA process as a first step to national reconciliation. In line with the NLD's policies and principles, Myanmar's first NLD president, Htin Kyaw, delivered a speech at his inauguration on 30 March 2016 in which four policies were prioritised: national reconciliation, internal peace, constitutional reform and improvements in the quality of life (Global New Light of Myanmar 2016). These policies were confirmed by Myanmar's state counsellor Aung San Suu Kyi in her New Year message to Myanmar in April 2016.

To achieve national reconciliation and peace, four rounds of the 21CP Conference—a forum that all peace stakeholders could attend to exchange political views and settle conflicts—were convened by the freshly elected NLD government. The four sessions would take place in August 2016, May 2017, July 2018 and August 2020. Central to the rebranded Panglong Conference was the government's insistence on all-inclusive participation in formulating the basic principles required to build the democratic federal union. Attendance by seven organisations within the Federal Political Negotiation and Consultative Committee (FPNCC)[3] (see Figure 8.1) as well as the Karenni National Progressive Party (KNPP) and the National

---

3   The FPNCC's seven members are: the United Wa State Army, the National Democratic Alliance Army, the Shan State Progress Party, the Kachin Independence Army, the Arakan Army, the Myanmar National Democratic Alliance Army and the Ta'ang National Liberation Army.

Socialist Council of Nagaland–Khaplang,[4] was a historically significant achievement for the third session of the 21CP Conference in July 2018. This was the first time that 19 (of 21) EAGs participated in the conference. Such positive developments were of course welcome, but the Panglong Conference was nonetheless criticised as being essentially symbolic, with no key results in terms of the unresolved political questions.[5]

Table 8.1 Ethnic armed group signatories and non-signatories to the NCA

	Remarks
NCA signatories	
All Burma Students' Democratic Front	Joined under the USDP government.
Arakan Liberation Party	
Chin National Front	
Democratic Karen Benevolent Army	
KNU	
KNU/KNLA Peace Council	
Pa-O National Liberation Organisation	
RCSS	
New Mon State Party	Joined under the NLD government.
Lahu Democratic Union	The USDP government allowed the Lahu Democratic Union to participate in the political dialogues without having to sign the NCA because it had no active conflicts on the ground (Author's interview).
NCA non-signatories	
KIA	These groups were formally invited to sign the NCA by the USDP government.
KNPP	
NDAA	
Shan State Progress Party	
UWSA	
National Socialist Council of Nagaland–Khaplang	

---

4   The Naga armed group has a different story in relation to the NCA due to its firm stance on self-determination. Although it was invited to join the NCA proceedings, the group refused, preferring to insist on full independence. In April 2012, the Naga armed group signed a bilateral ceasefire agreement at the state level committing it to no active fighting against the Tatmadaw (Myanmar's armed forces). According to the government's spokesperson, no proposal on dividing the country was accepted.

5   Information provided during interviews with various participants during fieldwork research in Myanmar (in Kayin, Kayah, Mon, Kachin, Chin and Shan states as well as in Naypyidaw) in 2016, 2018, 2019 and 2020.

	Remarks
Wa National Organisation	The USDP government allowed the Wa National Organisation and Arakan National Congress to participate in the political dialogues without having to sign the NCA because they had no active conflicts on the ground (Author's interview).
Arakan National Congress	
NCA non-signatories: A special case	
Arakan Army	These three groups were treated differently by the USDP government for the NCA process. The government ordered them to disarm unconditionally, but they were later told that if they wanted to join the government-led peace negotiations, they would temporarily have to surrender their arms (Author's interview).
MNDAA	
Ta'ang National Liberation Army	

Source: Created by the author based on public statements, interviews and the list of NCA signatory and non-signatory EAGs released by the Myanmar Peace Center (2016).

Indeed, there were many challenges connected to the NLD government's policy priorities that could threaten its regime legitimation. First among these, Aung San Suu Kyi's promise to bring all the EAGs into the Panglong Conference remained unfulfilled. Second, the UWSA delegates walked out on the second day of the first meeting in August 2016.[6] The discussion over non-secession from the union was a major stumbling block and no outcome resulted, although all negotiating parties agreed to the idea of integration into the union as long as their demands for democratic norms and federal principles were guaranteed (Latt 2017). At the beginning of 2018, the remilitarisation in Kachin and Shan states and a certain amount of armed friction in Kayin and Rakhine states during the NCA dialogues led to significant delays in convening the third meeting of the 21CP. Later in 2018, the KNU and the RCSS, the major ethnic signatories to the NCA, announced their temporary withdrawal from the peace talks due to constraints over key principles, feelings of fatigue, dissatisfaction over intangible results and continued fighting in ethnic areas that violated the terms of the NCA. In addition, the emergence of new alliances among some of the non-signatory groups represented a serious challenge to Aung San Suu Kyi's peace process.

---

6   According to local media, these delegates were given observer passes to enter the conference. As a reconciliatory move, the members of the UWSA-led FPNCC were invited to attend the opening ceremony of the 21CP Conference's second meeting in May 2017 as special guests.

In December 2016, the KIA joined with the Arakan Army (AA), the MNDAA and the Ta'ang National Liberation Army (TNLA) to form the active military Northern Alliance and, in early 2017, this group allied itself with the UWSA. In April 2017, the UWSA formed the FPNCC, incorporating the four members of the Northern Alliance as well as the NDAA and the Shan State Progress Party. The FPNCC's desire to implement a new peace approach outside the NCA was causing significant problems for the central government in the peacemaking process.

The disintegration of the United Nationalities Federal Council[7] over the signing of the NCA, which had been brewing since 2013, was merely the final setback in a long series of major challenges for the Union Peace Dialogue Joint Committee chaired by Aung San Suu Kyi.

From the time it took office, the NLD government made clear its hopes for establishing a democratic federal union, and this focus largely determined its domestic policy decision-making. It was because it wished to draw attention to the ethnic groups constantly demanding equal ethnic rights in Myanmar that the NLD government renamed the Union Peace Conference that had been initiated by the USDP government as the Twenty-First-Century Panglong. However, the use of the word 'Panglong' caused the NLD government considerable difficulties in its negotiation process as some of the EAGs anticipated achieving full autonomy that had not been implemented after the Panglong agreement of 1947. Most of the issues they raised at the talks centred on the question of full autonomy. One USDP officer commented in an interview that the choice of the word 'Panglong' and the NLD's actions in the 21CP Conference triggered challenges because the original Panglong Conference had been so strongly associated with the federal solution promised to the key ethnic leaders by Aung San Suu Kyi's father in 1947.[8]

---

7   Formed on 16 February 2011, the United Nationalities Federal Council (a coalition group comprising 16 EAGs) was a key negotiating body in the political negotiations of the Union Peace Working Committee set up by the Tatmadaw and the USDP government. The Karen National Union withdrew from the council as a fully fledged member in September 2014, and both the Pa-O National Liberation Organisation and the Chin National Front were excluded in 2015 because of their refusal to honour the all-inclusive principle or to sign up to the NCA. The Myanmar National Democratic Alliance Army and the Ta'ang National Liberation Army resigned from the council in 2016, followed by the Kachin Independence Army, the Wa National Organisation and the Shan State Progress Party in 2017. Although the New Mon State Party and the Lahu Democratic Union became new NCA members in 2018, they continue to be members of the council as well. In February 2018, the Chin National Front and the Karen National Union were accepted back into the council.
8   Interview with a USDP officer in Shan State, March 2020.

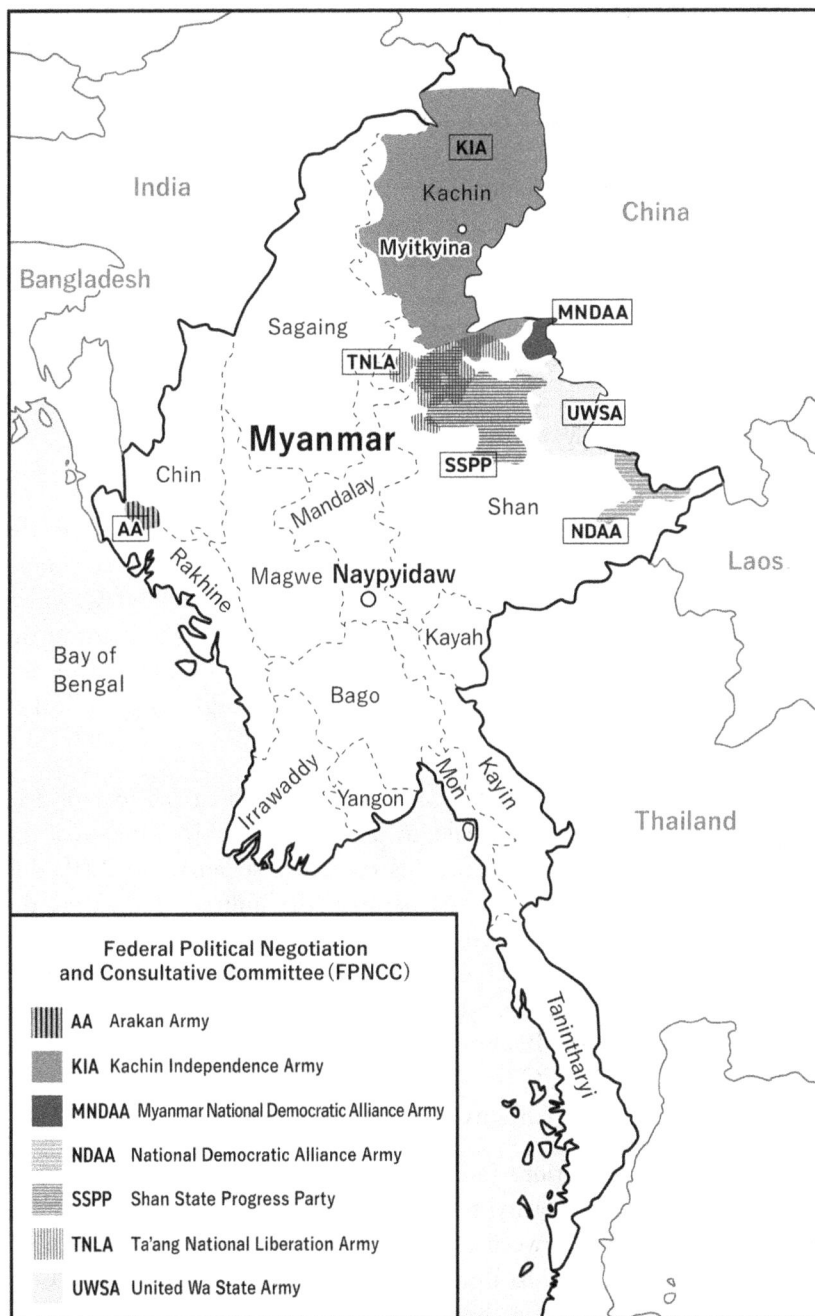

India

China

Bangladesh

KIA

Kachin

Myitkyina

Sagaing

MNDAA

TNLA

Myanmar

UWSA

Chin

SSPP

Mandalay

Shan

AA

NDAA

Laos

Rakhine

Magwe **Naypyidaw**

Bay of
Bengal

Kayah

Bago

Irrawaddy

Yangon

Mon

Kayin

Thailand

Taninthayi

Federal Political Negotiation
and Consultative Committee (FPNCC)

AA Arakan Army

KIA Kachin Independence Army

MNDAA Myanmar National Democratic Alliance Army

NDAA National Democratic Alliance Army

SSPP Shan State Progress Party

TNLA Ta'ang National Liberation Army

UWSA United Wa State Army

**Map 8.1 Ethnic armed groups in the Federal Political Negotiation and
Consultative Committee**

Source: Created by the author.

In another interview, a political commentator suggested the NLD government should focus on socioeconomic issues rather than the complex peace process because Thein Sein's USDP government, itself a midwife of the NCA, had already struggled hard to achieve a nationwide ceasefire.[9] Nitta (2017) states that the NLD government faced public criticism for its lack of focus on important infrastructure development while prioritising political and security concerns. The government's actions in pursuing the peace process meant there was a greater likelihood of challenge and dispute. In general, opinion suggests that it was highly questionable whether such an uncertain policy choice could consolidate the NLD government's power and influence within the ethnic borderlands. Indeed, Barany (2018) claims pursuing ethnic peace as a priority was Aung San Suu Kyi's most serious strategic mistake and biggest risk.

At the time of convening the high-profile 21CP Conference, Aung San Suu Kyi's government faced many practical challenges. While the signing of the NCA by two EAGs, the New Mon State Party and Lahu Democratic Union, was welcome, the formation of a new military alliance—the FPNCC, which later became a political body—to deal with the central government at the talks, together with the UWSA's departure from the 21CP Conference's first meeting and the deadlock over the issue of secession, added a great deal of complexity to the talks.

The decision by the KNU and RCSS to postpone their participation in the government-led political dialogue also considerably hampered the peace process. The formal negotiations reached a stalemate in 2019 due to renewed military confrontations between the military, known as the Tatmadaw, and three of the EAGs from the Northern Alliance (the AA, MNDAA and TNLA, but not the KIA); the first conflicts were in northern Shan State in December 2016, followed by fighting between the Tatmadaw and the AA in northern Rakhine and southern Chin states from 2018. The absence of the FPNCC from the 21CP Conference severely damaged the NLD government's credibility and caused a decline in its legitimacy.

These challenging conditions indicated that the NLD government was in danger of losing its popularity and domestic political legitimacy. As Kuik (2008) states, the link between domestic politics and regime legitimation motivates national leaders to find a way to engage with rising powers to consolidate their authority at home. In the case of Myanmar, the NLD

---

9   Interview with a political commentator in Yangon, July 2019.

government had no choice but to find a rising power as it focused on minimising loss (rather than maximising gain) for the sake of its regime legitimation. Under these conditions, the government's advances in China were influenced by its norms-oriented political goals and challenging domestic issues, as it hoped to retain stable relations of authority and improve sociopolitical conditions.

Rethinking the China factor and the significance of the CMEC

This section will outline the key role played by China and the CMEC in Myanmar's domestic politics. Before the launch of the BRI, bilateral relations between China and Myanmar had reached a turning point due to an increase in public opposition to Chinese-led investment projects such as the Myitsone Dam. Halting the Myitsone Dam project in 2011 and stopping the Kyaukphyu–Kunming high-speed railway (HSR) project in 2014 were clear signals that the USDP government had no desire to engage with China or its infrastructural projects. Cooling relations with China was seen as an attempt to decouple the mutual interdependence between Myanmar and China and reintegrate the former with the international community, especially the United States, in the hope of receiving international support for the government (Myoe 2015, 2016). By contrast, the NLD government formally aligned itself with China within the BRI framework. This caused public anger among people in the regions affected by the project and, as a result, the NLD government looked to China to enhance its regime legitimacy internally.

It is my argument that the government's approach to China, and to the BRI more specifically, was provoked by the NLD leaders' perception that the China factor could help them overcome some of their domestic challenges—particularly the participation of the UWSA-led FPNCC in the 21CP Conference and demilitarisation in Shan, Kachin and Rakhine states, which are the homelands of the EAGs within the FPNCC. To illustrate this argument, I will briefly outline the CMEC plan before discussing the major criticisms raised against it by a wide range of people in Myanmar and then analysing why the NLD government went ahead with the CMEC plan despite these criticisms.

The CMEC plan

Before the official announcement of the China–Myanmar Economic Corridor, the NLD government attended the First BRI International Cooperation Forum held in Beijing in May 2017. This was followed by a state visit by Chinese foreign minister Wang Yi, to Naypyidaw in November 2017, during which he met with Aung San Suu Kyi to discuss the BRI and proposed establishment of the corridor. In February 2018, Myanmar's Cabinet reviewed an MoU containing 15 provisions on establishing the CMEC plan (2019–30), which was then signed in Beijing on 9 September that year.

The CMEC plan consists of only nine projects, rather than the 38 originally proposed by China. The NLD government's decision to adopt just nine of the projects was based on discussions about Myanmar's overall capacity and mutual benefits. The government proceeded to formally announce the launch of three of these nine projects: the construction of three economic cooperation zones in Kachin and Shan states, the Muse–Mandalay HSR project and the Kyaukphyu Special Economic Zone (SEZ) (Lwin 2019b).

The NLD government did not identify the remaining six projects, called the 'early harvest', which means by 'putting basic infrastructure in place … [the] payoff happens later' (Kean 2019). However, it is worth noting that the New Yangon City Development project has been promoted as one of the three pillars of the CMEC, announced as part of 33 cooperative arrangements before a state visit to Myanmar by President of China Xi Jinping in January 2020. By greenlighting the CMEC, which is worth an estimated USD2 billion, Myanmar became a major partner in the BRI's beneficial projects under Aung San Suu Kyi's NLD government. Thus, Myanmar gave a public vote of confidence to China's BRI.

Before initiating the BRI, China had developed various projects in Myanmar under the USDP government, such as building oil and gas pipelines and similar infrastructure development projects. These have since been rebranded as part of the BRI (Zhuang 2017). In particular, the dual gas (in use since 2014) and oil (since 2017) pipeline represents one such ongoing project along this economic corridor. Myanmar has adopted China's CMEC plan for establishing a strategic SEZ at Kyaukphyu, three border economic zones and the Muse–Mandalay HSR project. These three projects have become crucial for Myanmar's strategic alignment with China as part of its domestic political strategy.

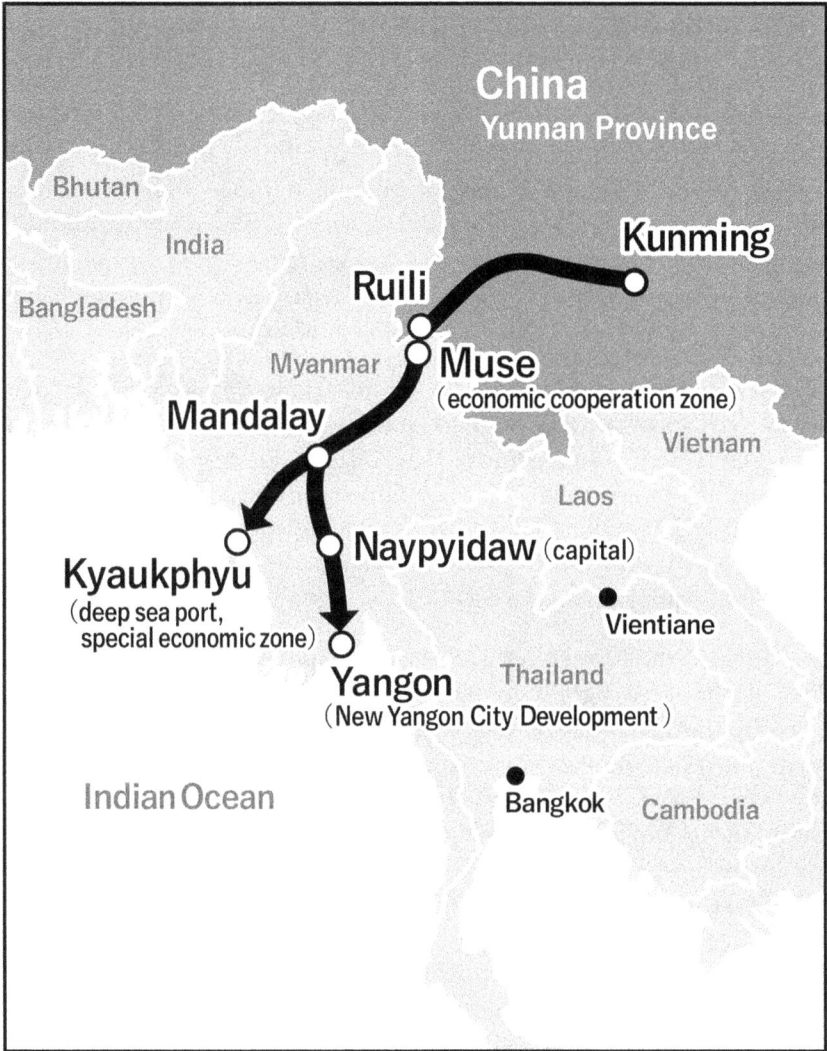

Map 8.2 The China–Myanmar Economic Corridor
Source: Created by the author.

The route of the CMEC (see Map 8.2) is an estimated 1,700 kilometres, with a Y-shaped design that runs from Kunming, the capital of China's Yunnan Province, to Muse, a key trading city on Myanmar's border with China. From there it runs through Mandalay, a major trading city in central Myanmar, then either west to the strategic deep-sea port of Kyaukphyu in Rakhine State or south to Yangon, Myanmar's commercial capital. Hence, the CMEC connects China's Yunnan Province and Myanmar's remote ethnic states with Yangon to enhance mutual economic growth.

Criticisms of the CMEC plan

The Myanmar Government's embrace of China's BRI is one thing, but its evaluation of the opportunities and challenges posed by China—Myanmar's immediate neighbour and a rising power—in terms of its national interest is quite another. A long history of bilateral relations and geographical proximity favour the CMEC, but public concern presents a real obstacle to implementing CMEC-related projects. There have been several critical nationwide protests against Chinese-led projects since Myanmar halted construction of its major China-led project at Myitsone in 2011.

Given the public's negative attitudes towards Chinese projects in Myanmar, several Myanmar political activists and civil society actors are sceptical about the CMEC plan. Myint (2019a, 2019b), for example, claims that, while the BRI can sustainably increase China's infrastructure investments in Myanmar and Myanmar will benefit from a growing economic hinterland in western China, the NLD government should have provided much more public information about the BRI.

In particular, the Kyaukphyu Deep-Sea Port project signed in November 2018 has received significant public criticism. According to one source (Russel and Berger 2019), China's investment in the port exceeds Myanmar's needs and what the nation can afford; this critique prompted the NLD government to renegotiate its shareholder agreement with the Chinese Government. As one step towards reducing public anxiety, in October 2017, Myanmar negotiated with China over the unfair shareholder agreement for the Kyaukphyu project. Consequently, the 85–15 per cent stake was changed to 70–30 per cent (Yhome 2018). As a further step to decrease financial risk in connection with the CMEC's investment projects, Myanmar scaled down the value of the Kyaukphyu port project, from USD7.3 billion to USD1.3 billion, in August 2018 (Anand 2019). Set Aung, former deputy finance minister, stated: 'No sovereign guarantees would be given for any loans financing the project, and [this ensures] that there is no debt burden for the Myanmar government, and these concerns are now quite limited' (Reuters 2018).

Another response was a public statement that China and Myanmar would adhere to three conditions to reduce public anxiety about debt threats: 1) international financial institutions would be allowed to participate to avoid the 'debt trap' issue; 2) non-Chinese investors and companies would be invited to bid for open tenders; and 3) Myanmar would make the final decision on all proposed projects (Lwin 2019a). Aung San Suu Kyi (2019) asked China to deliver projects that were politically transparent, socioeconomically responsible, publicly acceptable and environmentally sound. These actions demonstrated the NLD's careful scrutiny of all the provisions in the CMEC's MoU to ensure that all proposed projects provided genuine cooperation in line with the BRI's principle of mutually beneficial partnerships. Despite this, people still lack information about how they will benefit from Myanmar agreeing to the CMEC plan.

To reduce domestic concerns, the two countries' discussions of the CMEC involved mutual consultations and Chinese adaptation (Sun 2019). China has also been more cautious when implementing the projects to avoid provoking any changes to Myanmar Government policy that could generate uncertainty and endanger its projects (Zhu 2019).[10] Specifically, China decreased its foreign investment in Myanmar following the public protests and its approach to the elections held in Myanmar in November 2020 was noticeably conservative and low-profile (Zhu 2019).

Why did the NLD government continue to favour the CMEC plan?

Despite strong national resistance to China's development and infrastructure projects in Myanmar, particularly domestic concerns about the impact of the CMEC on the country, the NLD government decided to develop this economic corridor. There are two reasons the NLD accepted China's proposal for the CMEC. The first relates to peacemaking in Myanmar: building the CMEC could increase the prospects of a ceasefire because of the locations of CMEC-related projects across the most active and frequently fought-over conflict zones. The second is the economic development the CMEC can bring to Myanmar and the hope that through this the government could achieve its goal of consolidating its authority to govern.

From the peacemaking perspective, China's support for a ceasefire and, more specifically, its role as a conflict mediator are indispensable. Cooperation with China on the CMEC was designed to strengthen relations between the NLD government and China, which would help it make more substantial

---

10   How and whether China's position changes following the military takeover in February 2021 remain to be seen.

progress in ceasefire agreements with non-NCA EAGs, such as the Kachin, Wa and Kokang, as China could put pressure on these groups. The NLD government knew that persuading the UWSA and other non-signatory groups to take part in future peace conferences would be a key challenge. To achieve its policy commitments, it accepted China's engagement in the peace talks as a facilitative mediator, which also influenced the NLD leaders' decision-making regarding the CMEC. China can persuade or pressure some EAGs because various Chinese actors are involved in legal and/or illegal trading and arms smuggling due to their common ethnic heritage. The NLD was therefore relying on China to use its leverage to bring these groups to the negotiating table.

To obtain this support from China, Aung San Suu Kyi paid her first visit to China as state counsellor of the NLD government on 17 August 2016, two weeks before the inaugural session of the 21CP Conference. During her five-day visit to Beijing, Aung San Suu Kyi said that achieving peace and unity was her government's most important goal, adding that China was a good neighbour and would do everything possible to promote Myanmar's peace process (Xinhua 2016). In response, the Chinese leadership reaffirmed its constructive stance on Myanmar's peace efforts, its hope for the success of the 21CP Conference, its role in promoting Myanmar's peace process and the two countries' joint efforts in safeguarding peace and stability along their shared border (Bai 2016). Hunting for a peace mediator able to exert power and influence over non-NCA EAGs and increase their confidence in the peace process was one of the main objectives of Aung San Suu Kyi's state visit to Beijing.

On 24 August, two days after Aung San Suu Kyi's return from Beijing and a week before the 21CP Conference's first round started, Sun Guoxiang, then Chinese special envoy for Asian affairs, met with two EAGs, the UWSA and the Mong La–based NDAA, near the border with China (Gleeson 2016). Under pressure from China's high-level delegation, the UWSA and NDAA attended the first meeting of the 21CP Conference, although it was clear that the former was very unhappy about it (Myint 2016). One source stated that China was aware of the FPNCC's opposition to the whole process but used its diplomacy (as well as providing funds) to persuade these groups to participate (Inkey 2018).

An agreement to establish three border economic zones was signed in July 2018, comprising Kanpiketi in Kachin State, Muse in Muse Township and Chinshwehaw in Laukkai Township in Shan State. These locations are home to seven of the non-NCA groups. In addition, Muse is on the Myanmar–China border and the Muse–Mandalay trade route is vital for cross-border trade relations. Consequently, the Muse–Mandalay HSR project was signed in October 2018 and involves building a parallel road and railway from Ruili (Shweli in Burmese) through Muse to Kyaukphyu. The proposal has its roots in security concerns and is occasionally a target of attack by local EAGs. The Chinese-backed Kyaukphyu SEZ in Rakhine State has also experienced communal conflicts between ethnic Rakhines and Muslim communities, as well as intensified armed clashes between the Tatmadaw and the AA.

Given that all the CMEC development projects are situated in these conflict zones—that is, northern Myanmar (home to seven non-NCA EAGs) and Rakhine State (held by the AA)—durable political stability is essential for the smooth execution of the CMEC projects. Both China and Myanmar recognise that the concrete implementation of these projects will be impossible if there is no stability or security in Myanmar or across their shared border. Hence, for the NLD government, the CMEC was a way to generate a ceasefire utilising China's diplomatic support and persuasion of the non-NCA EAGs closest to its border.

In terms of economic development, the NLD government placed the CMEC within the framework of its Myanmar Sustainable Development Plan (MSDP), a single national strategy for a 'peaceful, prosperous and democratic Myanmar', which was issued in August 2018. Before formulating this plan, the government presented a 12-point economic policy program on 29 July 2016, focusing on economic priorities alongside its political vision of a united Myanmar. As part of this policy, the government stated that an economic framework would be established in support of national reconciliation (Kyaw and Hammond 2016).

Many business stakeholders objected that this economic plan also indicated that the government was prioritising national reconciliation to balance the interests of all ethnic groups (EIU 2016). The MSDP framework clearly indicated that the government was positioning peace and stability as its first pillar, setting peace, national reconciliation, security and good governance as its primary goals, followed by economic stability and strengthened macroeconomic management (Ministry of Planning and Finance 2018). Myanmar's embrace of China's BRI is linked with the government's

MSDP strategy, which offered huge opportunities, despite some challenges (Zhou 2019). In short, the NLD government identified China as a crucial development partner to enable it to achieve its economic goals.

In the domestic context, internal peace and economic development became key motivators for the government to maintain the status quo, which would depend on negotiating a ceasefire and achieving economic development, so the NLD government reformulated these two policies as associated elements within its policy program. This was succinctly articulated by Aung San Suu Kyi during her first visit to Beijing when she said: 'Without peace, there can be no sustained development' (Xinhua 2016). Both countries perceive Myanmar's domestic instability and ethnic unrest as major threats to the CMEC plan because the project sites are within the most restive conflict zones.

Based on these two considerations, the NLD government viewed China's involvement as a strategic requirement not only for peacemaking, but also for the state-building process so that it could achieve its primary policy goal of ethnic reconciliation alongside regime legitimation. China's role was fundamental to Myanmar's national interests, not simply as a mediator in concluding the NCA, but also as a reliable partner for national economic development, given China's economic and geopolitical power.

Conclusion

By viewing the CMEC as a feasible political prospect for Myanmar, the NLD government looked on it as the harbinger of a domestic ceasefire and internal security, which it prioritised over the country's economic prosperity, believing that economic development and increased investment would follow through cross-border economic connectivity. Achieving this stable position was associated with China's power and economic cooperation, which is why the NLD government approached China to support the ceasefire initiative and help consolidate the government's power and influence. Peace and security were key targets for the NLD government to create wealth in line with the MSDP and its goal of a 'peaceful, prosperous and democratic Myanmar'.

To sum up, the NLD government appeared to be tackling its three key objectives of peace, economic development and democracy within the single framework of the China–Myanmar Economic Corridor under the umbrella of the BRI. This is why the NLD government led by Aung San Suu Kyi welcomed China's diplomatic facilitation in Myanmar's peacemaking process and its financial engagement in economic cooperation to sustain domestic regime legitimation. However, given the fall of the NLD government in 2021, it is impossible to say whether this was a rational course of action for the government of Aung Sang Suu Kyi.

References

Anand, Bring V. 2019. 'A Perspective on China Myanmar Economic Corridor and Internal Dynamics.' 5 July. New Delhi: Vivekananda International Foundation. www.vifindia.org/article/2019/july/05/a-perspective-on-china-myanmar-economic-corridor-and-internal-dynamics.

Aung San Suu Kyi. 2019. 'Statement by Daw Aung San Suu Kyi, State Counsellor of the Republic of the Union of Myanmar at the High Level Meeting of the Second Belt and Road Forum for International Cooperation.' Beijing, 27 April. Naypyidaw: Ministry of Information of the Republic of the Union of Myanmar.

Bai, Tiantian. 2016. 'Suu Kyi Moves to Expand China Ties.' *Global Times*, 19 August.

Barany, Zoltan. 2018. 'Burma: Suu Kyi's Missteps.' *Journal of Democracy* 29, no. 1: 5–19. doi.org/10.1353/jod.2018.0000.

Economist Intelligence Unit (EIU). 2016. *Twelve-Point Economic 'Plan' Disappoints*. Report, 4 August. London: The Economist Intelligence Unit. country.eiu.com/article.aspx?articleid=1004473884&Country=Myanmar&topic=Economy&subtopic=Forecast&subsubtopic=Policy+trends.

Gleeson, Sean. 2016. 'Beijing Reps Meet with Border Armed Groups as Peace Conference Nears.' *Frontier Myanmar*, 29 August. frontiermyanmar.net/en/beijing-reps-meet-with-border-armed-groups-as-peace-conference-nears.

Global New Light of Myanmar. 2016. 'Transition Complete: U Htin Kyaw Sworn in as President.' *The Global New Light of Myanmar*, 31 March. www.burmalibrary.org/sites/burmalibrary.org/files/obl/docs21/31_Mar_16_gnlm.pdf.

Inkey, Mark. 2018. 'China's Stake in the Myanmar Peace Process: Why Is Beijing Providing Funds for Ethnic Armed Groups to Join a Government-Backed Peace Conference?' *The Diplomat*, 15 August. thediplomat.com/2018/08/chinas-stake-in-the-myanmar-peace-process.

Kean, Thomas. 2019. 'Myanmar Sets a Slower Pace for the Belt and Road.' *Frontier Myanmar*, 24 May. frontiermyanmar.net/en/myanmar-sets-a-slower-pace-for-the-belt-and-road.

Kuik, Cheng-Chwee. 2008. 'The Essence of Hedging: Malaysia and Singapore's Response to a Rising China.' *Contemporary Southeast Asia* 30, no. 2: 159–85. doi.org/10.1355/CS30-2A.

Kyaw, Aye T., and Clare Hammond. 2016. 'Government Reveals 12-Point Economic Policy.' *Myanmar Times*, 29 July. www.mmtimes.com/business/21664-nld-12-point-economic-policy-announcement.html [page discontinued].

Kyee, Khin Khin K. 2019. *Finding Peace along the China–Myanmar Economic Corridor: Between Short-Term Interests and Long-Lasting Peace*. Myanmar–China Research Project Working Paper No. 3. Chiang Mai: Institute for Strategy and Policy.

Latt, Lwin Cho. 2017. 'Myanmar Stumbling over Non-Secession.' *East Asia Forum*, 30 June. www.eastasiaforum.org/2017/06/30/myanmar-stumbling-over-non-secession. doi.org/10.18356/15645304-2017-1-14.

Lwin, Nan. 2019a. 'Gov't Spells Out Conditions for Signing BRI Deals with China.' *The Irrawaddy*, 30 May. www.irrawaddy.com/business/govt-spells-conditions-signing-bri-deals-china.html.

Lwin, Nan. 2019b. 'In Myanmar, China's BRI Projects Are Old Wine in a New Bottle.' *The Irrawaddy*, 8 November. www.irrawaddy.com/news/burma/in-myanmar-chinas-bri-projects-are-old-wine-in-a-new-bottle.html.

Ministry of Planning and Finance. 2018. *Myanmar Sustainable Development Plan (2018–2030)*. Naypyidaw: The Government of the Republic of the Union of Myanmar. cdn.climatepolicyradar.org/navigator/MMR/2018/myanmar-sustainable-development-plan-2018-2030_64d1d4e6f97c1daf22c3fecd3690a658.pdf.

Myanmar Peace Center. 2016. 'List of NCA Signatory and Non NCA-Signatory Ethnic Armed Groups.' Unpublished memo. Yangon.

Myint, Sithu Aung. 2016. 'Panglong and the Wa Walkout.' *Frontier Myanmar*, 25 September. frontiermyanmar.net/en/panglong-and-the-wa-walkout.

Myint, U. 2019a. 'Myanmar: Going from Pause to Fast Forward with China's Belt and Road Initiative (BRI).' *Republic of the Union of Myanmar Federation of Chambers of Commerce and Industry (UMFCCI) Centennial Magazine*, 30 July. ispmyanmarchinadesk.com/wp-content/uploads/2019/10/UMFCCI_Centennial-Magazine_Myanmar-from-Pause-to-Fast-Forward-with-BRI.pdf.

Myint, U. 2019b. '"Thinking, Fast and Slow" on the Belt and Road: Myanmar's Experience with China.' *ISEAS Perspective* 90. Singapore: ISEAS–Yusof Ishak Institute. www.iseas.edu.sg/wp-content/uploads/pdfs/ISEAS_Perspective_2019 _90.pdf.

Myoe, Maung A. 2015. 'Myanmar's China Policy since 2011: Determinants and Directions.' *Journal of Current Southeast Asian Affairs* 34, no. 2: 21–54. doi.org/ 10.1177/186810341503400202.

Myoe, Maung A. 2016. 'Myanmar's Foreign Policy under the USDP Government: Continuities and Changes.' *Journal of Current Southeast Asian Affairs* 35, no. 1: 123–50. doi.org/10.1177/186810341603500105.

Nitta, Yuichi. 2017. 'Myanmar and China to Cooperate on Economic Corridor.' *Nikkei Asian Review*, 2 December. asia.nikkei.com/Politics-Economy/International-Relations/Myanmar-and-China-to-cooperate-on-economic-corridor?page=1.

Perlez, Jane, and Wai Moe. 2016. 'Visiting Beijing, Myanmar's Aung San Suu Kyi Seeks to Mend Relations.' *New York Times*, 17 August. www.nytimes.com/2016/ 08/18/world/asia/visiting-beijing-myanmars-aung-san-suu-kyi-seeks-to-mend-relations.html.

Ramachandran, Sudha. 2018. 'China–Myanmar Economic Corridor Ambitions Meet Hard Reality.' *China Brief 18*, no. 15.

Reuters. 2018. 'Myanmar Scales Back China-Funded Kyauk Pyu Port Project in Rakhine State Due to Debt Concern.' *South China Morning Post*, 2 August. www.scmp.com/news/asia/southeast-asia/article/2158015/myanmar-scales-back-china-funded-kyauk-pyu-port-project.

Russel, Daniel R., and Blake Berger. 2019. *Navigating the Belt and Road Initiative*. A Report of the Asia Society Policy Institute, June. New York: Asia Society. asiasociety.org/sites/default/files/2019-06/Navigating%20the%20Belt%20and %20Road%20Initiative_2.pdf.

Sun, Yun. 2019. 'Slower, Smaller, Cheaper: The Reality of the China–Myanmar Economic Corridor.' *Frontier Myanmar*, 26 September. frontiermyanmar.net/en/ slower-smaller-cheaper-the-reality-of-the-china-myanmar-economic-corridor.

Xinhua. 2016. 'China Focus: Suu Kyi Says Peace Is Top Aim in M8yanmar.' *Xinhua*, 20 August. www.xinhuanet.com//english/2016-08/20/c_135618503.htm.

Yhome, K. 2018. 'The BRI and Myanmar's China Debate.' *Expert Speak*, 11 July. New Delhi: Observer Research Foundation. www.orfonline.org/expert-speak/bri-myanmar-china-debate.

Zhou, Taidong. 2019. 'Aligning the Belt and Road Initiative with Myanmar's Sustainable Development Plan: Opportunities and Challenges.' *IDS Bulletin: The Belt and Road Initiative and the SDGs—Towards Equitable, Sustainable Development* 50, no. 4: 69–88. doi.org/10.19088/1968-2019.139.

Zhu, Xianghui. 2019. 'China's Mega-Projects in Myanmar: What Next?' *ISEAS Perspective 84* (17 October). Singapore: ISEAS–Yusof Ishak Institute. www.iseas.edu.sg/wp-content/uploads/pdfs/ISEAS_Perspective_2019_84.pdf.

Zhuang, Beining. 2017. 'Spotlight: China–Myanmar Oil, Gas Project Benefits Both.' *Xinhua*, 10 May. www.xinhuanet.com/english/2017-05/10/c_136272395.htm.

9

The impact of domestic politics on BRI projects: The case of the China–Pakistan Economic Corridor

Filippo Boni

Introduction

When President of China Xi Jinping announced between September and October 2013 his plans to establish the Silk Road Economic Belt and the Twenty-First-Century Maritime Silk Road (which later became known as the Belt and Road Initiative), Pakistan was one of the first countries to embrace China's ambition to redefine relations between Asia and Europe. With a business-oriented leadership emerging from the 2013 elections, and the control of the Port of Gwadar handed over by the Pakistan Government to the China Overseas Ports Holding Company earlier that year, the political will was present on both sides to kickstart the China–Pakistan Economic Corridor (CPEC). CPEC has since come to represent a key test for China's global ambitions, given the amount of investment (about USD25 billion) and political capital that Beijing has invested in Pakistan. While early analyses focused on the geopolitical motivations behind CPEC, it was clear from the beginning that Pakistan's domestic politics were going to be a key variable in assessing the evolution of the projects. The federal nature of the Pakistan state, the precarious equilibrium between elected representatives and military officials and the relatively young democratic institutions have all become key factors in determining CPEC's trajectory. The aim of this chapter is therefore to provide an assessment of how CPEC has been internalised within Pakistan and how its domestic dynamics absorbed and, in turn, shaped the evolution of CPEC.

CPEC is an ideal case study to assess the internalisation of the BRI for several reasons. First, Pakistan has in recent years been one of the key flashpoints in which the competition between the United States and China has materialised (Boni 2021b). A case in point was the remarks made in November 2019 by then principal deputy assistant secretary of the US Bureau of South and Central Asian Affairs, Ambassador Alice Wells, who publicly criticised CPEC for its lack of transparency and debt implications (US Department of State 2019). Along similar lines, in May 2020, Ambassador Wells asked China to waive Pakistan's debt during the Covid-19 pandemic (Kamran 2020). Both sets of remarks were rejected by the Chinese Embassy and Pakistan's Foreign Office. As these instances show, understanding the domestic politics behind CPEC has wider regional and global implications as part of the Sino-US rivalry. Second, CPEC has by far the most advanced set of projects under the aegis of the Belt and Road Initiative (BRI) and the coordination mechanism between Pakistan and China is one of the most institutionalised, as it occurs through a joint decision-making body, the Joint Cooperation Committee.[1] Third, the myriad complex interests in the decision-making process within Pakistan, with CPEC becoming a cause of disagreements between civilian and military leaders, provide an ideal springboard to analyse how local stakeholders interacted with Chinese projects and how the latter have been internalised. As Senator Sherry Rehman (2019), former convener of the Senate Special Committee on the China–Pakistan Economic Corridor, clearly stated, 'the divergence in processes between a centralised Chinese Communist party government and Pakistan's nascent democratic parties and governance structures' has been one of the 'major roadblocks' of CPEC. This was also echoed by an editorial published in China's *Global Times* by Liu Zongyi (2019), who unequivocally claimed that 'the largest difficulty' in the construction of CPEC had 'to do with Pakistan's domestic politics'. It is therefore key to investigate this further.

The internalisation of the projects across the more than 148 countries that have in various shapes and forms joined China's initiative is also becoming increasingly important in the wider academic literature. While several

---

1   The Joint Cooperation Committee is jointly headed by the Minister for Planning, Development and Reform of Pakistan and the head of China's National Development and Reform Commission.

works are primarily focused on dissecting the geopolitical dynamics and motivations behind the initiative (Li 2020; Zhou and Esteban 2018; Clarke 2017; Ferdinand 2016; Callahan 2016), the focus is progressively shifting towards the domestic implications in BRI recipient countries. Going beyond monolithic interpretations of 'China', scholars within this strand have looked at the interests involved in the making of the BRI, including local governments, SOEs and, more broadly, Chinese politics (Jones and Hameiri 2021; Jie and Ridout 2021; Chen at al. 2019; Jones and Zeng 2019; He 2019). There is also a growing strand of literature that places greater emphasis on the domestic politics in countries receiving Chinese investments across South and South-East Asia as well as Latin America (Abb et al. 2024; Adeney and Boni 2024; Safdar 2021, 2022; van der Zwan 2022; Adeney and Boni 2021a; Boni and Adeney 2020; Leiva 2020; Liu and Lim 2019; Rowedder 2020). In their analysis of Malaysia, Liu and Lim (2019: 222) identify three key variables 'undergirding the BRI'—namely, the 'intertwining of [a] domestic ethno-political agenda with Chinese objectives', 'state–federal contestation' and 'convergence of geopolitical goals'. They argue that 'only when these three variables are properly addressed' can the projects 'be rolled out successfully'.

Building on this analytical framework, this chapter introduces one additional variable, change in leadership, which is crucial to understand BRI projects and the way they are internalised in the recipient countries. Analyses of CPEC have so far focused on the first two of Liu and Lim's three key variables (Abb 2022; Boni and Adeney 2020; Ahmed 2019) and the third (Garlick 2022; Boni 2019, 2021a), but to understand the factors undergirding the implementation of CPEC, 'change in leadership' is also key. It describes the alternation in power at the federal level between different political parties and leaders. Examples across other BRI countries—notably, Malaysia and Sri Lanka—have shown that leadership change does matter for the way in which BRI projects are taken forward. Sir Lanka halted projects for a year after Maithripala Sirisena came to power in the 2015 elections, then restarted them on the condition that some terms of the projects were changed. Similarly, Malaysia, following Mahathir Mohamad's election in 2018, negotiated a reduction in the cost of the East Coast Rail Link by one-third (Mitchell and Woodhouse 2019). In light of these examples, it is therefore important to trace how the evolution of CPEC was impacted by the July 2018 elections, in which Pakistan Tehreek-e-Insaf (PTI; 'Pakistan Justice Movement') defeated then prime minister Nawaz Sharif's party, the Pakistan Muslim League (Nawaz) (PML-N), and became the leading party.

By bringing this additional variable into the discussion, this chapter helps to develop a more comprehensive heuristic analytical framework to understand how domestic politics have become a determining factor in BRI projects. Moving beyond systemic analyses dissecting the geopolitical implications of the BRI, this chapter contributes to the still limited literature that underlines the importance of analysing how the BRI is unfolding on the ground. Rather than a top-down endeavour, the BRI is a complex mechanism of intertwined interests, whereby local actors have an important stake in the way in which the projects are implemented, alongside Chinese interests.

To investigate the internalisation of BRI projects in Pakistan, this chapter presents a longitudinal study of CPEC-related dynamics between 2017 and 2020 as these three years represent a critical juncture in Pakistan's domestic politics and, consequently, in its relations with China. The empirical analysis draws on interviews conducted with Pakistani analysts and journalists, triangulated with official statements from Chinese and Pakistani officials. The chapter proceeds as follows: section one contextualises CPEC within the 2018 elections in Pakistan and discusses the political and economic implications of the leadership change for the implementation of the projects. Section two looks at the institutional cohesion in Pakistan's civil–military relations and its implications for CPEC, before moving to the concluding section, which revisits the initial claim of the need to foreground leadership change in assessing the BRI.

Pakistan's 2018 elections and CPEC

The 2018 elections represented an important milestone in Pakistan's democratic history, as it was the second consecutive election in which a government was voted out of office and replaced with a democratically elected one. While democratic continuity was ensured by elections, the fate of Pakistan's prime minister was more in line with the position's chequered historical record, as no prime minister since 1947 had been able to complete a full term. One year before the elections, in July 2017, then prime minister Nawaz Sharif was disqualified by the Supreme Court of Pakistan on corruption grounds in what was largely regarded as a politically motivated ruling, allegedly endorsed by Pakistan's army, which was at loggerheads with Sharif over several domestic and foreign policy issues. As the domestic political situation was heating up in the months before the election, CPEC's 'early harvest' projects—those being prioritised between 2015 and 2020—

were well underway. In the immediate wake of the disqualification, China's Ministry of Foreign Affairs representatives reassuringly stated that neither the ties between the two countries nor CPEC would be affected by the ruling, adding that they were ready to cooperate with the new prime minister, Shahid Khaqan Abbasi (Dawn 2017).

Despite the confidence expressed publicly, the situation was in fact met with concern in Beijing. According to Andrew Small (2018), 'Chinese officials and experts privately indicated that domestic political issues had become the principal source of anxiety' about the successful development of CPEC. Evidence of these concerns can be also found in an opinion piece by Lan Jiang (2017), a professor at China West Normal University, published in the state-run *Global Times*, in which he suggested that 'the disqualification of Nawaz Sharif would likely bring some uncertainties to the ongoing CPEC project', concluding that 'the Pakistan leadership change will not affect China–Pakistan ties, but perhaps will bring some variable factors to the CPEC project'. These comments point to the fact that, since 2013, China has made no secret of its preference for the PML-N and its leaders. In 2016, praising the performance of the Punjab Government in executing CPEC projects, chairwoman of the Export–Import Bank of China Hu Xiaolian said that 'Punjab speed' was rapidly replacing 'Shenzhen speed'— a term used in China to epitomise rapid development (Rehman 2016). In addition, in a letter sent before the elections, former Chinese ambassador to Pakistan Sun Weidong expressed his appreciation for the support received by then chief minister of Punjab and brother of the former prime minister Shehbaz Sharif, who was addressed in the letter as a 'dear friend and brother' (Firstpost 2018).

Of a very different nature were relations between China and the PTI— the fiercest opponent of the PML-N government and its development practices. Some of the PTI's most prominent members, including its then leader and prime minister, Imran Khan, had been vocal in their concerns about CPEC while in opposition. President Xi Jinping's visit to Pakistan, in which CPEC was to be officially launched, was delayed in 2014 because of the *dharna* ('sit-in') staged by the PTI in the late summer–early autumn of that year.[2] In February 2016, Khan and then chief minister of Khyber Pakhtunkhwa Province Pervez Khattak visited the Chinese ambassador to convey their reservations about CPEC (Nation 2016). At a political

---

2   President Xi Jinping eventually visited Pakistan in April 2015 and officially launched CPEC. For an analysis of the visit, see Boni (2015).

convention held in Khyber Pakhtunkhwa in 2016, Khan stated that his province was 'being deprived of its due share from the CPEC' (Dawn 2016), referring to controversy about the corridor's route. Finally, before starting the sit-in against corruption in November 2016, Khan had to reassure then-Chinese ambassador Sun that the protest was directed at the government and not CPEC.

As these instances demonstrate, by the time the 2018 election campaign had started, CPEC had already become a regular staple of public debate in Pakistan and a key item of the government–opposition divide. It is therefore not surprising that in the run-up to the July elections all the main political parties were politicising CPEC for their own electoral goals. As a close observer of Pakistan's politics noted in an email interview with the author before the elections, the:

> CPEC is the buzzword and political parties claim credit for CPEC. The PML-N in public gatherings say that it is their idea and gift for Pakistani nations. While on the other hand Pakistan People's Party (PPP) claims that it's the initiative of Asif Ali Zardari [the president of Pakistan and head of the PPP until 2013]. (Author's interview, 2018)

The PML-N portrayed itself as the party that delivered on development and on the promises made during the 2013 campaign. The latter were centred on ending the electricity shortages that were affecting the country, and the PML-N was elected on its pledge to improve living conditions within Pakistan. It is thus not entirely surprising that the PML-N's message during the 2018 election campaign was aimed at showcasing the government's track record in completing energy projects financed under CPEC.

Like the PML-N, the PPP also tried to capitalise on CPEC by claiming ownership of and credit for its development, on the grounds that it was during the PPP's years in government (2008–13) that the plans for the corridor were laid out. As a party member told me in an email interview, Bilawal Bhutto Zardari 'claims that Asif Ali Zardari is the architect' of the CPEC project (Author's interview, May 2018). Notwithstanding the fact that the PPP repeatedly accused the government of taking undue political ownership of the projects, the PPP's support for CPEC has always been strong; further, Sindh, the PPP's historical electoral power base, is the province with the largest share of CPEC projects (Boni and Adeney 2020).

The results of the July 2018 elections saw the PTI emerge victorious. Given the cautious approach it had taken towards CPEC, it was clear that the change in leadership would bring new priorities and a new vision for the projects—one that required some course correction. The Chinese consul-general in Karachi Liu Zongyi argued that there may have been 'some confusion in the party that assumed power after the 2018 general elections' (Subohi 2020). Along similar lines, Liu listed the adjustment of 'the original blueprint' of CPEC 'after Pakistani Prime Minister Imran Khan's administration came to power … focusing more on economic and social development, industrial parks and agricultural cooperation' as one of the main reasons behind the difficulties in implementing CPEC projects after 2018 (Liu 2019).

The implications of leadership change

In the very first meeting between then Chinese ambassador to Pakistan Yao Jing and the newly elected prime minister Imran Khan, Yao stated that the 'PTI pursues the notion of governing for the well-being of its people, and hopes that China will keep on supporting Pakistan's economic and social development' (Embassy of China 2018a). This message was reiterated during Yao's meeting with the minister of railways, in which he reaffirmed that 'China is determined to expand its investment into people's livelihood in Pakistan and give full play of CPEC's role in promoting Pakistan's economic and people's livelihood development' (Embassy of China 2018c). To understand how the narrative around CPEC has changed and how the change in leadership in Pakistan influenced the shift in priorities, it is useful to compare these remarks with those made by then Chinese ambassador to Pakistan Sun Weidong in the immediate aftermath of the 2013 elections. In his first speech on arrival in Pakistan, Ambassador Sun stated that China and Pakistan should 'pay more attention to the pivot projects of the transportation infrastructure and the economic zones along the corridor', adding that the two sides would 'take energy and infrastructure cooperation as a top priority' (Embassy of China 2013). On the other hand, the prime minister's adviser on commerce and investment Abdul Razak Dawood stated in his first meeting with the Chinese ambassador that he was hoping 'that China will keep on supporting Pakistan's industrialization and improve the imbalanced trade between Pakistan and China', highlighting the trade imbalance between the two countries (Embassy of China 2018b). In the typically florid language accompanying the statements by the two countries' representatives, it was unusual to find a mention of this aspect of the relationship. A few days later, Dawood was reported by the *Financial Times* as saying that 'the previous government did a bad job negotiating with China on CPEC—they didn't do their homework correctly and didn't negotiate correctly so they gave away a lot'. He added that:

> Chinese companies received tax breaks, many breaks and have an undue advantage in Pakistan; this is one of the things we're looking at because it's not fair that Pakistan companies should be disadvantaged.

Dawood concluded with a rather unprecedented statement for a Pakistan Cabinet member, suggesting that 'we should put everything on hold for a year so we can get our act together. Perhaps we can stretch CPEC out over another five years or so' (Anderlini et al. 2018).

In addition to the main claims made by prominent members of the new government, it is essential to look at the financing of CPEC projects to assess the impact of the leadership change. A perusal of the outcomes of the eighth and ninth meetings of the Joint Cooperation Committee—the chief decision-making body of CPEC—provides evidence that the focus changed and project financing was reduced. While there was a range of bilateral exchanges within the various joint working groups, including on socioeconomic cooperation, and the two sides agreed to move forward with poverty alleviation demonstration projects in all regions of Pakistan, no new mega-projects were agreed to—a clear discontinuity with the previous rounds of negotiations, in which projects were added to the CPEC portfolio.[3]

The evolution of Pakistan's Public Sector Development Program, the main annual source of development funding from the government, provides further evidence of how the change in leadership affected CPEC. There were two versions of the 2018–19 budget devoted to projects coming under the program, in April 2018 (presented by the PML-N) and in September 2018 (revised by the new government). While the PML-N's development program was a pre-election one and was certainly driven by largely unsustainable electoral pledges, between the PML-N version and the PTI one in September there was a drop in the number of projects, from 1,284 to 829 (Monitoring Desk 2018). CPEC projects were also affected by the cuts. In particular, 12 schemes in Gwadar were dropped from the Public Sector Development Program (Rana 2018); for the following year (2019–20),

---

3   For a summary of the eighth and ninth Joint Cooperation Committee meetings, see CPEC Secretariat (2018); Rana (2019a, 2019b).

while priority was given to the completion of the projects already underway, only one CPEC scheme (Zhob to Kuchlak Highway) was approved and one (Mirpur–Mangla–Muzaffarabad–Mansehra Expressway) was classified as 'in process'. Apart from these two, no new projects were added to the Public Sector Development Program's CPEC portfolio. The 2020–21 program prioritised the ML-1 project as well as the Zhob–Kuchlak Highway, but no new significant scheme was added, including the special economic zones that are one of the main areas of future collaboration between Pakistan and China under the aegis of the BRI (Government of Pakistan 2020).

To be sure, while the change in leadership played a decisive role in the shifting of priorities, other factors should also be considered to explain CPEC's trajectory. The main contributing factor to the CPEC's slowdown was Pakistan's financial predicament. Its economic growth dropped from 6.2 per cent in 2018 to 2.5 per cent in 2019, dropping further during the Covid-19 pandemic to –1.3 per cent. In addition, the country agreed in May 2019 to a USD6-billion bailout package from the IMF, aimed at strengthening Pakistan's finances. Under the deal, Pakistan would repay its external debt, including the USD14.6 billion it owed to China, in large part related to CPEC (IMF 2019). According to some observers, given the United States' pre-eminence within the IMF and the growing Sino-US rivalry, the deal was a way to push Pakistan to disclose some of the CPEC agreements and, more generally, an attempt to drive a wedge into Sino-Pakistani relations (Shahid 2019).

Additional evidence of Pakistan's financial predicament came in March 2020, when then president Arif Alvi visited China. While the visit was a sign of solidarity with China during the Covid-19 pandemic and of overall strength in Sino-Pakistani ties, his delegation included Minister for Planning, Development, Reforms and Special Initiatives Asad Umar, and the two governments signed an MoU establishing joint working groups on science, technology and agriculture under the CPEC umbrella.[4] During the visit, CPEC and its financing were high on the agenda, as Pakistan had 'formally taken up its difficulties with China for relief in purchase prices'. Pakistan had paid about USD615 million of its debt to China between May 2020 and June 2021 and the visit was also aimed at requesting 'relaxations in the existing agreements' (Dawn 2020).

---

4   For an assessment of the official visit and Sino-Pakistani relations during the Covid-19 pandemic, see Boni (2020).

Analysing the evolution of CPEC against the backdrop of Pakistan's domestic politics before and after the 2018 general election, this section has demonstrated two important aspects: first, leaders' priorities matter when it comes to the focus and nature of the projects being implemented under the wider BRI umbrella. While the focus of CPEC shifted from energy generation and connectivity to social development, the financing of the projects also changed, both those financed with Chinese loans and those funded by Pakistan's Public Sector Development Program. Second, while official claims suggest that Chinese Government actors and firms are not affected by who is in power, this section has shown that this is patently not the case. China enjoyed very good relations with the PML-N and its leaders, but a cordial, yet more cautious relationship with the PTI, which translated into a partial reorientation and slowdown of CPEC projects.

CPEC and civil–military relations

Another visible outcome of the change in leadership was the way in which the CPEC decision-making process was organised. This point is important as it demonstrates the internalisation of BRI projects and how they become enmeshed in the complexities of domestic politics in recipient countries. CPEC has been a cause of disagreement between civilian and military leaders in Pakistan's often tense civil–military relations, especially under the PML-N government (2013–18). At the centre of the civil–military tussle were the overall management of the projects and the creation of an authority tasked with overseeing the implementation of roads, power plants and other infrastructure projects of CPEC. On the one hand, the PML-N leadership was not willing to dilute its control over the initiative, whereas the Pakistan military was advocating for a greater say in the decision-making process. According to a seasoned observer of Pakistani politics, there was 'a demand that some sort of overarching authority be created under which all of CPEC should be executed. This demand came from the military, although they never said it themselves officially' (Author's interview, May 2018).

After the power transition between the PML-N and the PTI, we observed a progressive entrenchment of the military's role in the CPEC-related decision-making process. The first sign of the dilution of civilian control was the establishment of the National Development Council, which included the chief of army staff as one of its members. Interestingly, the council's remit included the formulation of 'policies to achieve accelerated economic growth' as well as to approve 'long-term planning in relation to national and regional connectivity. Furthermore, it shall set out guidelines for regional cooperation' (Khan 2019). While including the chief of army staff as a member of this newly formed council was the first step towards a greater role for the military, it was the establishment of the CPEC Authority in October 2019 through the 'China Pakistan Economic Corridor Authority Ordinance 2019' that represented the culmination of the wider process of increasing the military's role in CPEC, given that the authority is headed by a retired three-star Pakistan Army general. In the run-up to the ordinance, the proposal to establish the authority was met with scepticism by both the Cabinet Committee on CPEC and the Parliamentary Committee on CPEC. In the Cabinet Committee, questions were raised by Ishrat Hussain, adviser to the prime minister on institutional reform and austerity, and by Abdul Razak Dawood, adviser on commerce, textiles and industry, about 'the appointment of a large number of staff for the CPEC Authority saying it will hurt the austerity drive of the government, given the proposed number of new employees was around 70' (Yousafzai 2019). Along similar lines, when the Parliamentary Committee on CPEC voted on the proposal to establish the CPEC Authority it was 'unanimously rejected' (Nation 2019). More generally, there were concerns that the Planning Commission's functions would overlap with those of the CPEC Authority, including interprovincial and interministerial coordination as well as sectoral research for informed decision-making and long-term planning (Shahid 2020).[5]

The establishment of the CPEC Authority shows the progressive dilution of civilian control over the military in the country as well as how CPEC has become an area of contestation between elected representatives and the military.

Conclusion

At the beginning of 2020, a statement by the Chinese Embassy in Pakistan said the BRI 'was connected with the "Naya Pakistan" vision … focused on social-economic, industrial and agricultural cooperation' (Embassy of China 2020). Along similar lines, in February 2020, then Chinese ambassador Yao Jing outlined that 'the new real aspects of the CPEC basically demonstrate

---

5   Another important point is that Section 12 of the ordinance exempts the authority and its members from suit prosecutions and other legal proceedings, as a way to protect the staff to carry out their duties without hindrance.

Mr Imran Khan's vision of the economy', adding that the prime minister had pushed for the formation of a joint working group on agriculture, and concluding that 'Prime Minister Imran Khan pays special attention to the poverty alleviation, education, [and] health … so we have started … social sector cooperation', implementing 17 fast-tracked cooperation projects, including building hospitals and vocational training centres (BRI TV 2020).

Yao's remarks are a potent reminder of how the focus of CPEC shifted after the change in leadership in 2018. As this chapter demonstrated, while the focus in the early harvest projects was on energy generation and connectivity, most of the rhetoric about and financing of CPEC since 2018 has shifted towards social development. More broadly, this chapter has shown that leadership priorities matter in the implementation of the BRI and that, despite the huge amount of investment and political will to push projects forward, the projects under the BRI umbrella require coordination by and understanding of local stakeholders. Another important aspect is how debates about BRI projects have become internalised and interacted with the complexity of Pakistani politics. From government–opposition skirmishes about political ownership of CPEC to civil–military tensions over project management, the analysis demonstrated how CPEC has become enmeshed in Pakistan's public discourse.

Looking beyond Pakistan, the analysis presented in this study and the inclusion of 'leadership change' as a key variable in the assessment of BRI projects have the potential to be applied comparatively across other countries involved in Beijing's initiative. As mentioned in the introduction, Malaysia and Sri Lanka represent two important cases in which new leaders coming to power sought to modify the terms of engagement with Chinese projects. Another example is the Maldives—historically in India's orbit of influence—which in the 2013–18 period, under the leadership of Abdulla Yameen, was very keen to accept investment from China under the BRI and to align itself closely with Beijing. As in Malaysia and Sri Lanka, in the Maldives, Yameen's successor as president, Ibrahim Mohamed Solih, questioned the nature and extent of the Maldives' debt exposure to China and sought to renegotiate terms on some of the projects previously agreed to. This chapter is therefore the first attempt to bring 'leadership change' into academic analyses of BRI projects. It is hoped that by considering this variable, it will be possible in future to devise a comprehensive analytical framework to assess the way in which BRI projects are implemented in recipient countries, including the complexities of domestic political dynamics as part of Beijing's endeavour to project its global influence.

References

Abb, Pascal. 2022. 'All Geopolitics Is Local: The China–Pakistan Economic Corridor Amidst Overlapping Centre–Periphery Relations.' *Third World Quarterly* 44, no. 1: 76–95. doi.org/10.1080/01436597.2022.2128329.

Abb, Pascal, Filippo Boni, and Hasan Karrar. 2024. *China, Pakistan and the Belt and Road Initiative: The Experience of an Early Adopter State.* London: Routledge. doi.org/10.4324/9781032633411.

Adeney, Katharine, and Filippo Boni. 2021. *How China and Pakistan Negotiate.* Paper. Washington, DC: Carnegie Endowment for International Peace. carnegie endowment.org/2021/05/24/how-china-and-pakistan-negotiate-pub-84592.

Adeney, Katharine, and Filippo Boni. 2024. 'Global China and Pakistan's Federal Politics: 10 Years of the China–Pakistan Economic Corridor.' *Commonwealth & Comparative Politics*: 1–21. doi.org/10.1080/14662043.2024.2354568.

Ahmed, Zahid S. 2019. 'Impact of the China–Pakistan Economic Corridor on Nation-Building in Pakistan.' *Journal of Contemporary China* 28, no. 117: 400–14. doi.org/10.1080/10670564.2018.1542221.

Anderlini, Jamil, Henny Sender, and Farhan Bokhari. 2018. 'Pakistan Rethinks Its Role in Xi's Belt and Road Plan.' *Financial Times*, 10 September. www.ft.com/content/d4a3e7f8-b282-11e8-99ca-68cf89602132.

Boni, Filippo. 2015. 'Xi Jinping's Pakistan Visit: What's Left Behind?' *UoN Blogs*, 18 May. Nottingham: Institute of Asia and Pacific Studies, University of Nottingham. blogs.nottingham.ac.uk/asiapacificstudies/2015/05/18/xi-jinpings-pakistan-visit-whats-left-behind.

Boni, Filippo. 2019. *Sino-Pakistani Relations: Politics, Military and Regional Dynamics.* Abingdon: Routledge. doi.org/10.4324/9780429431982.

Boni, Filippo. 2020. 'Sino-Pakistani Relations in the Time of COVID-19.' *South Asia @ LSE Blog*, 8 April. London: London School of Economics and Political Science. blogs.lse.ac.uk/southasia/2020/04/08/sino-pakistani-relations-in-the-time-of-covid-19.

Boni, Filippo. 2021a. 'Caught between the U.S. and China: Critical Junctures in Pakistan's Foreign Policy.' In *Routledge Handbook on South Asian Foreign Policy*, edited by A. Pande, 311–23. New York: Routledge. doi.org/10.4324/9780429054808-25.

Boni, Filippo. 2021b. *The US–China Rivalry in South Asia and Pakistan's Hedging Dilemma*. RSC Policy Briefs 2021/60. Global Governance Programme, EU–Asia Project. Fiesole: Robert Schuman Centre for Advanced Studies, European University Institute. hdl.handle.net/1814/73436.

Boni, Filippo, and Katharine Adeney. 2020. 'The Impact of CPEC on Pakistan's Federal System: The Politics of the CPEC.' *Asian Survey* 60, no. 3: 441–65. doi. org/10.1525/as.2020.60.3.441.

BRI TV. 2020. 'Public Talk of Chinese Ambassador H.E. Mr Yao Jing on CPEC at Institute of Strategic Studies Islamabad.' *BRI TV*, 22 February. www.youtube. com/watch?v=BMjepMoZaPc&feature=youtu.be.

Callahan, William A. 2016. 'China's "Asia Dream": The Belt Road Initiative and the New Regional Order.' *Asian Journal of Comparative Politics* 1, no. 3: 226–43. doi.org/10.1177/2057891116647806.

Chen, Jihong, Yijie Fei, Paul Tae-Woo Lee, and Xuezong Tao. 2019. 'Overseas Port Investment Policy for China's Central and Local Governments in the Belt and Road Initiative.' *Journal of Contemporary China* 28, no. 116: 1–20. doi.org/ 10.1080/10670564.2018.1511392.

China–Pakistan Economic Corridor (CPEC) Secretariat. 2018. 'CPEC 8th Joint Cooperation Committee (JCC) Meeting Held in Beijing, China on 20th December 2018.' News release, 20 December. Islamabad: CPEC Secretariat. cpec.gov.pk/news/147.

Clarke, Michael. 2017. 'The Belt and Road Initiative: China's New Grand Strategy?' *Asia Policy* 24: 71–79. doi.org/10.1353/asp.2017.0023.

Dawn. 2016. 'Dispute over CPEC Is with Nawaz-Led Govt, Not with China: Imran.' *Dawn*, 25 December. www.dawn.com/news/1304419.

Dawn. 2017. 'China Ready to Continue Working Jointly on CPEC Despite PM's Disqualification.' *Dawn*, 29 July. www.dawn.com/news/1348227.

Dawn. 2019. 'Dues, Faulty Design Delay CPEC Work.' *Dawn*, 3 December. www. dawn.com/news/1520096/dues-faulty-design-delay-cpec-work.

Dawn. 2020. 'High-Risk Countries Approach China for Debt Relief.' *Dawn*, 1 May. www.dawn.com/news/1553610/high-risk-countries-approach-china-for-debt-relief.

Embassy of China. 2013. 'Realize Our Common Dreams through Mutually Beneficial Cooperation: Speech by Ambassador Sun Weidong at the Arrival Reception.' News release, 17 July. Islamabad: Embassy of the People's Republic of China in the Islamic Republic of Pakistan.

Embassy of China. 2018a. 'Ambassador Yao Jing Called on Imran Khan: Chairman of the Pakistan Tehreek-e-Insaf.' News release, 30 July. Islamabad: Embassy of the People's Republic of China in the Islamic Republic of Pakistan. pk.chineseembassy. org/eng/zbgx/events/t1583481.htm.

Embassy of China. 2018b. 'Ambassador Yao Jing Met with Adviser to PM on Commerce and Investment.' News release, 30 August. Islamabad: Embassy of the People's Republic of China in the Islamic Republic of Pakistan.

Embassy of China. 2018c. 'Ambassador Yao Jing Met with Minister of Railways.' News release, 31 August. Islamabad: Embassy of the People's Republic of China in the Islamic Republic of Pakistan.

Embassy of China. 2020. 'Looking Forward to a New Chapter of China–Pakistan Friendship.' News release, 2 January. Islamabad: Embassy of the People's Republic of China in the Islamic Republic of Pakistan. pk.chineseembassy.org/eng/zbgx/ t1729328.htm [page discontinued].

Express Tribune. 2016. 'PTI Protest Not against CPEC, Imran Tells Chinese Ambassador.' *The Express Tribune*, 19 October. tribune.com.pk/story/1202724/ allaying-concerns-pti-protest-not-cpec-imran-tells-chinese-ambassador.

Ferdinand, Peter. 2016. 'Westward Ho—The China Dream and "One Belt, One Road": Chinese Foreign Policy under Xi Jinping.' *International Affairs* 92, no. 4: 941–57. doi.org/10.1111/1468-2346.12660.

Firstpost. 2018. 'Ahead of Elections, Former Ambassador of China to Pakistan Endorses CPEC, Praises Shehbaz Sharif.' *Firstpost*, 24 July. www.firstpost.com/ world/ahead-of-elections-former-ambassador-of-china-to-pakistan-endorses- cpec-praises-shehbaz-sharif-4808341.html.

Garlick, J. 2022. *Reconfiguring the China–Pakistan Economic Corridor*. Abingdon: Routledge. doi.org/10.4324/9781003018377.

Government of Pakistan. 2020. *Public Sector Development Programme 2020–21*. June. Islamabad: Planning Commission, Ministry of Planning, Development & Special Initiatives. www.pc.gov.pk/uploads/archives/PSDP_2020-21.pdf.

He, Baogang. 2019. 'The Domestic Politics of the Belt and Road Initiative and Its Implications.' *Journal of Contemporary China* 28, no. 116: 180–95. doi.org/ 10.1080/10670564.2018.1511391.

International Monetary Fund (IMF). 2019. 'Pakistan: Request for an Extended Arrangement under the Extended Fund Facility—Press Release; Staff Report; and Statement by the Executive Director for Pakistan.' *Country Report* no. 2019/212, 8 July. Washington, DC: IMF. www.imf.org/en/Publications/CR/Issues/2019/ 07/08/Pakistan-Request-for-an-Extended-Arrangement-Under-the-Extended- Fund-Facility-Press-Release-47092.

Jie, Yu, and Lucy Ridout. 2021. *Who Decides China's Foreign Policy*. Briefing Paper, Asia-Pacific Programme, November. London: The Royal Institute of International Affairs, Chatham House. www.chathamhouse.org/sites/default/files/2021-11/2021-11-01-who-decides-chinas-foreign-policy-jie-et-al.pdf_0.pdf.

Jones, Lee, and Shahar Hameiri. 2021. *Fractured China: How State Transformation Is Shaping China's Rise*. Cambridge: Cambridge University Press. doi.org/10.1017/9781009047487.

Jones, Lee, and Jinghan Zeng. 2019. 'Understanding China's "Belt and Road Initiative": Beyond "Grand Strategy" to a State Transformation Analysis.' *Third World Quarterly* 40, no. 8: 1415–39. doi.org/10.1080/01436597.2018.1559046.

Kamran, Yousaf. 2020. 'US Urges China to Waive Off Pakistan's Debt Amid Covid-19 Crisis.' *The Express Tribune*, 20 May. tribune.com.pk/story/2225775/1-us-urges-china-waive-off-pakistans-debt-amid-covid-19-crisis.

Khan, Sanaullah. 2019. 'PM Imran Establishes National Development Council.' *Dawn*, 18 June. www.dawn.com/news/1488948.

Kiani, Khaleeq. 2019. 'Govt Trying to Get $9bn Chinese Loan for Railway Project at 2pc.' *Dawn*, 6 December. www.dawn.com/news/1520698/govt-trying-to-get-9bn-chinese-loan-for-railway-project-at-2pc.

Lan, Jiang. 2017. 'Ouster of Nawaz Sharif Adds Variables to Economic Corridor Plan.' *Global Times*, 3 August. www.globaltimes.cn/content/1059537.shtml [page discontinued].

Leiva, Diego. 2020. 'BRI and Railways in Latin America: How Important Are Domestic Politics?' *Asian Education and Development Studies* 10, no. 3: 386–98. doi.org/10.1108/AEDS-08-2019-0127.

Li, Mingjiang. 2020. 'The Belt and Road Initiative: Geo-Economics and Indo-Pacific Security Competition.' *International Affairs* 96, no. 1: 169–87. doi.org/10.1093/ia/iiz240.

Liu, Hong, and Guanie Lim. 2019. 'The Political Economy of a Rising China in Southeast Asia: Malaysia's Response to the Belt and Road Initiative.' *Journal of Contemporary China* 28, no. 116: 216–31. doi.org/10.1080/10670564.2018.1511393.

Liu, Zongyi. 2019. 'How CPEC Hurdles Can Be Overcome.' *Global Times*, 19 December. www.globaltimes.cn/content/1174147.shtml.

Mitchell, Tom, and Alice Woodhouse. 2019. 'Malaysia Renegotiated China-Backed Rail Project to Avoid US $5bn Fee.' *Financial Times*, 15 April. www.ft.com/content/660ce336-5f38-11e9-b285-3acd5d43599e.

Monitoring Desk. 2018. 'Govt Drops 455 Projects from PSDP 2018–19.' *Profit by Pakistan Today*, 26 September. profit.pakistantoday.com.pk/2018/09/26/govt-drops-455-projects-from-psdp-2018-19.

Nation. 2016. 'Imran Khan, CM KP Convey CPEC Reservations to Chinese Ambassador.' *The Nation*, 11 February. nation.com.pk/11-Feb-2016/imran-khan-cm-kp-convey-cpec-reservations-to-chinese-ambassador.

Nation. 2019. 'Parliamentary Committee Gives Refusal to Establish "CPEC Authority".' *The Nation*, 6 September. nation.com.pk/06-Sep-2019/no-cpe.

Rana, Shahbaz. 2018. 'Austerity Axe Falls on CPEC, Gwadar Projects.' *The Express Tribune*, 26 September. tribune.com.pk/story/1811585/1-austerity-axe-falls-cpec-gwadar-projects.

Rana, Shahbaz. 2019a. '8th JCC Meeting: "Missing Paperwork" Delays CPEC Mass Transit Schemes.' *The Express Tribune*, 9 January. tribune.com.pk/story/1884162/2-8th-jcc-meeting-missing-paperwork-delays-cpec-mass-transit-schemes.

Rana, Shahbaz. 2019b. 'Pakistan, China Agree to Expand CPEC Scope.' *The Express Tribune*, 6 November. tribune.com.pk/story/2094342/2-pakistan-china-agree-expand-cpec-scope.

Rana, Shahbaz. 2020a. 'PTI Govt Approves CPEC's US$7.2b Strategic Project.' *The Express Tribune*, 7 June. tribune.com.pk/story/2237291/2-pti-govt-approves-cpecs-7-2b-strategic-project.

Rana, Shahbaz. 2020b. 'CPEC's Strategic ML-1 Project Gets Final Nod.' *The Express Tribune*, 6 August. tribune.com.pk/story/2258237/cpecs-strategic-ml-1-project-gets-final-nod.

Reed, Tristan, and Alexandr Trubetskoy. 2019. *Assessing the Value of Market Access from Belt and Road Projects*. Policy Research Working Paper 8815, April. Washington, DC: International Finance Corporation, World Bank Group. documents1.worldbank.org/curated/en/333001554988427234/pdf/Assessing-the-Value-of-Market-Access-from-Belt-and-Road-Projects.pdf. doi.org/10.1596/1813-9450-8815.

Rehman, Huzaifa. 2016. 'China Discards "Shenzhen Speed" for "Punjab Speed".' *The News International*, 26 July. www.thenews.com.pk/print/137730-China-discards-Shenzhen-speed-for-Punjab-speed.

Rehman, Sherry. 2019. *Special Committee on the Project of China–Pakistan Economic Corridor (CPEC): First Interim Report (July 2018 – June 2019)*. Islamabad: Senate of Pakistan. senate.gov.pk/uploads/documents/1567600264_202.pdf.

Rowedder, Simon. 2020. 'Railroading Land-Linked Laos: China's Regional Profits, Laos' Domestic Costs?' *Eurasian Geography and Economics* 61, no. 2: 1–10. doi.org/10.1080/15387216.2019.1704813.

Safdar, Muhammad Tayyab. 2021. *The Local Roots of Chinese Engagement in Pakistan.* Report, June. Washington, DC: Carnegie Endowment for International Peace. carnegieendowment.org/files/Safdar_Pakistan_and_China_final.pdf.

Safdar, Muhammad Tayyab. 2022. 'Domestic Actors and the Limits of Chinese Infrastructure Power: Evidence from Pakistan.' *Journal of Contemporary Asia* 54, no. 2: 317–41. doi.org/10.1080/00472336.2022.2145576.

Shahid, Jamal. 2020. 'Govt Defends Establishment of CPEC Authority.' *Dawn*, 1 January. www.dawn.com/news/1525566/govt-defends-establishment-of-cpec-authority.

Shahid, Kunwar Khuldune. 2019. 'The IMF Takeover of Pakistan.' *The Diplomat*, 18 July. thediplomat.com/2019/07/the-imf-takeover-of-pakistan.

Small, Andrew. 2018. 'Buyer's Remorse: Pakistan's Elections and the Precarious Future of the China–Pakistan Economic Corridor.' *War on the Rocks*, 27 July. warontherocks.com/2018/07/buyers-remorse-pakistans-elections-and-the-precarious-future-of-the-china-pakistan-economic-corridor.

Subohi, Afshan. 2020. 'CPEC: The Ball Is in Pakistan's Court.' *Dawn*, 10 February. www.dawn.com/news/1533449.

US Department of State. 2019. 'A Conversation with Ambassador Alice Wells on the China–Pakistan Economic Corridor: Remarks, The Wilson Center, Washington, DC, 21 November.' Washington, DC: US Department of State. www.state.gov/a-conversation-with-ambassador-alice-wells-on-the-china-pakistan-economic-corridor.

van der Zwan, G. 2022. 'Chinese Linkage and Democracy in Pakistan.' In *Securitization and Democracy in Eurasia: Transformation and Development in the OSCE Region*, edited by A. Mihr, P. Sorbello, and B. Weiffen, 329–43. Cham: Springer. doi.org/10.1007/978-3-031-16659-4_23.

Yousafzai, Fawad. 2019. 'Cabinet Committee Approves Setting Up CPEC Authority Despite Objections.' *The Nation*, 27 August. nation.com.pk/27-Aug-2019/cabinet-committee-approves-setting-up-cpec-authority-despite-objections.

Zhou, Weifeng, and Mario Esteban. 2018. 'Beyond Balancing: China's Approach Towards the Belt and Road Initiative.' *Journal of Contemporary China* 27, no. 112: 487–501. doi.org/10.1080/10670564.2018.1433476.

10

The winners and losers of the BRI in the Middle East

Mina Tadrous Milad Tadrous

Introduction

The Belt and Road Initiative (BRI) has a significant impact on the Middle East—a region of special importance to the initiative's maritime element. This region matters to China due to its dependency on seaborne energy imports from the region and the Middle East's strategic location at the crossroads of Asia, Europe and Africa (Watanabe 2019). Chinese investment in rivalrous countries such as Iran and Saudi Arabia is believed to have an impact on those countries' relationships, and could call into question China's concept of non-intervention based on its different levels of investment and involvement. China has greatly expanded its interests in the Middle East in the past decade, which has been marked by instability and a series of conflicts.

Although the BRI creates opportunities for economic growth and development in the Middle East, it also brings challenges and the risk of provoking further conflict and instability in the region. Even though the initiative was presented as being based on a mutually advantageous strategy, aiming to benefit all countries along its land and maritime routes, some countries seem to have been losing out. This loss of opportunities for some could become increasingly controversial, as it widens disparities between rivalrous countries. For example, in the context of rivalry between Saudi Arabia and Iran, Iran could lose potential business opportunities when Saudi Arabia receives more investment.

The literature has discussed the significance of the BRI for the Middle East as a whole and for each country within the region (Kamel 2018; Watanabe 2019; Evron 2019; Amineh 2022). While these studies assume that the countries of the Middle East accrue benefits from the BRI, they pay little attention to the fact that these states have conflicting relationships, which brings the potential that the BRI could lead to relative gains and relative losses—in other words, winners and losers. This means that even though a country receives BRI projects, if the level of benefit is less than that of its rival countries, that could mean a relative loss. This issue is compounded by another problem in the literature—that is, small states such as Syria, Yemen and Bahrain are overlooked. What does the BRI mean to these states, where it could further widen the disparities with their bigger neighbours? A regional approach, rather than a country-specific approach, matters a great deal to the discussion of the BRI in the Middle East due to the intensity of the rivalrous relationships in the region (Al Jazeera 2023). One country's economic development and diplomatic relations with a great power such as China impact its relations with a regional rival, and the extent of this impact is especially significant in the Middle East (Birringer 2010).

This study will examine why some countries lose BRI opportunities in comparison with other countries. Is it because of the power dynamics in the region or because of China's intentional or unintentional prioritisation of some countries over others in the context of the BRI? Moreover, by looking at the nature of the BRI as a new strategy for securing China's national interests, as well as the initiative's connectivity aspect, the analysis will discuss China's investment across the whole Middle East and how it relates to the serious conflicts and instability in the region. The study will analyse two primary investment sectors, energy and transport, and compare the level of Chinese investment with the degree of insecurity in the relevant countries.

The chapter is divided into three parts. The first will review the literature on the BRI in the Middle East and suggest that it pays only limited attention to the reasons for establishing winners and losers in the region, or the impact this has on regional power dynamics. The second section will define the 'winners' and 'losers' by drawing on neorealism and neoliberalism, with a particular focus on the concept of relative gain. The third section will concentrate on six countries, forming three sets of rivalrous relationships— Saudi Arabia versus Iran, Iraq versus Syria, and Egypt versus Türkiye— and consider the degree of investment China has made in the energy and transport sectors. Using this approach, the chapter assesses which country has experienced greater relative gains in terms of China's BRI investment from 2013 to 2019.

The chapter concludes by arguing that China's investment has been made in areas where it can prioritise the energy sector as first choice or the transport sector as second choice, and the degree of insecurity within, or between, countries does not affect China's level of investment. Further, it argues that the implementation of the BRI could inflame present conflicts and instabilities in the region due to China's choice to invest in some countries rather than others, which could lead to increased interstate rivalry.

The BRI and the Middle East: Mutual benefits

Most previous studies have considered the mutual benefits of the BRI, for both China and the Middle East; however, there is a lack of research exploring the implementation of the BRI in the Middle East from the perspective of regional power dynamics and the incentives that encourage China to invest more in some countries than in others.

There are three main aspects to the importance of the Middle East for the BRI: its huge energy reserves, its significant geostrategic location and its large markets for both products and investment. First, the Middle East is one of China's most important sources of energy and hence is essential to China's rapid industrialisation; imports to China from members of the Organization of the Petroleum Exporting Countries reached 4.7 million barrels a day in 2017 (Paraskova 2018). Second, the region's location at a geostrategic crossroads enables China to enhance its BRI strategies and thus connect to West Asia, Africa and Europe. Moreover, the Middle East is considered an extended neighbourhood for the western parts of China, as the region has long related to China via the Silk Road—a connection that was intentionally revived through the BRI (Sharma 2019). Last, the Middle East is a thriving market for Chinese products and investment initiatives, including infrastructure and energy-based projects, as it includes some countries considered to be less industrially developed with outdated infrastructure.

Previous research has considered China's intentions for the BRI in the Middle East. The BRI features prominently in China's foreign policy (as well as being part of its geo-economic policy) with the aim of strengthening its economic leadership through investment in infrastructure projects in its neighbouring regions. At the same time, the Middle East plays a key part in BRI plans due to its rich energy resources and the need to develop its infrastructure (Sharma 2019). Anu Sharma (2019) argues that, within the BRI context, China is actively presenting itself to the Middle East as an alternative to traditional great-power politics, in an attempt to increase its economic reach and its involvement in Middle Eastern politics. Maha Kamel (2018) argues that the BRI not only presents an opportunity for the Middle East based on a win-win strategy, but also opens a new phase of Chinese involvement in Middle Eastern issues.

As the literature suggests, the BRI has the potential to benefit the Middle East in various ways. The first is that it enables the region's authoritarian states to obtain foreign investment without having to consider political conditionality. Before China increased its investments in the Middle East, the region had to rely on Western investment. However, that came with the conditionality that recipient countries had to meet strict ethical standards, such as having a positive impact on society and not adversely impacting the environment.

China's investment, mostly offered through loans, comes with far fewer conditions. Therefore, it is unsurprising that the BRI has been popular among non-democratic governments in the region. For example, China started concluding MoUs on the BRI with Saudi Arabia and Iraq in 2013, and with Egypt and Iran in 2014, at the same time strengthening its bilateral relations with the region. China raised its 'strategic partnerships' to 'comprehensive strategic partnerships' for Egypt in 2014 and for Saudi Arabia and Iran in 2016 (Li and Ye 2019).

Beijing has characterised the BRI as a beneficial opportunity for all countries involved. It is noticeable that many countries in the Middle East are taking the BRI seriously as part of their development strategy, including it in their national planning. For example, Saudi Arabia aligned the BRI within its 'Saudi Vision 2030' (Chen et al. 2018), with the expectation that the BRI would bolster its oil exports to China, allowing the country to maintain its exports to the Chinese market as a substitute for falling exports to the United States.

Iran considers its collaboration with China within the BRI as an alternative for its sanctions-torn economy (Saleh and Yazdanshenas 2020). Iran also regards the BRI as a unique opportunity for improving its infrastructure (Tehran Times 2020). This is significant as Iran needs at least USD200 billion to invest in its energy industry over the next five years to raise its energy production to the required level (Xinhua 2016a).

Egypt has shown keen interest in the BRI in terms of infrastructure development—in particular, it has become an important element in the development of the Suez Canal Corridor, as China has become the primary investor in this Egyptian mega-project (Xinhua 2019). Egypt's Suez Canal Economic Zone (SCZONE) integrates with the BRI to interconnect and boost global trade (Belt and Road News 2019). Providing a good example of the cooperation between Egypt and China within the BRI framework, the China–Egypt TEDA Suez Economic and Trade Cooperation Zone is considered an important platform for promoting economic and trade cooperation between the two countries (Xinhua 2019).

As for the second benefit, some of the literature claims that the BRI provides an opportunity to promote peace processes in the Middle East through infrastructure development and economic reforms. After the Arab Spring in 2011, Middle Eastern governments aimed to stabilise their countries by pursuing various opportunities for economic growth and development. Thus, since the launch of the BRI in 2013 and the establishment of the AIIB in 2015, many Middle Eastern countries have been eager to take part (Weiss 2017).

While some of the literature focuses on the potential benefits the BRI can offer the Middle East, other research pays closer attention to the problems associated with the initiative. Rebecca Harding (2019) argues that the BRI will add complexity to the region's already pressing issues, including unemployment and high levels of debt. Because the region suffers from popular uprisings and insurgencies, inward investment from China may not be the best option, especially for countries in which China invests heavily, such as Saudi Arabia and Egypt. Bonnie Girard (2018) argues that the BRI will raise immediate concerns about debt sustainability among poorer countries; she references Sri Lanka, which was forced to hand over majority control of its Hambantota Port to China after being unable to repay its loans. Girard also points to the lack of transparency in BRI projects, especially regarding Chinese funds that are distributed to countries already high on Transparency International's Corruption Index.

Thus, to increase understanding of the problems the BRI could bring to the region, this study assesses the implications of the initiative in relation to the regional power dynamics in the Middle East. The following question is posed: could the BRI be accused of inflaming conflict and instability in the region and, if so, in what way? Meanwhile, the Chinese Government claims that the BRI has the power to promote peace in the Middle East by helping regional states develop their economies. President Xi declared the following in his speech to the Arab League in January 2016:

> Instead of looking for a proxy in the Middle East, we promote peace talks; instead of seeking any sphere of influence, we call on all parties to join the circle of friends for the Belt and Road Initiative; instead of attempting to fill the 'vacuum', we build a cooperative partnership network for win-win outcomes. (Xinhua 2016b)

Despite this claim, investments are being made in a region in which rivalrous relationships abound. China's investment could thus affect already fraught relationships. Rather than benefiting all the countries in the region, the BRI could leave some behind and increase the level of inequality as a result. In other words, the BRI may create winners and losers from its investment opportunities, which could then exacerbate existing rivalries.

Defining winners and losers

It is apparent from an analysis of the level of investment and its implementation that certain countries gain a great deal from utilising the BRI, while others lose the chance to employ it for their benefit. Thus, defining the winners and losers is important for a discussion of the challenges the BRI could bring to some countries in the Middle East and for considering regional power dynamics.

I will begin by defining the concepts of relative and absolute gain. The neorealist assumption is that while states will always pursue their interests, these interests can be defined by either relative gain or absolute gain. Relative gain refers to a state's attempt to achieve more than others, particularly in terms of international influence. Relative gain is connected to the idea of the zero-sum game, which maintains that total wealth cannot be increased and the only way for one state to gain capital is to take wealth away from other states (Waltz 1979). In contrast, an absolute gain— a classic realist and neoliberal concept—is not compared with the gains or losses of others. Neoliberalism stresses the importance of cooperation and believes that all states can attain peace, prosperity and wealth. Absolute gain is interrelated with the idea of the non-zero-sum game, which emphasises that states can enlarge their wealth through peaceful engagement and cooperation with other states.

To understand what is meant in the context of the BRI, states will be described as units to help determine whether they should be characterised as winners or losers. In this vein, 'absolute' versus 'relative' terms will be used to determine into which category they fit (Gruber 2000). Absolute wins or losses are determined based on a comparison of a state's situation before and after a specific event. In other words, if the state is better off after an event, it is considered an absolute winner, while if it is not better, or is even worse, off after an event, it is considered an absolute loser. Meanwhile, relative wins or losses mainly rely on a comparison of one state with another. If two states are both improved by a specific event, the state that gains more will be considered the relative winner, while the other state is the relative loser.

Among the various definitions of winners and losers, the above discussion shows that dynamic characterisations best reflect the identification of winners and losers following a specific event or in conjunction with long-term processes such as the BRI. In addition, this approach may reflect prior or existing inequalities between small countries due to rivalrous relationships with bigger countries. In discussing rivalrous relationships between specific countries, relative gains matter more than absolute gains.

In the following empirical analysis, the relative gains are determined using two main indicators: the total value of Chinese investment in each country and the value of investment in the energy and transport sectors. Finally, the analysis will illustrate the impact of Chinese investments as part of the BRI by discussing relative gains vis-a-vis Middle Eastern power dynamics across three sets of countries with rivalrous relations: Saudi Arabia versus Iran, Iraq versus Syria and Egypt versus Türkiye.

Three sets of rivalrous relations and the relative gains of the BRI

This section presents the empirical analysis, focusing on the case studies of six Middle Eastern countries in three sets of rivalrous relationships. Each case study is divided into three parts: the first examines the nature of the rivalry; the second assesses the relative gains each country has accrued from the BRI, looking at the number of projects and the size of the investment, especially in the energy and transport sectors; and the third section discusses the impact of the BRI's implementation on regional power dynamics.

The reason for selecting energy as an important indicator for relative gain stems from the fact that the Middle East has long been an important source of energy resources for China. The reason for choosing transport as one of the indicators is related to the nature of the BRI, in which connectivity is one of its main pillars. In fact, energy and transport are the two main Chinese investment interests in the Middle East.

Saudi Arabia and Iran

The nature of the rivalry

The rivalry between Saudi Arabia and Iran is partly reflected in the indirect conflicts between the two countries as they engaged in proxy wars in other states, including Syria, Iraq, Yemen and Bahrain. This rivalry has had significant effects on these states, resulting in the loss of various opportunities to benefit from the BRI. As will be discussed later in the case of Iraq and Syria, both Saudi Arabia and Iran have proven involvement in those countries' civil wars.

For instance, after the Iraq War began in 2003, a security vacuum was created and Iraq fell into civil war. Sunni and Shia militia groups organised across the country and, until the eruption of the Arab Spring in 2011, the Saudis sent funds and weapons to the Sunni groups while the Iranians supported the Shias. This trend continued even after the Arab Spring began. In Syria, the Iranian military fought side by side with militias—some of which were extremist groups like Hezbollah—in support of dictator Bashar al-Assad. In other words, the Iranians were actively supporting the militias in their fight against rebel Sunni groups, who were Saudi proxies.

Discussion of relative gains

For Saudi Arabia and Iran, relative gains carry significance, especially in their continuous rivalry—often referred to as the 'Regional Cold War'. Regarding the total value of BRI investment, Saudi Arabia has seen more relative gains, with USD19.79 billion in investments compared with Iran's USD12.24 billion (see Figure 10.1, Table 10.1 and Table 10.2).

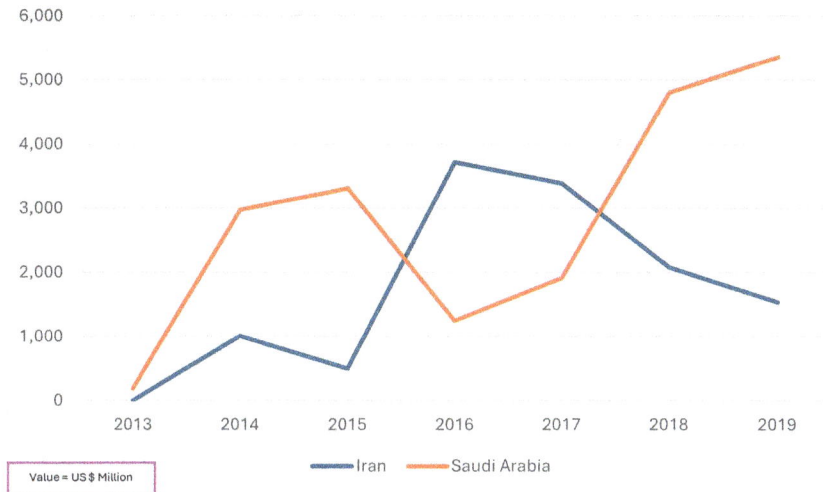

Figure 10.1 Total value of BRI investments in Saudi Arabia and Iran, 2013–19
Source: Compiled by the author based on data from AEI (2020).

Table 10.1 List of all BRI investments by China in Saudi Arabia, 2013–19

Year	Month	Chinese entity	Transaction party	Sector	Subsector	Value (USD m)
2013	November	China National Building Material Corporation	Southern Province Cement Company	Real estate	Construction	190
2014	February	China Communications Construction Company	–	Transport	Shipping	200
2014	April	Sinopec	Aramco	Energy	Oil	190
2014	May	China Communications Construction Company	Aramco	Utilities	–	500
2014	November	CRCC	–	Real estate	Construction	1,980
2014	November	Power Construction Corporation of China	–	Energy	Oil	100
2015	April	Sinopec	–	Chemicals	–	450
2015	April	China National Building Material Corporation	Arabian Cement	Real estate	Construction	100

189

Year	Month	Chinese entity	Transaction party	Sector	Subsector	Value (USD m)
2015	June	Sinopec	–	Energy	Oil	140
2015	October	Power Construction Corporation of China	Aramco	Energy	Gas	700
2015	October	Power Construction Corporation of China	Aramco	Energy	Gas	1,290
2015	December	Sinopec	–	Utilities	–	430
2015	December	Sinopec	–	Agriculture	–	200
2016	January	Power Construction Corporation of China	–	Real estate	Construction	390
2016	February	China Minmetals	–	Real estate	Construction	230
2016	March	China National Machinery Industry Corporation (Sinomach)	Advanced Tyre	Transport	Autos	180
2016	May	Wison Energy	–	Chemicals	–	120
2016	July	China National Petroleum Corporation	Aramco	Energy	Oil	330
2017	February	Sinopec	Aramco	Energy	Gas	250
2017	May	Power Construction Corporation of China	–	Utilities	–	1,370
2017	September	China National Petroleum Corporation	Aramco	Energy	Gas	190
2017	December	China National Petroleum Corporation	Aramco	Energy	Oil	100
2018	March	Sinopec	SABIC (Saudi Basic Industries Corporation)	Energy	Gas	270
2018	July	China National Petroleum Corporation	Aramco	Energy	Oil	560
2018	August	China National Chemical Engineering	–	Chemicals	–	410

Year	Month	Chinese entity	Transaction party	Sector	Subsector	Value (USD m)
2018	September	Sinopec	–	Chemicals	–	100
2018	October	Wison Energy	SABIC	Real estate	Construction	150
2018	December	Power Construction Corporation of China	Aramco-led consortium	Transport	Shipping	3,020
2018	December	Sinopec	Aramco	Energy	Oil	290
2019	January	Sinopec	Aramco	Energy	Oil	270
2019	February	State Construction Engineering Corporation	–	Real estate	Construction	670
2019	May	China Communications Construction Company	–	Energy	Oil	120
2019	June	State Administration of Foreign Exchange	ACWA Power	Energy	Alternative	960
2019	July	China Energy Engineering Corporation	–	Other	Industry	780
2019	August	China Railway Construction Corporation	Aramco	Utilities	–	260
2019	August	CRCC	–	Transport	Rail	100
2019	October	China National Offshore Oil Corporation	–	Energy	–	700
2019	November	Sinopec	Aramco	Energy	Gas	400
2019	December	State Grid Corporation of China	Saudi Electricity Company	Utilities	–	1,100
Total value of investments						**19,790**

Source: Compiled by the author based on data from AEI (2020).

Table 10.2 List of all BRI investments by China in Iran, 2014–19

Year	Month	Chinese entity	Transaction party	Sector	Subsector	Value (USD m)
2014	March	China Communications Construction Company	–	Real estate	Construction	160
2014	May	China Metallurgical Group Corporation	–	Metals	Steel	350
2014	November	China National Machinery Industry Corporation (Sinomach)	–	Transport	Rail	320
2014	December	Sinosteel Corporation	Zarand	Energy	Coal	180
2015	September	China Communications Construction Company	–	Transport	Autos	500
2016	January	Sinosteel Corporation	Bafgh Kasra	Metals	Steel	470
2016	January	China North Industries Group Corporation Limited (Norinco)	Golbahar New Town Development	Transport	Rail	330
2016	May	China Energy Engineering Corporation	–	Utilities	–	1,960
2016	August	Power Construction Corporation of China	–	Energy	Gas	360
2016	November	China National Petroleum Corporation	Total	Energy	Gas	600
2017	February	Sinomach	–	Metals	–	220
2017	February	China Petroleum and Chemical Corporation (Sinopec)	–	Energy	Oil	590
2017	November	Norinco	–	Chemicals	–	1,530

Year	Month	Chinese entity	Transaction party	Sector	Subsector	Value (USD m)
2017	December	Sinopec	–	Energy	Oil	1,050
2018	January	CRCC	–	Transport	Rail	540
2018	March	Sinomach	–	Transport	Rail	840
2018	March	Sinomach	–	Transport	Rail	700
2019	August	China General Technology Group (Genertec), Beijing Power Equipment Group	–	Transport	Rail	1,540
Total value of investments						**12,240**

Source: Compiled by the author based on data from AEI (2020).

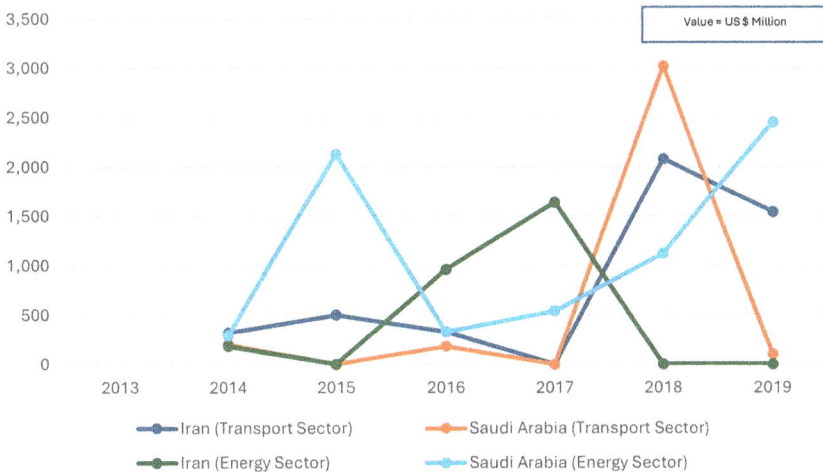

Figure 10.2 Total value of BRI investments in Saudi Arabia and Iran in the energy and transport sectors, 2013–19
Source: Compiled by the author based on data from AEI (2020).

Through China's investments in the energy and transport sectors, it can be seen (Figure 10.2) that Iran has acquired more relative gains than Saudi Arabia in the transport sector, with a total of USD4.77 billion compared with Saudi Arabia's USD3.5 billion. In contrast, Saudi Arabia has achieved approximately two and a half times more investment gains (USD6.86 billion) than Iran (USD2.78 billion) in the energy sector. The largest single investment for Saudi Arabia was in the transport sector in December 2018, with a total of USD3 billion. This investment can be considered a relative gain for Saudi Arabia since this project aims to establish marine facilities for the mega-shipyard King Salman International Complex for Maritime Industries and Services, which is part of Saudi Arabia's national industrial strategy with a focus on economic diversification. The complex is on the Persian Gulf coast in eastern Saudi Arabia and covers an area of 4.96 square kilometres (Si 2018).

In the Saudi versus Iran rivalry, both sides have achieved relative gains within specific sectors and have attracted Chinese investments, thus both can be considered winners from China's BRI. Saudi Arabia has aligned its 'Saudi Vision 2030' with the BRI. This strategic framework was formed with the aim of reducing Saudi Arabia's economic dependency on oil by diversifying its export markets and developing other sectors such as education, infrastructure, innovation and tourism. Similarly, Iran, which has been hurt by US sanctions, with its economy consequently partly paralysed, has found in China a strategic partner able to help it improve its shattered economy.

Impact on the rivalry

Saudi Arabia and Iran are the countries in the Middle East where China has concentrated most of its investment. Achieving economic benefits and securing the flow of energy necessary for its rise as a great power were part of China's goals. However, its support in these areas could result in further conflict, especially as Iran has been working for decades to build its dominance and influence in the region, despite being damaged by US sanctions. The large scale of Chinese investment can be considered a lifeline for the Iranian economy, following the sanctions imposed by the Trump administration in 2018 to isolate the Iranian Government because of its military and nuclear ambitions.

Economic development supported by China will enable Iran to increase its power and influence within the region by enhancing its military power and developing its nuclear program. This could escalate the level of conflict, especially with Saudi Arabia and its allies. Therefore, China has been criticised for not promoting stability and peace through its continued investment in Iran and for its support of Iran's nuclear agenda. Moreover, China's firm support for the Iran nuclear deal, the Joint Comprehensive Plan of Action, indicates that it may be fuelling regional conflicts, especially after the United States' withdrawal from the joint plan (Xinhua 2020). It should not be forgotten that the US State Department has named Iran 'the world's largest state sponsor of terrorism' (Fassihi and Myers 2020).

On the other hand, aligning the BRI with the Saudi Vision 2030 will help the Saudis to diversify their economy by engaging in projects in sectors including transport, construction, agriculture, chemicals and utilities. Rather than relying on oil for economic growth, this will increase Saudi Arabia's economic power, reflecting its hegemony in the region, and allow it to build its military with increased capabilities to support the Sunnis against the Shias in the countries where Saudi Arabia is heavily involved, including Syria, Iraq, Yemen and Bahrain.

Relative gains from the BRI may ultimately add fuel to the region's conflicts, due to the disproportionate Chinese investments in rival countries. Both Saudi Arabia and Iran have benefited from BRI investments and can thus continue accumulating power to use against each other, enhancing their military forces and engaging in regional conflicts and proxy wars. The state of rivalry between Saudi Arabia and Iran and the regional inequalities this has created are an important factor in the relative gains of both Syria and Iraq, while at the same time resulting in relatively low Chinese engagement in countries like Yemen and Bahrain. This will lead to a situation where many countries miss out on the opportunities offered by the BRI due to their continuing civil wars, border threats and insecurity.

Iraq and Syria

The nature of the rivalry

As Table 10.3 shows, China has chosen to invest significantly in Iraq and not at all in Syria. A particularly perplexing feature of the BRI is that China invests in some countries more than others, despite apparent similarities between them, which means that many countries miss out on the opportunities the initiative provides. For example, the situation in Iraq is not unlike that in Syria in terms of violence, instability, levels of insecurity, civil war and the spread of terrorist groups, yet Iraq has achieved relative gains by attracting Chinese investments in the energy and construction sectors, which should lead to a resurgence in its economy.

Iraq and Syria both suffered at the hands of the Islamic State of Iraq and Syria (ISIS) terrorist group. ISIS seized several Iraqi cities, including Mosul, and many parts of Syria in 2014. With its transnational jihadist agenda, ISIS attempted to unite the two countries under an Islamic caliphate, and it made a public display of removing the borders between the two countries in a blatant rejection of the Sykes–Picot Agreement established by the Western powers (Barnes-Dacey 2014). This agreement was a secret treaty made between France and the United Kingdom in 1916 that defined their mutually agreed spheres of influence in an eventual partition of the Ottoman Empire after World War I (Fromkin 1989).

The relationship between Iraq and Syria cannot be considered a serious rivalry, but it is a cautious relationship, nonetheless. The Iraq War in 2003 raised fears in Syria about the insecurity and chaos that would follow the invasion of Iraq by US forces, in particular because of the countries' shared border. The political relationship between these two countries has often been hostile—for example, during the last years of Saddam Hussein's rule in the early 2000s, the relationship was tense. It was restored in November 2006 (BBC News 2006). Additionally, being the targets of Saudi Arabia and Iran in their proxy wars has weakened the relationship between Iraq and Syria and increased their mutual distrust. In sum, their fraught relationship is based on these continuing insecurities and instabilities, especially those awakened by the Arab Spring in 2011 and the rise of ISIS in 2014.

Table 10.3 List of all BRI investments by China in Iraq, 2013–19

Year	Month	Chinese entity	Transaction party	Sector	Subsector	Value (USD m)
2013	November	China National Petroleum Corporation	Exxon Mobil	Energy	Oil	1,250
2013	November	China Communications Construction Company	–	Utilities	–	170
2013	December	China Communications Construction Company	–	Utilities	–	160
2014	January	Sinoma International Engineering	Hewa Holding	Real estate	Construction	190
2014	May	China National Petroleum Corporation, Power Construction Corporation of China	–	Energy	Oil	790
2014	July	China National Petroleum Corporation	–	Energy	Oil	610
2015	May	Zhongman Petroleum	–	Energy	Oil	530
2015	July	Anton Oilfield Services Group	–	Energy	Oil	140

Year	Month	Chinese entity	Transaction party	Sector	Subsector	Value (USD m)
2016	February	China National Petroleum Corporation	–	Utilities	–	270
2016	October	China National Machinery Industry Corporation (Sinomach)	Kar Electrical Power Production Trading	Energy	Gas	1,010
2016	October	Sinomach	KAR Group	Real estate	Construction	240
2016	November	China National Petroleum Corporation	–	Energy	Gas	280
2017	June	Norinco	–	Real estate	Construction	450
2018	May	China National Offshore Oil Corporation	–	Energy	Oil	220
2018	May	Norinco	–	Energy	Oil	1,350
2018	November	China National Petroleum Corporation	Lukoil	Energy	Oil	160
2018	November	Zhongman Petroleum	Petronas	Energy	Oil	100
2019	January	China National Building Material Corporation	–	Real estate	Construction	250
2019	February	China National Petroleum Corporation	Petronas	Energy	Oil	150
2019	March	China National Petroleum Corporation	Basrah Gas Company	Energy	Gas	170
2019	May	China National Petroleum Corporation	–	Energy	Gas	1,070
2019	May	Sinomach	–	Real estate	Construction	260
2019	September	Power Construction Corporation of China	–	Energy	Oil	110
2019	November	China National Petroleum Corporation	–	Energy	Oil	120
2019	November	Sinomach	–	Energy	Oil	140
Total value of investments						**10,190**

Source: Compiled by the author based on data from AEI (2020).

Discussion of relative gains

Table 10.3 shows that China has invested USD10.19 billion in Iraq, while there has not been a single BRI project focused on Syria. The most surprising thing of all is that China began implementing its BRI projects in Iraq immediately after its launch in 2013 and before the rise of ISIS, and it continued to invest in further projects throughout 2014 and 2015 when destruction and chaos at the hands of ISIS were at their peak in Iraq. Syria presents some golden opportunities for China in reconstruction projects, as it is strategically located at the crossroads of Africa, Europe, Central Asia and the Caucasus (Belt and Road News 2019). In addition, it is at the juncture of oil and gas pipelines connecting resource fields in the Arabian Peninsula, the Persian Gulf and Iran with European markets, which would help China to promote the BRI as a revival of the ancient Silk Road.

Of China's investments in Iraq between 2013 and 2019, USD8.2 billion was in the energy sector alone. This means that, regardless of Syria's strategic location and its reconstruction opportunities, China is focusing on Iraq's energy sector and is apparently unfazed by the level of violence in the country. Syria is losing out on any relative gain in comparison with Iraq (Barnes-Dacey 2014).

Impact on the rivalry

Due to China's substantial investments in Iraq's energy sector, compared with zero investments in Syria, Iraq will ultimately play a more central role in the BRI than Syria. Moreover, due to the endless conflicts in the country, Iraq has fallen behind in terms of economic diversification and its dependency on oil exports will motivate China to invest further in the transport sector to secure flows of oil and gas. As President of China Xi Jinping made clear: 'Cooperation between Iraq and China would focus mainly on oil and infrastructure' (OBOR Europe 2019).

Hence, China intends to continue investing in Iraq's infrastructure, making it one of the key countries along the BRI routes, especially if it also invests in the transport sector in Iran and Türkiye. This would make Iraq a main connection point between Türkiye and Iran and all the way to Europe. Such a development would leave Syria behind and could weaken its economy further, despite its strategic location. China's greater investment in Iraq and the increased level of inequality could raise tensions between the two countries.

Egypt and Türkiye

The nature of the rivalry

In the eastern Mediterranean, tensions between Egypt and Türkiye have been on the rise since July 2013, and their relationship has reached high levels of mutual hostility. There are two main causes of the tension. The first is related to Türkiye's plans to explore for oil and gas in the region. Türkiye has not acknowledged the maritime boundary between Egypt and Cyprus that gives Egypt the right to explore for oil and gas in the territorial waters around the island. Türkiye does not formally recognise the Government of Cyprus (which is backed by Greece) but does recognise the Turkish Republic of Northern Cyprus. Hence, Türkiye has been accused of breaching Egyptian sovereignty in the eastern Mediterranean (Megahid 2018).

The second factor is Türkiye's engagement in Libya at both the political and the military levels. This involvement has taken the form of sending ships to deliver aid to the internationally recognised government in Tripoli, for example. After recognising Fayez al-Sarraj's government of national accord in Libya, Türkiye increased its military visibility and deterrence there, just as Libyan Field Marshal Khalifa Haftar's supporters intensified their military deployment and activity *against* the government of national accord. The Turkish presence in Libya has led the Egyptian Government to build a 'security alliance' with Libya in response, and these tensions have had implications for the stability of the Middle East and North Africa (Al-Anani 2020).

Discussion of relative gains

China has been investing in both countries on a significant scale. For Egypt and Türkiye, the relative gains matter, especially regarding their hostile relationship and the rising tensions in the eastern Mediterranean. In terms of BRI gains, both countries can be considered winners; however, Egypt stands out as the most successful, with total investments reaching about USD17.41 billion, compared with Türkiye's USD5.96 billion (see Tables 10.4 and 10.5).

As Figure 10.3 shows, Chinese investments in Egypt are much higher than those in Türkiye. In 2018, China made its largest investment in Egypt across various fields such as energy, textiles and construction, with the total value reaching USD8.7 billion. This compares with no investments in Türkiye in that year. Although the total value of Chinese investment in Egypt fell in 2019, it is still the relative winner over Türkiye when comparing Chinese investments as part of the BRI.

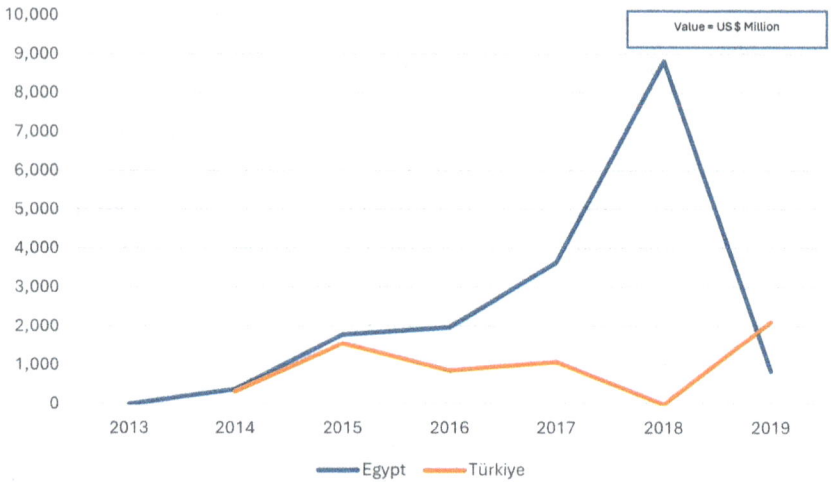

Figure 10.3 Total value of BRI investments in Egypt and Türkiye, 2013–19
Source: Compiled by the author based on data from AEI (2020).

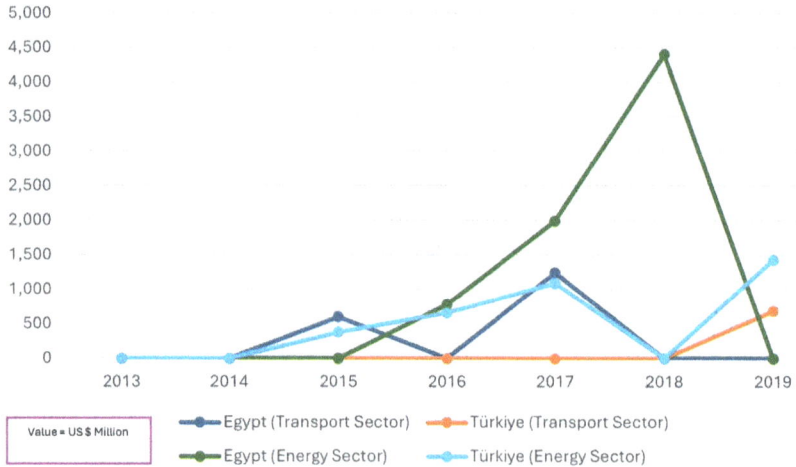

Figure 10.4 Total value of BRI investments in Egypt and Türkiye in the energy and transport sectors, 2013–19
Source: Compiled by the author based on data from AEI (2020).

As shown in Figure 10.4, Egypt had greater relative gains in the energy sector with a total investment of USD7.17 billion, compared with USD3.56 billion for Türkiye. For the transport sector, Egypt attracted investments of USD1.84 billion, compared with USD1 billion for Türkiye. It is worth noting that China made one single investment in the transport sector in Türkiye in 2019 with a total value of USD690 million. This was not aimed at improving the Turkish transport sector, however, such as building railways and ports. Rather, it came from a consortium led by China Merchants Group wishing to purchase a majority stake in Türkiye's ICA Construction to gain access to its expressway assets in Istanbul (Liao 2019).

Impact on the rivalry

Investment in the energy sector has benefited China's relations with Egypt at the expense of Türkiye, especially since one of the main tensions between the two countries concerns exploration for oil and gas in the Mediterranean Sea. As Chinese foreign minister Wang Yi's visit to Cairo in early 2020 revealed, China might not support Türkiye in these current crises. The visit clarified that China considers Egypt a new international centre for shipping and logistics in the Mediterranean, and Wang stated that China would cooperate with Egypt to ensure an early political settlement of the crisis in Libya (Nordic Monitor 2020).

In a similar vein, China has paid increased attention to the Suez Canal as the maritime gateway to Europe, and it has become the largest investor in Egypt's SCZONE mega-project (Xinhua 2019) following the completion of the Suez Canal expansion in 2015 (BBC News 2015). Although China is building a network of railways and connecting roads between cities in Central Asia, Türkiye and all the way to Europe, it still relies heavily on the Suez Canal due to its strategic location and because of its importance for China's merchandise exports to Europe (van der Putten 2016). Thanks to China's attention and various investments in the SCZONE, the canal will ultimately increase its capacity and strengthen Egypt's position of power in world trade through Europe and the eastern Mediterranean. As a result, China is entering the playing field of the eastern Mediterranean, which has long been full of both great power and regional geopolitical tensions, especially (though not exclusively) between Egypt and Türkiye (van der Putten 2016).

Table 10.4 List of all BRI investments by China in Egypt, 2014–19

Year	Month	Chinese entity	Transaction party	Sector	Subsector	Value (USD m)
2014	July	Sinoma International Engineering	–	Real estate	Construction	370
2015	April	China Railway Construction Corporation	Egyptian National Railways	Transport	Rail	600
2015	May	China National Building Material Corporation	–	Other	Industry	190
2015	May	China Energy Engineering Corporation	–	Utilities	–	990
2016	March	State Grid Corporation of China, Power Construction Corporation of China	–	Energy	–	780
2016	June	Sinoma International Engineering	–	Real estate	Construction	1,190
2017	May	China National Machinery Industry Corporation (Sinomach)	–	Agriculture	–	400
2017	August	Aviation Industry Corporation of China, China Railway Engineering Corporation	–	Transport	Rail	1,240
2017	October	Power Construction Corporation of China	Soukhna Refinery and Petrochemicals Company	Energy	Oil	1,990
2018	March	China Communications Construction Company	–	Logistics	–	120
2018	August	China National Building Material Corporation	–	Other	Industry	180
2018	September	Dongfang Electric, Shanghai Electric	–	Energy	Coal	4,400

Year	Month	Chinese entity	Transaction party	Sector	Subsector	Value (USD m)
2018	September	China Minmetals Corporation	–	Other	Textiles	670
2018	September	China State Construction Engineering Corporation	–	Real estate	Construction	3,450
2019	July	China State Construction Engineering Corporation, Wengfu	–	Chemicals	–	840
Total value of investments						**17,410**

Source: Compiled by the author based on data from AEI (2020).

Table 10.5 List of all BRI investments by China in Türkiye, 2014–19

Year	Month	Chinese entity	Transaction party	Sector	Subsector	Value (USD m)
2014	April	Industrial and Commercial Bank of China	Tekstil Bank	Finance	Banking	320
2015	February	China National Machinery Industry Corporation (Sinomach)	OEDAS, OEPAS	Energy	–	380
2015	May	Sinoma International Engineering	Limak Holdings	Real estate	Construction	160
2015	May	Sinoma International Engineering	Votorantim Cimentos	Real estate	Construction	100
2015	September	China Merchants Group, China Investment Corporation, China Ocean Shipping (Group) Company	Fina Liman	Logistics	–	920
2016	January	Dongfang Electric	Hattat Holding Energy Group	Energy	Coal	660

Year	Month	Chinese entity	Transaction party	Sector	Subsector	Value (USD m)
2016	May	Bank of China	–	Finance	Banking	110
2016	December	ZTE	NETAŞ Telekomunikasyon	Technology	Telecom	100
2017	November	Power Construction Corporation of China	TEYO	Energy	Coal	1,090
2019	September	State Power Investment Corporation, Aviation Industry Corporation of China	–	Energy	Coal	1,320
2019	November	China Electronics Technology Group Corporation	Kalyon Holding	Energy	Alternative	110
2019	December	China Merchants Group–led consortium	–	Transport	Autos	690
Total value of investments						**5,960**

Source: Compiled by the author based on data from AEI (2020).

Comparison of the three rivalrous relationships

Table 10.6 demonstrates that China is prioritising cooperation and investment in countries with a developed energy sector (as its first choice) and transport sector (as its second choice). Furthermore, it shows that the selection of countries for significant investment is not dependent on that country's level of security or political stability. This is most apparent where China has been investing in the Iraqi energy sector since the launch of the BRI in 2013, which coincided with the rise of ISIS and the consequent chaos and violence across the country. In contrast, China has not invested in Syria, which has suffered similar levels of instability since 2013, even though Syria's geostrategic location could have a positive impact on the connectivity aspect of the BRI and there are golden opportunities for reconstruction projects throughout the country. More than anything else, the situation in each of the three sets of countries examined here proves that China is focusing its investment primarily in states with leading energy and transport sectors, regardless of the level of insecurity that prevails or the relationships between these states.

Table 10.6 Winners and losers from China's prioritisation of investment

Factors	Saudi Arabia versus Iran	Iraq versus Syria	Egypt versus Türkiye
Energy	Saudi Arabia: USD6.86 billion Iran: USD2.78 billion	Iraq: USD8.2 billion Syria: None	Egypt: USD7.17 billon Türkiye: USD3.56 billion
Transport	Saudi Arabia: USD3.5 billion Iran: USD4.77 billion	Iraq: None Syria: None	Egypt: USD1.84 billion Türkiye: Less than USD1 billion
Insecurity	Saudi Arabia: Stable Iran: Partly unstable	Both: Mostly unstable	Both: Partly unstable

Source: Created by the author.

Conclusion

This study has examined the implications of the BRI on rivalrous relationships in the Middle East by locating the power dynamics of the region within the context of the BRI and its implementation. It has shown that, for various reasons, there are clear winners and losers from the BRI. It presented two factors as potential causes: the nature of the power dynamics in the region and China's intentional or unintentional favouring of some countries over others for its BRI investments.

The findings of this study show that China's investment program is focused on areas where it can cooperate with the host country in the energy sector, as a first choice, or the transport sector, as second choice. It further showed that the target country's degree of insecurity does not affect China's investment decisions, which means the BRI could offer an advantage to countries with abundant energy resources. Another finding is that, despite the expectation that conflict would deter China from investing in a country, that did not prove to be the most important factor when it comes to differentiating BRI winners from losers.

These findings show that the BRI has unintended consequences for rivalrous relationships in the Middle East based on China's decision to invest in some countries rather than others. Considering the relative gains, this could exacerbate existing conflicts and instabilities within the region by altering the regional power dynamics.

References

Al-Anani, Khalil. 2020. 'Egypt–Turkey Strained Relations: Implications for Regional Security.' *Policy Analysis*, 18 March. Washington, DC: Arab Center Washington DC. arabcenterdc.org/policy_analyses/egypt-turkey-strained-relations-implications -for-regional-security.

Al Jazeera. 2023. 'How Has the Saudi–Iran Divide Affected the Middle East?' *Al Jazeera*, 7 April. www.aljazeera.com/news/2023/4/7/how-has-the-saudi-iran-divide-affected-the-middle-east.

American Enterprise Institute (AEI). 2020. 'Worldwide Chinese Investments and Construction.' *China Global Investment Tracker*. Washington, DC: AEI. www. aei.org/china-global-investment-tracker.

Amineh, M.P. 2022. *The China-Led Belt and Road Initiative and its Reflections: The Crisis of Hegemony and Changing Global Orders*. London: Routledge. doi.org/ 10.4324/9781003256502.

Barnes-Dacey, Julien. 2014. 'Syria and Iraq: One Conflict or Two?' *Commentary*, 27 June. Berlin: European Council on Foreign Relations. www.ecfr.eu/article/ commentary_syria_and_iraq_one_conflict_or_two280.

BBC News. 2006. 'Iraq and Syria Restore Relations.' *BBC News*, 21 November. news.bbc.co.uk/2/hi/middle_east/6167968.stm.

BBC News. 2015. 'Egypt Launches Suez Canal Expansion.' *BBC News*, 6 August. www.bbc.com/news/world-middle-east-33800076.

Belt and Road News. 2019. 'Egypt's Suez Canal Economic Zone Integrates with China's BRI: Minister.' 20 March. Beijing: State Council Information Office. english.scio.gov.cn/beltandroad/2019-03/20/content_74593769.htm.

Birringer, T. 2010. *Four Scenarios and No Recourse? Saudi Arabia and Iran's Nuclear Program*. Research Report, 1 January. Bonn: Konrad Adenauer Foundation. www.jstor.org/stable/resrep10015.

Chen, Juan, Shu Meng, and Wen Shaobiao. 2018. 'Aligning China's Belt and Road Initiative with Saudi Arabia's 2030 Vision: Opportunities and Challenges.' *China Quarterly of International Strategic Studies* 4, no. 3: 363–79. doi.org/ 10.1142/S2377740018500203.

Current Affairs Correspondent West Asia. 2019. 'Syria to Become Part of Belt & Road Initiative: Bashar al-Assad.' *Belt and Road News*, 17 December. www.belt androad.news/2019/12/17/belt-road-initiative-is-built-on-consistency-bashar-al-assad [page discontinued].

Evron, Y. 2019. 'The Challenge of Implementing the Belt and Road Initiative in the Middle East: Connectivity Projects under Conditions of Limited Political Engagement.' *The China Quarterly* 237: 196–216. doi.org/10.1017/S030574 1018001273.

Fassihi, Farnaz, and Steven L. Myers. 2020. 'Defying U.S., China and Iran Near Trade and Military Partnership.' *The New York Times*, 11 July. www.nytimes.com/2020/07/11/world/asia/china-iran-trade-military-deal.html.

Fromkin, David. 1989. *A Peace to End All Peace: The Fall of the Ottoman Empire and the Creation of the Modern Middle East*. New York: Owl Books.

Girard, Bonnie. 2018. 'China's BRI Bet in the Middle East.' *The Diplomat*, 18 July. thediplomat.com/2018/07/chinas-bri-bet-in-the-middle-east.

Gruber, Lloyd. 2000. *Ruling the World: Power Politics and the Rise of Supranational Institutions*. Princeton: Princeton University Press. doi.org/10.1515/9781400 823710.

Harding, Rebecca. 2019. 'China's Belt and Road Initiative and Its Impact on the Middle East and North Africa.' *International Banker*, 20 September. international banker.com/finance/chinas-belt-and-road-initiative-and-its-impact-on-the-middle-east-and-north-africa.

Kamel, Maha S. 2018. 'China's Belt and Road Initiative: Implications for the Middle East.' *Cambridge Review of International Affairs* 31, no. 1: 76–95. doi.org/10.1080/09557571.2018.1480592.

Li, Quan, and Ye Min. 2019. 'China's Emerging Partnership Network: What, Who, Where, When and Why.' *International Trade, Politics and Development* 3, no. 2: 66–81. doi.org/10.1108/ITPD-05-2019-0004.

Liao, Shumin. 2019. 'CMET-Led Group to Pay USD689 Million for Turkish Expressway Assets.' *Yicai Global*, 24 December. www.yicaiglobal.com/news/cmet-led-group-to-pay-usd689-million-for-turkish-expressway-assets.

Megahid, Ahmed. 2018. 'Tensions Rise between Egypt and Turkey over Eastern Mediterranean Resources: Analysts Warned the Latest Controversy over Sovereignty Could Lead to War over Vital Resources.' *The Arab Weekly*, 11 February. thearabweekly.com/tensions-rise-between-egypt-and-turkey-over-eastern-mediterranean-resources.

Nordic Monitor. 2020. 'China Strengthens Ties with Egypt at the Expense of Turkey.' *Nordic Monitor*, 14 January. Stockholm: Nordic Research and Monitoring Network. www.nordicmonitor.com/2020/01/china-strengthens-ties-with-egypt-at-the-expense-of-turkey.

One Belt One Road (OBOR) Europe. 2019. 'The BRI, A Renaissance for Iraq?' *OBOR Europe*, 1 October. www.oboreurope.com/en/bri-renaissance-iraq.

Paraskova, Tsvetana. 2018. 'China Becomes World's Next Top Oil Importer.' *OilPrice.com*, 6 February. oilprice.com/Energy/Crude-Oil/Chinas-Becomes-Worlds-Next-Top-Oil-Importer.html.

Saleh, Alam, and Zakiyeh Yazdanshenas. 2020. 'Iran's Pact with China Is Bad News for the West.' *Foreign Policy*, 9 August. foreignpolicy.com/2020/08/09/irans-pact-with-china-is-bad-news-for-the-west.

Sharma, Anu. 2019. 'An Analysis of "Belt and Road" Initiative and the Middle East.' *Asian Journal of Middle Eastern and Islamic Studies* 13, no. 1: 35–49. doi.org/10.1080/25765949.2019.1586179.

Si, Katherine. 2018. 'PowerChina Wins US$3bn Construction Project for Saudi Mega-Yard.' *Seatrade Maritime News*, 30 November. www.seatrade-maritime.com/asia/powerchina-wins-3bn-construction-project-saudi-mega-yard.

Tehran Times. 2020. 'Tehran–Beijing Partnership is "A Turning Point", Says Iran's Ex-Ambassador to UN.' *Tehran Times*, 25 July. www.tehrantimes.com/news/450468/Tehran-Beijing-partnership-is-a-turning-point-says-Iran-s.

van der Putten, Frans Paul. 2016. 'Infrastructure and Geopolitics: China's Emerging Presence in the Eastern Mediterranean.' *Journal of Balkan and Near Eastern Studies* 18, no. 4: 337–51. doi.org/10.1080/19448953.2016.1195978.

Waltz, Kenneth. 1979. *Theory of International Politics*. New York: Random House.

Watanabe, Lisa. 2019. 'The Middle East and China's Belt and Road Initiative.' *CSS Analyses in Security Policy* 254: 1–4.

Weiss, Martin A. 2017. *Asian Infrastructure Investment Bank (AIIB)*. CRS Report, R44754(6). Washington, DC: Congressional Research Service.

Xinhua. 2016a. 'Closer Partnership as "Belt and Road" Meets Suez Canal Corridor.' *People's Daily*, 20 January. en.people.cn/n3/2016/0120/c90780-9006923.html.

Xinhua. 2016b. 'Work Together for a Bright Future of China–Arab Relations: Speech by H.E. Xi Jinping President of the People's Republic of China at the Arab League Headquarters, Cairo, 21 January 2016.' *China Daily*, 22 January. www.chinadaily.com.cn/world/2016xivisitmiddleeast/2016-01-22/content_23191229.htm.

Xinhua. 2019. 'Spotlight: China, Egypt Join Hands to Write New Chapter of Suez Canal Development.' *Xinhua*, 17 November. www.xinhuanet.com/english/2019-11/18/c_138563688.htm.

Xinhua. 2020. 'China Reiterates Firm Support for Iran Nuclear Deal: FM Spokesperson.' *Xinhua*, 14 July. www.xinhuanet.com/english/2020-07/14/c_139211499.htm.

Part III: Conclusion

11

The globalisation of Chinese actors and the transformation of the BRI into a domestic issue: Implications for global and domestic governance and for Japan

Miwa Hirono[1]

Focusing on China and developing countries along the route of the Belt and Road Initiative (BRI), this book has examined the three central questions set out at the beginning of Chapter 1:

1. How have the key Chinese actors operationalised their transition from local to global actors?

2. How have the key actors in the host countries interpreted, utilised or coopted BRI projects into the political, economic and social environments of their countries, and how have the BRI projects been established as domestic issues within the host countries as a result?

3. What are the implications of the BRI for global and domestic governance generally, and for Japan's role in countries where the BRI projects take place, in particular?

1   The research used in this chapter was supported by JSPS Grant-in-Aid for Scientific Research JP17K03606 and JP21K01380.

In this concluding chapter, I will synthesise and reflect on the analysis provided in each of the preceding chapters to provide a response to these three questions.

Aspects of the global development of the BRI

First and foremost, this book emphasises that the global development of the BRI has been both centralised and decentralised. There is no denying that since Xi Jinping came to power in 2013, the degree of centralisation and top-down decision-making in the Communist Party regime has been strengthened. At the same time, it is also true that governance has been decentralised within China and among the Chinese actors themselves, and the implementation of the BRI has been carried out in a bottom-up manner. In other words, the way the initiative is being developed globally means that both vectors operate simultaneously. Effectively, while it is true that the Chinese Government and the CPC are strategically and systematically promoting the BRI, it is also true that various Chinese actors are operating in their own interests, with or without engaging in the government strategy.

Some years ago, Scott Kennedy used the metaphor of a Christmas tree to describe the BRI, arguing that it is little more than a collection of policies displayed together (Kennedy, cited in Clover and Hornby 2015). Given the passage of time since Kennedy introduced this idea, a fresh look at the BRI shows that it has gone beyond the stage of being a mere 'collection' of policies and has become increasingly centralised at the policy level. These changes are salient in China's 'planned diplomacy', which formulated some centralised direction of how the BRI should be elaborated and implemented (outlined by Aoyama in Chapter 3). Furthermore, Mori's discussion of the way the Chinese Government is strengthening its ties with Chinese companies (Chapter 5) reveals how its governance has been centralised and has affected the corporate actors involved in the BRI. Arguably, the Chinese Government and the CPC have been decorating the Christmas tree in a very systematic way since the BRI was first established.

While there is clearly a planned aspect to the BRI, the various actors—as ornaments on the Christmas tree—are getting on and off the tree of their own volition. Moreover, their activities are not limited to the Christmas tree, but extend into the surrounding area, which is the reality of the current global development of the BRI. For example, the exclusion of China's provincial governments from the national strategy, the over-compartmentalisation of administrative structures (Aoyama, Chapter 3) and the important role played by the global network of Chinese entrepreneurs (Mori, Chapter 5) are not necessarily elements 'planned' by the Chinese Government; they have existed for a long time and have been developed by actors pursuing their own interests. Provincial governments, Chinese enterprises and China-based networks, as willing 'ornaments', will use the BRI or whatever other business opportunity is available to them, just as governments and leaders in the countries in which China invests will use the BRI if it is advantageous to their political interests (Chapters 6–10). The book shows how these various actors pursue their own interests, both on and off the 'Christmas tree'. This means that it is difficult to position ornaments in accordance with China's national strategy.

Another 'unplanned' element is the very negative image of the BRI that has emerged through the 'debt trap' and other factors, even though improving China's image is very important for its national strategy. The debt trap does not apply to all emerging economies, but it does apply particularly to those in Africa in terms of stifling industrialisation. However much China tries to foster a positive image, unless it fully understands the circumstances of the countries along the BRI and carefully integrates their interests, it will be difficult to achieve truly mutual benefits.

What does the existence of this twin process of centralisation and decentralisation imply? Even if we assume that all these activities are planned by the Chinese Government, the fact remains that each of these 'ornaments' has its own agenda and is developing in various (potentially unplanned) ways. It is not necessarily the case that the Chinese Government's intentions will be reflected in the global development of the BRI, and the reality of the initiative will be greatly influenced by the actions of the 'ornaments'. Depending on how the Chinese network operates within any one BRI country (Chapters 6–10), there is a good chance the initiative will develop its own trajectory, away from the planned objectives of the Chinese Government. What that will mean is a difficult question to answer, but at the very least we cannot rule out the possibility that it will lead to developments not envisaged by China. Moreover, if we look at the 'ornaments' of the destination countries, as we have seen in the cases of Thailand, Indonesia, Myanmar and Pakistan (and also in the examples of the Maldives and

Malaysia, which do not feature in this book), it is clear that if the BRI is re-examined from the perspective of local needs, local actors have the power to change what the BRI entails for them.

Domestic issues in countries along the Belt and Road route

Regarding the second central question—that of the domestic impact in countries along the route—several situations were discussed in this book. It was pointed out that although the BRI may be proceeding smoothly thanks to close connections between Chinese elites and central governments in some countries, anti-China sentiment could become an issue when opposition to the elites increases in these countries (Ang, Chapter 6 on Thailand; Wijaya, Chapter 7 on Indonesia). We also saw that the BRI is being used to resolve domestic conflicts (Cho Latt, Chapter 8 on Myanmar). And while the BRI is contributing to the economic development of the Middle East, the imbalance in the volume of investment in different countries could have a negative impact on regional hostilities (Tadrous, Chapter 10). Each of these chapters analyses the way in which the BRI is becoming interlinked with domestic politics, domestic economic policy and regional power relations and is being exploited by local political and economic actors. Their combined analysis reveals that China, as a superpower, does not dominate the countries and regions in which it invests, but the BRI is being used and incorporated as a pawn in local dynamics.

In the light of this analysis, the argument considered in Chapter 1, which sees the BRI as a form of 'neo-colonialism' or a '*Pax Sinica*', is a specious one that ignores the actual situation in the countries along the route. As China steps up its international presence in the realms of politics and economics, enhances its military and its role in multilateral organisations such as the United Nations, and becomes more involved in space exploration and the information technology sector, and as relations between the United States and China become ever more strained, it is often argued that China is trying to establish its hegemony in the world through the BRI. However, there is a wide gap between the fact that China's power is increasing in international politics in general and the argument that China is trying to establish global hegemony. To fully understand the complex nature of the

BRI, we must consider the reality on the ground in the countries where China is investing—as the authors have done in this book—and the views of local people.

Attending to the views of local people offers a form of decolonisation in research terms, with more emphasis placed on the actors implementing the project. Researching the BRI purely from the perspective of China and other major powers effectively means neglecting the emerging economies. In this sense, the earlier metaphor of the Christmas tree is in fact problematic and should be treated with caution. The 'ornaments' here—that is, the Chinese actors and the actors in the destination countries who get on and off the BRI Christmas tree—are not placed on the tree by someone else. As already noted, they are actors who, like the toys in the Disney film *Toy Story*, can move of their own volition.

Implications for global and domestic governance

What are the implications of the above discussion for global and domestic governance, as touched on in the third key question? Adachi posed this question in Chapter 2, querying the extent to which the promotion of the BRI is shaking the fundamental principles of an open economy, multilateralism and liberal democracy. He argued that the BRI seems to follow the same economic policy that China has pursued since Deng Xiaoping's reform and opening—namely, the promotion of a capitalist economy within a planned one. In the current version of the BRI, there are many planned aspects: the Chinese Government promotes 'planned diplomacy' to implement its economic policy (Aoyama, Chapter 3), which prepares the ground for the integration of the 'trinity' of trade, investment and aid—the Chinese Government's preferred approach to developing economies. Such planning also provides the basis for success in the open economy.

Chinese networks have also been active in promoting capitalist business relations (Mori, Chapter 5). While China is not an 'open economy' from the perspective of its increasing role at the state level when working with other countries, it is nonetheless true that the BRI is based on the active participation of key actors in an open international economy. In the same way that the contradictory elements of 'centralisation' and 'decentralisation' are mixed up in the BRI, the contradictory elements of 'planning' and an 'open economy' are also intertwined. In other words, the promotion of the BRI has strengthened one aspect of global governance, the 'open economy', while at the same time fostering the Chinese nuance of 'planning'.

Regarding liberal democracy, a Chinese-style approach to state management and investment without political conditions could set back democratisation efforts in emerging economies. Certainly, the cases of Thailand (Ang, Chapter 6) and Indonesia (Wijaya, Chapter 7) reveal a situation in which the power of the common people is relatively weak, as the elites in these countries use the BRI to increase and entrench their own power. At the same time, both in these two countries and in Myanmar (Lwin Cho Latt, Chapter 8) and Pakistan (Boni, Chapter 9), there are clearly groups that are opposed to or sceptical about the BRI. These groups have been able to utilise general elections to elect new leaders whose stance is not necessarily pro-China, as in the case of Pakistan, or they have tried to use the BRI to increase the power of their own elites, as in Thailand. In other words, the people of the countries along the route are not necessarily pro-China or even pro-elite. Consequently, they are not 'ornaments placed by someone else' (much less by China), but instead are seriously considering how to use the BRI for the benefit of their own country and on their own terms. In this sense, the BRI does not necessarily undermine liberal democracy. On the contrary, the analysis in this book confirms that there are cases where the BRI has given rise to a renewed sense of democracy in the countries in which China has invested.

Regarding domestic governance in these countries, Adachi (Chapter 2) notes that although there are concerns that China's infrastructure projects are having a negative impact on corruption, human rights and financial sustainability, governments risk losing their mandate if they fail to win over voters in support of such projects. As described above, the groups that oppose or are sceptical about the BRI reveal a situation where voters are demanding accountability so that domestic governance can be more democratic and beneficial to society. This question of the benefits and disadvantages that the BRI entails for the whole of society—not just the elites—is an issue that must be examined further in future research.

In addition, an important question for the domestic situation is how countries along the route will re-evaluate the BRI in the new context of Covid-19. The pandemic had wide-ranging effects on all countries, including people's health, the stoppage of industrial operations due to restrictions on the movement of people, unemployment, damage to tourism and the cessation of social life. How will the BRI in the post-Covid era cope with the various problems in these countries that have arisen, or been accelerated, by the virus? It is no exaggeration to say that in future the BRI will need to incorporate a better understanding of the local context of the countries receiving investment, particularly how to provide assistance that is more relevant to the needs of diverse local populations. While this may be seen as a risk to the success of the project in the short term, such careful considerations will be extremely important for the continuation of the project and its long-term success.

The significance of the BRI for Japan

The Japanese Government's response: Cooperation and differentiation

Given the foregoing analysis, I would like to conclude this book by considering the implications of the BRI agenda for Japan. For some time after the launch of the BRI in 2013, the Japanese Government did not show support for the initiative. However, at a Japan–China summit held during the Asia-Pacific Economic Cooperation (APEC) meeting in Vietnam in November 2017, then prime minister Shinzo Abe agreed for the first time with President Xi Jinping that Japan would discuss the contributions of China and Japan to the world, 'including the Belt and Road Initiative' (MoFA 2017). At the same time, the meeting:

> agreed that it is important to cooperate to build a free, open and mutually beneficial rule-based relationship, and that promoting business between private enterprises and developing business between China and Japan in third countries would be beneficial not only for the development of those two countries but also for the target countries. (MoFA 2017)

As Prime Minister Abe told the Japanese Diet in 2019, the Japanese Government:

> is willing to cooperate with the project if it incorporates the 'four conditions' of openness, transparency and economy of the project, and financial stability of the target country through appropriate financing. We are not totally in favour of it. (Nikkei 2019)

Thus, while the Japanese Government has expressed its willingness to cooperate with the BRI, it has also tried to maintain a certain degree of distance—for example, by outlining these 'four conditions'. Nonetheless, there has been substantial economic cooperation between China and Japan in third countries, even before the government's formal announcement of its (albeit tentative) support for the BRI in 2017. As Kenichi Kokubo, then managing director of Hitachi Limited, explained in December 2017, his company frequently worked with third countries other than Japan and China (Okada 2017). This included the case where a Chinese corporation accepted, at the request of a third country, to use Hitachi-made key components in its HSR carriages. Kokubo also cited the example of a power station for which the company had contracted in Libya, where a Chinese company was used to reduce costs, emphasising that the 'Japan–China collaboration had led to a win-win situation' (Okada 2017). As Mori suggests in Chapter 5, the Chinese Chamber of Commerce in Japan, which facilitates relationship-building between Chinese merchants in Japan and representatives of Japanese companies, is also a member of the Advisory Committee of the WCEC. It is, therefore, possible to promote further on-the-ground cooperation between Chinese and Japanese enterprises in countries along the BRI routes.

In addition, following the APEC meeting, third-country market cooperation was considered in Thailand and, during Prime Minister Abe's visit to China in October 2018, Japanese and Chinese companies and others concluded 52 memorandums of cooperation, including the development of smart cities in Thailand (Sankei Shimbun 2019).[2] This expectation of cooperation between Japan and China in third countries is an opinion I have heard expressed in several interviews in both Japan and China. When I interviewed people connected with Japanese companies in Myanmar, Kyrgyzstan and the Maldives, they told me that the scale of the BRI is so large that Japanese companies will not be able to survive if they do not participate in it and will therefore be obliged to cooperate at some level. It is certain that Japan–China cooperation in third countries comes in response to such voices on the ground.

---

2   While the Chinese side positions this as part of the BRI, in Japan, the then minister for economy, trade and industry Hiroshige Seko stated that 'basically it has nothing to do with the Belt and Road Initiative', illustrating a difference in position (Sankei Shimbun 2019).

Alongside this cooperative attitude, Japan is trying to 'differentiate' its projects from those of China to a certain extent. This can be seen both at the foreign policy level and at the level of practical cooperation. At the foreign policy level, the Japanese Government is promoting the 'free and open Indo-Pacific' with the United States, India and Australia. As discussed by Sato-Daimon in Chapter 4, the BRI is often seen as China's pursuit of hegemony or revisionist attitudes or the export of Chinese values. In contrast, through the 'free and open Indo-Pacific', Japan is advocating, among other things, strengthening connectivity in a way that complies with the rules of the international order. By emphasising these rules, Japan is seeking to create an alternative to the BRI at the policy level. Japan's rivalry with China in terms of foreign aid may also be relevant. There have been various discourses that seek to differentiate Japanese aid from Chinese aid by emphasising the 'quality' of the former (see, for example, Hirono 2019).

The impact of such differentiation is not necessarily negative. Differentiation also has the potential for Sino-Japanese investment and aid to become complementary and play an important role in the development of third countries. In this respect, the model case for Sino-Japanese cooperation as set out by the Japanese Government in 2019 has great potential. The Ministry of Economy, Trade and Industry set out three areas for Japan–China business cooperation in third countries—namely: the development and operation of solar and wind power plants in the field of 'energy saving and environmental cooperation'; the joint development of industrial parks in eastern Thailand in the field of 'industrial upgrading'; and improving the railway linkages between China and Europe in the field of 'logistics utilisation' (Sankei Biz 2017).

Policy recommendations for Japan

Japan has three contrasting standpoints on the BRI. The first is the position of Japanese companies, especially those operating in third countries, and actors involved in aid. For the former, China is no longer a 'rival' with which they can compete on a quantitative scale in terms of the BRI. Japan should use the BRI as an 'opportunity', while differentiating itself in the ways outlined above. The second standpoint relates to Japan's position as a member of the Organisation for Economic Co-operation and Development's Development Assistance Committee (DAC) in Asia, which has a different history from that of the West. As shown by Sato-Daimon in Chapter 4, Japan also used to engage in the 'trinity' of investment, trade and aid activities and was criticised internationally for so doing. Now, however, as a member of the DAC, it is engaging in investment, trade and aid activities that meet so-called international standards.

As a DAC member with a non-Western background, Japan must seriously consider how to maintain the international order based on democracy and the protection of human rights, and how to reflect the Sustainable Development Goals (SDGs) and human security in its investment activities in the future. There is no contradiction between Japan's position and the objectives of the BRI: even though China might regard the SDGs and human security as factors that slow infrastructure investment, it is extremely important to aim for and implement investments that incorporate the SDGs and human security to achieve a long-term return on investment and to benefit a diverse range of local elites as well as non-elites.

The third standpoint, which is rarely discussed by analysts but is implied by this book, is how Japan, China and other donor states can be utilised by host-state actors to benefit their domestic political and economic status. Great-power politics exists internationally, but once these donor countries operate in host countries, those politics are 'reproduced' in the host state's domestic context. Donor countries can be drawn into unnecessary domestic rivalry, which does not help the betterment of people's livelihoods.

So how should Japan respond to the BRI from the perspective of these three standpoints? First, Japan must take careful note of the debate about China's 'pursuit of hegemony' and the growing anti-China sentiment that can be seen in Japan, in host states and around the world, and aim for a relationship that is free from prejudice. At the root of these debates is a wariness of the 'hardening' of China, brought about by the centralisation of power by the CPC and by President Xi in particular. Bearing in mind China's military actions in the South and East China seas as well as its 'wolf warrior', hardline diplomatic stance in its confrontation with the United States, the use of 'mask diplomacy' to expand its global influence, enforcement of the National Security Law in Hong Kong and the suppression of human rights in Xinjiang, there is a view that China is indeed trying to use the BRI to increase its hegemony and suppress human rights.

However, the application of this argument to the BRI needs much more substantial evidence. As the detailed analysis in this book reveals, the underlying reality of the BRI is that centralisation and decentralisation coexist within China. It is true that the BRI is a centralised initiative of President Xi's economic policy, but it is also true that the BRI is a decentralised activity, with a variety of actors motivated by purposes other than national strategy (that is, the pursuit of their own individual interests rather than China's national interests). Moreover, in the countries in which China invests, the existence of either the Belt and Road or China does not necessarily feature in local politics in terms of China's hegemony but is merely understood as a local political factor. Failure to heed this fact risks making erroneous judgements about how to respond to the many emerging economies that will be instrumental in determining the world's future development.

How can Japan make better use of the opportunity of the BRI, while also, as a member of the DAC in Asia, ensuring that projects provided under the initiative offer high-quality economic opportunities for people in third countries? The policy recommendations provided by this book are as follows.

1. Promote third-country market cooperation with China and reflect the Development Assistance Committee's principles and the SDGs in investment and aid projects

As noted above, the Japanese Government has differentiated itself from its Chinese counterpart in third-country market cooperation, claiming to implement 'high-quality' investment and aid. In so doing, it should consciously reflect Japan's standards as a DAC member to ensure that projects under the BRI receive investment and assistance from a long-term perspective and according to the interests of the different peoples in the investment destinations. The need to consider these perspectives also applies to Japan's technological cooperation with Chinese corporations working in third countries—an issue that adds a further complex dimension to third-country market cooperation because of potential security concerns (Onishi 2019). The US–China 'trade war' is developing into a 'tech war', which has serious implications for security. However, rather than waiting to see how the United States will react to China, re-examining the issue of technological cooperation from the perspectives of the Development Assistance Committee's principles and the SDGs could help Japan to devise its own approach to cooperation.

2. Differentiate Japan from China to provide diverse opportunities for third countries

Several economic powers are positioned to provide a variety of support packages for local economies by offering investment and aid activities that would fully utilise these economies' respective strengths. In so doing, the investment programs for these countries should be differentiated and coordinated so that they can truly contribute to the development of local economic policies.

3. Use local experts and listen to local voices

As the analysis presented in this book has shown, particularly that provided in Part III, the meaning of the BRI has been transformed in different local contexts. To understand the BRI, and for Japan to take advantage of the opportunities it presents, it is necessary to fully understand its local implications. To do this, it is important to use local experts and to 'listen' to local voices. Japan can utilise its existing human resource development efforts that have already strengthened collaborative networks with local bureaucrats. These include the Japan Law Education Centres that have been established in several countries in Central and South-East Asia, as well as human resource development programs such as JICA's legal aid program (Umirdinov 2019) and the Japanese Grant Aid for Human Resource Development program.

4. Promote joint research between China and Japan

Many of the criticisms that China now faces are similar to those once directed at Japan. China's aid activities have developed through observation and replication of Japan's experience (Brautigam 2011). The problems with China's development 'trinity' approach, 'debt trap' and other global issues that are examined in this book resemble the international criticisms Japan once faced. By sharing and examining the trajectory of Japan's activities as a DAC member following that criticism, as well as the results of Japan's aid program, it should be possible to understand the impact of aid programs under the BRI. In this context, joint research and study between China and Japan should be conducted on how to reflect the SDGs and safeguard human security as part of the BRI. A comparative analysis of investment and aid approaches between Japan and China would also provide an opportunity to reflect on the East Asian approach, which is intentionally different from that of the West.

References

Brautigam, Deborah. 2011. *The Dragon's Gift: The Real Story of China in Africa.* New York: Oxford University Press.

Clover, Charles, and Lucy Hornby. 2015. 'China's Great Game: Road to a New Empire.' *Financial Times*, 13 October. www.ft.com/content/6e098274-587a-11e5-a28b-50226830d644.

Hirono, Miwa. 2019. 'Asymmetrical Rivalry between China and Japan in Africa: To What Extent Has Sino-Japan Rivalry Become a Global Phenomenon?' *The Pacific Review* 32, no. 5: 831–62. doi.org/10.1080/09512748.2019.1569118.

Ministry of Foreign Affairs (MoFA). 2017. 'Nicchū shunō kaidan [Japan–China Summit Meeting].' News release, 11 November. Tokyo: Ministry of Foreign Affairs of Japan. www.mofa.go.jp/mofaj/a_o/c_m1/cn/page1_000432.html.

Nikkei. 2019. 'Ittai ichiro, kyōryoku ni yon jyōken- shushō "zenmen sansei dehanai" [Prime Minister: I Do Not Fully Agree with Four Conditions for Cooperation on Belt and Road Initiative].' *Nikkei*, 25 March. www.nikkei.com/article/DGXMZO42874300V20C19A3000000.

Okada, Mitsuru. 2017. 'Abe seiken ga itten, chūgoku no "ittai Ichiro" shijide ugokidasu keizaikai [The Abe Administration Has Changed [Its Attitude], with the Business Community Moving to Support China's "Belt and Road" Initiative].' *Business Insider*, 13 December. www.businessinsider.jp/post-108346.

Onishi, Yasuo. 2019. *Ittai ichiro' kōsō no tenkai to nihon no taiō* [*The Development of the 'Belt and Road' Initiative and Japan's Response*]. Ajiken Porishī burīhu [Ajiken Policy Brief] 123. Tokyo: Institute of Developing Economy, Japan External Trade Organisation.

Sankei Biz. 2017. 'Seihu "ittai Ichiro" minkankyōryoku wo shien- shōene nado sanbunya reiji [Government Supports Private Sector Cooperation on "Belt and Road" in Three Areas, Including Energy Conservation].' *Sankei Biz*, 8 December. web.archive.org/web/20171209152333/http://www.sankeibiz.jp/macro/news/171208/mca1712080500007-n1.htm.

Sankei Shimbun. 2019. 'Tai de no nicchū kyōryoku jigyō- chūgoku "ittai ichiro no ikkan" [Japan–China Cooperation Project in Thailand: Part of China's "Belt and Road"].' *Sankei Shimbun*, 6 March. www.sankei.com/world/news/190306/wor1903060026-n1.html.

Umirdinov, Alisher. 2019. *Generating a Reform of the BRI from the Inside: Japan's Contribution Via Soft Law Diplomacy*. RIETI Discussion Paper Series, 19-E-076. Tokyo: Research Institute of Economy, Trade and Industry.

Index

*Page numbers in **bold** indicate figures and tables*

www.ingramcontent.com/pod-product-compliance
Lightning Source LLC
Chambersburg PA
CBHW051959270326
41929CB00015B/2718